O9-CFU-120

LONG BEFORE FORTY

C. S. FORESTER

Long Before Forty

LITTLE, BROWN AND COMPANY   BOSTON   TORONTO

On C. S. Forester's death, the archives of his bank revealed the autobiography of his first thirty-one years. It ends when he was established as a professional novelist but long before *The General* and the Hornblower novels had propelled him to the heights of recognition and success. To readers of his novels, and to would-be writers and those fascinated by the career of writing, it is an absorbing work.

The early years were spent in Camberwell. Cecil was the youngest of three brothers, all clever and precocious and clearly headed for scholarships. Together they shared an enthusiasm for lead soldiers and paper campaigns involving armies and fleets in serious tactical exercises. As a small boy, Cecil exploded an almost fatally successful mine, handmade in a back garden with three-pennyworth of gunpowder.

A weak heart set him apart from the war experiences of his contemporaries, and the ensuing restless and lonely period began his breaking away from the professional pattern of his family. Following unwillingly in the footsteps of a brilliant brother, he became a medical student, but persistently failed the School Examination in Bones. He compensated himself with pleasures he could ill afford and once sang in the street for the money for an evening out with a première danseuse. Soon afterwards the decision was made to earn his living by writing. The last part of the book recounts Forester's chastening early experiences with publishers and the desperate application to both serious literary effort and hack work which for the time being became his life.

Also reprinted in this volume are the autobiographical notes from *The Hornblower Companion*, written thirty years later when his success had reached its height. Possibly no novelist since Anthony Trollope has written so frankly about his working life and talents.

Chapter One

THE earliest recollection, perhaps, is of being on board a ship at sea in a fog. There was a good deal of bustle and excitement, bells ringing and sirens blaring and folk running about – very much to the taste of a small boy aged two and a half, but not to his mind indicative of anything really untoward. I was somewhere at the ship's side, peering through an opening which the first officer had had closed with string network for my especial benefit; before that precaution had been taken I had been in the habit apparently of hanging most of my small self out over the Mediterranean. Exactly whereabouts in the ship this entrancing opening was is more than I can say now. If I were to trust to my memory I should call it a porthole, but that only goes to show that my memory is distorted by later recollections. Presumably it was some sort of opening in the bulwarks.

Anyway, as I knelt there and fiddled with the network the fog suddenly lifted, almost as dramatically as the curtain rising at a theatre. That, too, was not specially marvellous to me; the most ordinary and the most extraordinary things are on much the same plane of the marvellous to the two and a half year old mind. We were at the entrance to Malaga harbour – there was a glimpse of hills and houses to be seen. Plenty of small boats were manoeuvring round us; a couple of hundred yards away or so a big steamer was aground on a sandbank: we were aground on the same sandbank, which sufficiently accounts for the bustle on board, but that meant nothing to me. Presumably it meant something to my mother, who was on board with a considerable number of her children – three at least and possibly five, all under thirteen years old; I do not know how many of my brothers and sisters were with us.

7

In fact I do not remember anything else to do with that voyage – I cannot say what on earth a passenger steamer from Egypt was doing at Malaga, nor how we got off the sandbank, nor what the rest of the journey was like. But that one recollection is vividly clear. Moreover, if ever nowadays I smell the peculiar sharp scent of tea made with condensed milk the whole picture of the hills and the houses and the wrecked steamer is conjured vividly up before my eyes in an instant. I suppose a canny steward was allaying panic among the women passengers by serving out cups of tea, and in those days – 1901 or so – fresh milk was unobtainable in small Mediterranean steamers.

Presumably the next recollection is of a time a month or two later. It shows a very small boy who could walk upstairs but not downstairs, standing outside a small house in Camberwell and finding the world a very strange place. I was all bundled up in woollen clothes and mufflers and things – very odd after the tussores and linens to which I was accustomed – and yet I was conscious of a new and most unpleasant sensation. What was the matter with me was cold, the raw cold of an English February, which was something quite out of the run of my previous experience, for the only two winters I had ever known had been passed in the benign sunshine of Egypt.

Moreover, the house decorators to whom I was talking were to my mind being extremely rude in not understanding what I was saying to them. That is easily explainable to me now, for I was persisting in addressing them in Arabic. I could speak English as well, of course – probably better – but to my mind then people of the social order of house decorators could not be expected to understand anything except Arabic. I told those house decorators over and over again that they were doing their work all wrong, that brick houses were not nearly as nice as white stone ones with walls two feet thick, that the smell of size and varnish was objectionable to me, and that I did not like England and was going straightaway with my mother to find a steamer back to Egypt; but they only laughed.

They laughed until more house decorators arrived, and among the newcomers was a man who had served in the English army and who had fought at Tel-el-Kebir under Wolseley. He actually managed to remember a few words of Arabic – that is another instance of unexpected memory, because Tel-el-Kebir

8

was fought twenty years before – and when he used them my sorrowing heart was comforted. What he said I cannot remember and cannot possibly imagine – what Arabic words which an English Tommy would pick up in the Cairo bazaars could possibly be of use in a conversation with a two and a half year old? – but whatever it was it reassured me until at last he was able to get me out of the men's way and indoors to where the warm-hearted Irish maid could take charge of me, and offer me the warmth of a kitchen fire and a wooden horse on wheels in exchange for the charcoal braziers and camels of Cairo.

The last I heard of that maid she had risen to the surprising position of cook to His Eminence the Cardinal Archbishop of Westminster, and I suppose no other raw Irish girl has made a similar success of life in the last thirty years. And she deserves every bit of it too. My regret is that His Eminence, *ex officio*, cannot possibly have any children or grandchildren to wander down into his kitchen and say 'I'll block up the pathway, Maggie' as I used to do, and ask infantile questions about boiling kettles and roasting joints. It would be nice for His Eminence, and I strongly suspect that Maggie would still like it, and I am quite sure that the grandchildren would.

That winter in Camberwell must have been a depressing period, all the same. I can remember my mother weeping over the cracked chilblains with which her poor hands were covered; and I have heard – although I did not observe it at the time – that our Camberwell neighbours refused to notice my mother's existence. It was far too suspicious, to their minds, that a strange woman should turn up from foreign parts with five children and no apparent husband. They turned up their noses and passed her on the other side of the street – whether my mother would have been glad if they had done otherwise is more than I can say. It must have been a dreadful time for my mother, spending her first winter in England after fifteen years of Egypt – fifteen years of warmth and sunshine, of willing servants and pleasant social life. Khedivial balls and Nile trips – arriving in a small suburban house with one maid; embarrassed with five children, and tormented by the cold and by the chilblains.

However, my memory is not burdened with recollections of that period, for practically the next picture I can recall is of being helped up into my high chair at the breakfast table and saying 'I'm three today, I'm three today' and feeling very satisfied with myself in consequence; that must have been several months after our arrival in England. A week after my third birthday I went to school.

Chapter Two

IT may be that those early years in a hot climate conduced to precocity; or it may be that as the youngest of five I tended to copy my seniors, but however it was at three years old I could read with ease and could make some sort of show at writing. I was never taught either – I learnt to read by studying the big bound volumes of *Chums* which my brothers read. They contained, among other things, most thrilling serials by S. Walkey, about pirates and Spaniards and shiploads of treasure. It was only later (probably under the influence of *The Scarlet Pimpernel*) that Mr Walkey turned his attention to the French Revolution. At that time he dealt with a period indefinitely post-Elizabethan; there are bits of his stories which I can remember now. In one story the villain was called Perefixe (Don Something Perefixe, I suppose), and in another story (possibly the same, although I do not think so) there were two low comedy but high mettled characters called Captain Slapper and Lieutenant Bang who turned out eventually to be Admirals in the Dutch navy. In one story the hero had the advantage of understanding the conspirators' conversation because he had learned Spanish at Leyden University – I had not the foggiest notion where or what Leyden University was, but I was entirely convinced by that bit of local colour. And in another story the hero and his faithful friend Brumby are being pursued by bloodhounds, when Brumby cuts his leg so that the blood running down leaves a trail behind him, and then, dashing away from his friend makes certain in this manner that the brutes will follow him and forsake the hero's trail. But the hero must have been caught by those bloodhounds sooner or later despite Brumby's action, for I can also remember his being traced by a pair of them, catching and killing one of them, and

11

escaping by distracting the attention of the remainder by throwing the dead bloodhound to them carved in slices 'the head to the biggest', I remember. The mental picture of cutting a bloodhound into slices with a rapier was one particularly pleasing to my mind at that time.

But when I went to school at three years and a week I do not think my reading had yet progressed to such heights. Yet I remember struggling with boredom when I found myself dumped in a class and taught to read and to write. Writing, as I say, had come to me naturally in the way that some people learn to swim, yet here was I being tactfully initiated into pothooks and pothangers, in a class where the production of one recognisable pothanger in five minutes was an achievement accorded praise. Nowadays, I understand, children do not begin to read or write at school until they are seven or so – if I had been sent to a school like that I shudder to think of the enormities my restlessness would have urged me into.

The school, by the way, was a Council school, for my father, thank God, had no snobbery in the matter. He had five children to educate, and although he had an income which was considered large in those days he had plenty to do with his money – himself to maintain in Egypt, and all of us in England, and the expenses of the voyages to and fro whenever leave came his way, and so on. If we went to a Council school when we were young there would be all the more money to spare when we grew up and needed it; moreover, and more important than all, we could win scholarships from a Council school at an earlier age than we could win scholarships from any other school. Christ's Hospital, for instance, offered scholarships to boys at L.C.C. schools; the lucky winner of one was fed and clothed and educated at quite a good public school at no cost whatever from the age of ten to that of seventeen. There was nothing to compare with this open to any child at a preparatory school – most of the scholarships at public schools still leave a large hiatus between the award and the total of fees and expenses, as I was to discover later.

So to a Council infants' school I went – first in a perambulator pushed by the faithful Maggie and later on my own legs escorted by bored sisters. Straightaway came the first introduction to a sensation which I came to know well later on, and to hate more powerfully every year – the sensation of being

12

different. I was not as the other children were – not because of
the beauty of my soul or my body, but because of circumstances.
I had no father (or old man or dad) at home. I had been born
in Egypt. I had travelled in big steamers, and I had looked
camels in the eye at other places than the Zoo. I wore better
clothes than most of the other children there, I was the only
Cecil among dozens of Tommies and Berts, and, try as I would,
I could not talk Cockney like them. All this marked me out in
the eyes of the children, just as my ability to read and write
marked me out in the eyes of the teachers. It is perfectly horrible
to feel different from one's fellows, although I cannot recall any
single example of ill treatment by the other children on account
of my difference. We were an astonishingly tolerant crowd. I
can remember a general knowledge lesson when the teacher
dissected a fresh herring in front of us, and later announced
that she would give the result to the child who answered her
recapitulatory questions best.

We all of us laid ourselves out to win that prize – as children
will do for any sort of prize – and we were mildly astonished
when it was given to one of the duller children in the class who
had not been asked a single question. It never occurred to a
single one of us that he was given that herring because he had
no boots to his feet and probably had not had a good meal in
his belly since the day of his birth, poor little devil. We never
realised in the least that the teacher had performed a prodigy
of tact in not asking him questions, because the poor stunted
little blighter could not have answered one of them. I don't
expect that any of us, for that matter, had ever paid any
attention (beyond an indifferent mental note) to the fact that
he was barefooted!

Rags and poverty made no difference to us, but curiously
enough my smart little suits and white socks, and most especially
my manner of talking (described as la-di-da or swanky) often
excited comment, scornful or amused, although public criticism
never went as far as blows or even the mildest physical annoyance. I was admitted as an equal into their games, and even as
a leader in times of war, but I was never allowed to consider
myself a normal human being. And as time went on and my
wretched family began to distinguish itself the difference
became more marked – my elder brother, too old for Christ's

13

Hospital, won a scholarship to a good secondary school (the Headmaster now is admitted to the Public Schools Headmasters' Conference, and so it calls itself a public school) and my next brother brought off the coup my father had planned for him and won a Christ's Hospital scholarship (one of twenty distributed among twenty thousand candidates) and went off to become a contemporary of Edward Blunden's and my sisters both won scholarships and I was clearly expected to do as well or better. The rumour had gone round that my brother and I were intended to become doctors – in a school where ninety-nine children out of a hundred had no ambition beyond becoming office boys or shop boys at fourteen this made me a phenomenon as remarkable as a pink tiger.

How I hated it! How I wished that I was not two years younger than anyone else in the class! At one period my child's mind deduced that the cause of the difference lay in the fact that I was not allowed to play in the streets as every other child did. I used to beg my mother to allow me to do so. I was firmly convinced that a course of top spinning in the gutters, or of kicking a tennis ball about in a quiet, side street, or of cricket against a lamp-post was a sure route to the paradise of the ordinary. But my mother would not see my point of view, and I soon came to realise that even if I could persuade her that playing in the streets would stop my becoming a doctor she would never agree to my playing in the streets.

I tried to gain my ends by stealth, of course, in the end – no child is ever going to brook without a struggle restrictions which he thinks unreasonable. On one occasion I climbed out of an upper bedroom window and scrambled down to ground level by way of the ornamental stonework round the front door. That won me a Saturday morning in the streets, but as the performance had been carried out in broad daylight under the eyes of at least twenty mothers, all of whom hurried to tell my mother about my terrible deed, my reception on reaching home did not encourage me to repeat the experiment.

My mother emerged victorious in the clash of wills eventually, and I had to resign myself to the amusements of a lonely child indoors. Long battles with lead soldiers on the playroom floor (my brothers had worked out the rules of a system of Little Wars long before H. G. Wells wrote his epoch-making monograph on the subject) or still more complicated naval campaigns with highly conventionalised paper ships (the game was devised by my elder brother who was a positive genius in such matters) representing battleships and frigates of Nelson's time. Before I was ten I had marched armies in dozens to Berlin and Moscow, and directed uncounted squadrons to places like Cape Coast Castle and Singapore, while expressions like 'turning a flank' and 'breaking the line' fell from my lips as mere commonplaces. Those brothers of mine, ten years or so older than myself, had indicated these possibilities to me, had even condescended to play with me on occasions when high and mighty eighteen year olds had nothing better to do than to play with a lonely eight year old, but for some obscure motive I concealed from them the results of this initiation – the Army Lists covering scores of pages of foolscap, the Naval Operation Orders beginning, in a style copied from the letters in Laughton's *Letters of Lord Nelson*, with 'I hereby require and command you', the newspapers and bulletins proclaiming the victories won on land or sea – masses and masses of scribbled paper stored with conscientious secrecy in my toy boxes, and of which I still have a very few samples remaining.

I read, of course, during those years, enormously, volu-minously. There were five tickets at the Public Library round the corner available for my use, and at least once a week (later on it became once a day, honestly) I would toil round there with an armful of books to change. Partly as a result of practice and partly by accident, I was able to read very fast; I suppose I was not more than seven years old when I formed the habit (which I have maintained ever since) of reading one book a day at least. No public library can stand that sort of strain very long. The standard authors like Henty and Ballantyne and Collingwood (a boy's author who does not seem to me to have been awarded his full meed of recognition) and Robert Leighton (one of his books, a good one, is called *The Thirsty Sword*, and naturally appealed to me) were devoured in enormous gulps. Circumstances forced me into new paths, such as I had heard my elders discussing. By the easy gradient of S. R. Crockett and Rider Haggard I ascended to the heights of Dickens (whose work I found I disliked intensely) and Thackeray (whom I enjoyed) and Mrs Henry Wood and Charlotte M.

Yonge and Jane Austen and G. P. R. James and Henry James and H. G. Wells (why, I thought, did a man who could write *The War of the Worlds* bother about stuff like *Kipps*?) – absurd stuff for a child to read. At first, I suppose (for I cannot remember clearly) I did not understand one sentence in three of what I read, but the pressure set up in an inelastic library remedied that, because inevitably I was forced into re-reading, again and again, until I had got hold of some glimmering of what the author was after. There is a very definite memory still remaining of how I felt when, sitting lonely in the quiet play-room, I first began to realise (I was ten years old or so at the time) that there was a meaning to that hitherto meaningless story *The Turn of the Screw*.

And on those occasions when nowhere in the library could I find any fiction which appealed to me, I was urged by slow degrees into reading non-fiction – some of it the oddest, most poisonous stuff imaginable according to some; Suetonius and Gibbon along with Cherry Kearton's nature books and W. H. Hudson and so on. Suetonius, of course, despite the fact that large chunks of his were left in the original Latin which I could not translate, exactly suited certain moods of mine. The fantasies of a child, especially a lonely child, centre frequently about omnipotent power. The maddest freaks of the Caesars roused neither horror nor surprise in my mind. They had my fullest approval and sympathy. The kind of thing they did when they found themselves (as no mortal has found himself since) at the head of the civilised world with absolutely no check, moral or political or religious, upon their actions, was just the sort of thing I had already considered doing were I ever to find myself (as I described it to myself) 'with no policemen and no God'. Caligula in one direction, and Vitellius in another, and Nero in another, as Suetonius represents them, are very good presentments of children freed from control.

When all else in the way of reading failed, there was always the Encyclopaedia – Harmsworth's, which was published when I was six or seven. It was good sound stuff, most of it – a far better production than the Harmsworth's Universal Encyclopaedia which appeared soon after the war – and eventually I was lured into reading most of the contents of its seven volumes. The study began, of course, by going to it for confirmation or explanation of things found in Suetonius and my other favourites, and the temptation to read the next article frequently overcame me, until an hour or two later I would find I had reached the end of the volume. Some of what I read stuck in my mind. I must have been a curiously horrid child – W. S. Gilbert reserved a place in his little list for 'children who are up in dates and floor you with them flat' and I was up in many subjects besides dates. The one solitary engaging trait I exhibited was my complete inability to pronounce three-quarters of the words I wanted to use.

Chapter Three

SOME of the infants' school memories – of a period doubtless antedating my introduction to the Encyclopaedia and Suetonius – are amazingly fresh and clear. There were half a dozen of us little boys who used to play pantomimic games in the playground during the breaks. In one I remember particularly that Tommy Turner used to climb to the top of the railings (he was the only one of us who could) and hang on these, while the rest of us, sitting on the asphalt, chanted, 'The man in the moon came down too soon'. At the right moment Tommy Turner would slide down the railings (from the moon, presumably), ask his way to Norwich in dumb show, devour cold plum porridge, burn his mouth, and then vomit realistically – that was his star turn, which made us laugh until we were weak.

Then there was the weekly sewing and drawing class, when all the little girls were put on one side of the room and set to sewing or knitting, and all the little boys on the other to draw leaves, or flowers, or watering cans, or allied subjects. Whenever a little girl got into a muddle with her wool she had to stand on her form for the mistress to come round and get her out of it. Invariably (at least, so it appears to me now) every single girl *did* get into a muddle, so quickly that the mistress could not possibly cope with the demand for her services. Soon twenty or thirty little girls would be standing dolefully waiting their turn, while the mistress went from one to another with 'Why, you've dropped a stitch,' or 'Carelessness! Sheer carelessness!' and giving to each who deserved it what she always described as 'a good hard smack' on hand or arm – it was a more drastic punishment to smack the arm. Meanwhile there was no attention to be spared for the twenty or thirty little boys at the other side of the room, and we, forgetting all

18

about our watering cans and daffodils, would revel in a sort of clubbish atmosphere, lolling about in our desks, chatting with each other in a high falutin style, and generally displaying our serene masculine superiority over the woebegone little girls standing dolefully on their forms waiting their turns to be smacked. Those Friday afternoons (or were they Tuesday afternoons? I am doubtful about it) offered splendid opportunities of demonstrating to the girls how hopelessly inferior they were to us lordly males.

For we felt like that about it. Girls were inconsiderable compared with us, although we all of us were very glad of opportunities of attracting their notice.

For courtships and friendships flourished among us six-year-olds. All the horrid things one reads about in psychoanalytic books, and in nasty little studies of the child mind, went on among us. Little intimacies might be laughed at but they were desired and coveted, and were never thought wrong in the least. I do not know whether what went on there is normal in infants' schools, but now, perhaps, I have come to believe not, but I cannot bring myself to forget some of the things I remember. Probably I should be horrified if I were to find my own child doing the same as I have done. And yet I cannot think that it did us any harm. The craze died away of its own accord, and later on, when we were moved up into classes where boys and girls were separated memory of the old days evaporated to a surprising extent. In most cases no impression was left at all, not even the haziest recollection, as I was surprised to discover when, returning to school after a three weeks' absence through an injury, I casually referred to previous experiences in conversation with a friend who had shared them with me. He really did not know what I was talking about, and I, too, lapsed into the same sort of condition quite readily.

Before very long I did not care two hoots about Millie (surname forgotten) who had once been about the fifth most important member of my universe. It was she whom I crowned Queen of the May on one memorable occasion of school ceremony, when, dressed in my smart white suit and white socks (much admired by the poorer parents) I laid a wreath upon her head (Dicky Graham, a bosom pal of mine, brought the wreath upon a cushion) and said

Bend thy beautiful head, my dear,
That I may crown thee Queen of the Year.
Spring is the queen of the year
May is the queen of the spring
Thou art the Queen of the May, my dear
Thou art the Queen of the year.

Who wrote those classic lines I don't know. It might have been our class mistress – but I had to say them, all the same, with the rest of the class in their best pinafores marshalled round by the staff, while an audience of bedazzled parents clapped applause.

That event was like the realisation of a dream and disappointing in consequence. I rather fancy that one of my most usual fantasies had been the picturing of myself posing and making brilliant speeches before an adult audience with Millie (what in the world was her surname?) somewhere associated with me, but the actual event was just rather tiresome and rather boring. I was a disillusioned, rather blasé individual by the time it was all over. I was cured completely for the time of all desire for social prominence – or for Millie Whateverhernamewas too, perhaps. Certainly it was with keen anticipation and with no sense of loss that I passed on to the Big Boys' school where no girl might set foot, and where pantomime games and maypole dances were eschewed in favour of football and other manly pastimes.

I have found by subsequent inquiry that this particular school (at that particular period, anyway) was rather exceptional in its educational achievements. At many council schools it was (and is) rather unusual for a scholarship to be won by one of the children – such an event often called for a holiday in celebration. With us it was otherwise. Half a dozen scholarships in a year was a poor figure – L.C.C. scholarships to secondary schools mainly, with a few foundation scholarships and a few to trade schools, although no one had succeeded in pulling off a Christ's Hospital scholarship since my brother's achievement of several years before. These remarkable results were attained by voluntary hard work on the part of the masters and involuntarily hard work on the part of the dozen or so bright boys who were early picked out for the scholarship class – with me, of course (a year and a half younger than anyone else in the school) among them.

For a year or two we went through the usual curriculum, and then we were moved into a special class, the ex-seventh (missing the fourth and the fifth and the sixth) and crammed in a manner which it hurts me to remember. I believe that nowadays the system is discarded; I honestly hope so. We were not conscious of any particularly severe treatment – it is my firm belief that it is impossible to injure a young boy by overwork because he instinctively refuses to be crammed beyond a certain capacity – but nowadays, looking back, I can realise how drastically we were dealt with. We children of nine or ten (I was only eight at my initiation) were called upon to learn arithmetic as far as arithmetic has ever gone with me, and algebra (fancy children of ten doing quadratic equations, as I well remember doing!) and French. We studied the hard parts of English grammar, we wrote essays for homework, we paraphrased great chunks of *The Lady of the Lake*, we studied Shakespeare painstakingly (I was inevitably cast for the part of Prince Arthur when we read *King John*) and we learned everything so thoroughly that later, when I was barely eleven and went to a good secondary school I held my own easily without doing any work in a class where the average age was fourteen.

We learned remarkably thoroughly everything we were taught and for a very good reason. If we did not the cane was called in. A boy will get six sums right out of six (a most unusual circumstance in normal cases) every time if he knows for certain he will get two on each hand if he has one wrong. He will toil for a couple of hours in the evening (if his parents allow it) to put together an essay which will please his master when he knows that if he does not he will be beaten next morning. As one of the army handbooks points out, certainty of speedy punishment is the mainstay of discipline – the *certainty* of it, not the severity. That was the ruling idea in our scholarship class. We were not caned with exceptional violence, but we were caned every time we were found wanting. It was a cast iron, rigid system, never relaxed on any excuse whatever, one mistake, one caning, and as a result of it we produced work of an inconceivable perfection. But nowadays the bare thought of a ten year old doing two hours' homework in the evening, or being beaten because he writes the second person plural present of 'faire' as 'vous faisez' sets all my humanitarian instincts in revolt.

Yet we none of us died, as far as I can remember, and none of us even went weak in the head, or suffered any permanent damage whatever – save for me; my eyesight, what with close school work and hours of daily reading, gave way so that at seven I had to wear spectacles (another blessed distinguishing mark) and I have worn them ever since.

The system, as I said, has been made impossible now. Quadratic equations and the theory of indices are not taught in elementary schools even to boys of fourteen, let alone to children of ten. French, too, has disappeared from the curriculum, I believe, which is much more of a loss. In my time we even had oral French – once a week a dear old white haired lady came and talked French to us, telling us stories of 1870. Thinking about it dispassionately, I cannot believe that the L.C.C. stood for that oral French; my personal theory is that the masters clubbed together and engaged our teacher out of their own pockets and without the knowledge of authority. They were quite capable of it; they were a happy band of fanatics with completely at their mercy a dozen bright boys who not only could be made to win scholarships under sufficient pressure, but could be coerced into learning all sorts of other subjects far more advanced than the scholarship examinations we would have to take. Yet I must repeat that none of us knew we were unhappy, and we were still capable of playing games and of doing things which really deserved caning, and we all of us (as far as I can guess; in this matter I can only speak for myself, of course) maintained flourishing inner lives and well developed fantasies. But it has just occurred to me that perhaps there is an explanation of why I was always so woefully thin in those days, and pasty faced, so that I was always being most unpleasantly tested for worms, with negative results.

I wish I knew what was the eventual destiny of my fellow bright boys in the Ex-seventh. Seeing that they were all a year or more older than me the fate of a large proportion of them can be guessed – killed or mutilated in the war. But the brightest of the lot of them had an unusual Christian name and surname, and several times lately when passing through Camberwell I have noticed that name written on the side of a builder's and decorator's carts. It must be the same individual – the same unusual name, the same district. If so, he must be doing well; a builder and decorator with three or four carts must be accounted a successful man. Does he, I wonder, find quadratic equations any use to him now, or does he owe his success to the way he was crammed at elementary school? I wish I had the courage to go into his office and ask him; but it is over twenty years since he saw me last, and I very much doubt if he would recognise in me the skinny bespectacled shrimp with the bristly hair who sat in the desk in front of him.

Chapter Four

THE outstanding incident of those years was the Big Bang. It seems to me now to be just as unbelievable as all the rest of it, but it really happened. Maxwell – Willie Maxwell – it was who first started it.

'Do you know,' he said to me one day, wide eyed, 'Cooper's sell *gunpowder* ?'

Cooper's was the oil and colourman in a side street near the school.

'Go on,' I said – not that I did not believe him, but because that was the conventional reply to any statement of fact unknown to the hearer.

'They do. *Reelly* they do. And you can buy a penn'orth of it in a big bag.'

That was real news. I had naturally believed that such a heavenly commodity as gunpowder could only be purchased for unattainable sums like sovereigns. But pennies were to me comparatively easily come by, with two big brothers and an indulgent mother. My soul yearned for gunpowder – a big bagful of that was all I could get, but gunpowder in pails, in barrels, in roomfuls, if possible. For days I must have thought and dreamed nothing but gunpowder. In the end a whole sixpence came my way, and on Saturday morning in the course of running domestic errands I went into Cooper's with my heart nearly bursting with excitement. Mr Cooper would not sell me sixpenn'orth of gunpowder. Three penn'orth was all he would run to – a monstrous bluepaper cornucopia of it. I nearly died with disappointment when, reaching home with my pocket bulging with gunpowder, I could not slip upstairs straightaway to gloat over my purchase in the solitude of the playroom. I had instead to go back to Cooper's to buy all the things I had been told to buy there and had forgotten in the excitement of the moment.

But at last I was alone with my gunpowder. I ran my fingers through it lovingly like Midas with a cornucopia of gold-dust. I went off into day dreams wherein that pound of gunpowder expanded into the barrels-full of my ambition. It must have been an hour or two before I really started playing with it. Some benevolent spirit over me must have guarded me from harm when I did so. I put pinches of it into the fire, I hit pinches of it with a hammer, I did most of the things a small boy can be expected to do with a pound of gunpowder. Yet there was still some left on Monday for me to take to school to display proudly to my friends.

An epidemic of gunpowder-fever broke out instantly. Everyone who could raise a penny expended it on gunpowder. But it was unsatisfactory somehow. We could not get a real big bang out of it. Even when a small group of the more daring of us lit quite a little pile of it in a secluded corner of the playground it did not make much noise. It merely went up with a gratifying flare and a mild roaring sound and a mass of smoke.

Despairingly at home I read up the subject in the Encyclopaedia, digging out facts from a whole series of fascinating articles on Gunpowder and Explosives and Guns and so on. The reason was there to be found, and I found it at length – gunpowder will not explode, as opposed to mere rapid burning, unless it is confined. The first idea suggested by this discovery was to obtain a bit of iron tubing, cram it with gunpowder, and put it into the fire. Fortunately my guardian angel saw to it that no iron tubing was to be found. As a substitute there promptly grew up the idea of a mine – dig a hole in the ground, put in your powder, cover it well up, and set it off. The Encyclopaedia had some interesting data about mines, and the more I debated the idea the more marvellously beautiful it appeared to me. Life was utterly imperfect until I had achieved a mine.

But a mine called for the use of slow match; slow match sent me back to the Encyclopaedia. Probably it was not for another day or two that the method was worked out. Slow match is made by soaking cord in a strong solution of saltpetre and allowing it to dry. Saltpetre? That was one of the three constituents of gunpowder, here, ready to my hand – it never occurred to me that perhaps Mr Cooper could have sold me saltpetre out of his shop.

Next there comes on the scene the figure of Stanley Williams, the only son of his mother and she a widow, one of the 'nicer' boys of the school, one of the few with whom my mother countenanced my associating. I cannot remember whether I decided that his help was necessary or whether his presence in my home on one of the rare occasions when I was allowed to have a friend to play with my lead soldiers was a mere coincidence. Anyway, one Saturday there he was in the playroom with me. Already I had stolen a gallipot full of water and recklessly I poured some of my new three-penn'orth of gunpowder into it. We stirred it, first hopefully, then desperately. To all appearance the gunpowder was unchanged save to become a mere messy mud. But I saw it with the eye of faith. Even though the charcoal and the sulphur still remained to constitute that mud, the saltpetre must have passed into solution. I soaked string in the liquid. I hung it before the fire to dry. Hopefully I tried it. It would not burn properly. It gave a splutter or two, but it would not burn smoothly or continuously. Not even when it was properly dried would it burn. Stanley Williams sniggered, and I could have killed him. But I would not despair; my faith in the Encyclopaedia, though shaken, was still living. Fiercely I poured still more gunpowder into the gallipot and stirred it up.

Somehow before the new solution could be tried Stanley Williams had to go home, and my experiments were interrupted. It must have been only by a series of miracles that our investigations remained undetected – I can picture, even if I cannot remember, the sort of mess two boys with a jar of water and a pound of gunpowder and some experimental fuses could make. It must have been some practical difficulty connected with parents and sisters which prevented me, on my discovery next day that the new slow match worked simply perfectly, from going into the garden and digging a mine there and then. It actually was not until next Saturday that I put the scheme into practice, in Stanley Williams' garden.

For this choice of site I can suggest several reasons. I must have wanted to prove to Stanley that my plans were not as chimerical as he thought them. Mine digging in my own garden must have appeared impractical because a sister or someone must have been digging at her silly old pansies or something just where a mine would be most effective. Stanley Williams' garden, on the other hand, was convenient in having a door on to the street – his mother rented the top of a corner house and Stanley had the run of the garden.

Be all this as it may, Saturday morning found me (at a time when I was supposed to be running errands) in Stanley's garden explaining what we were going to do. I had a yard of the new fuse, a box of matches, and my pockets simply bulged with gunpowder – the result of several purchases, which must have been made (I greatly fear) only with pennies obtained by means not strictly legitimate. I paraphrased the Encyclopaedia as I explained that we must dig a hole, put in the powder, and ram earth well down on top, with a bit of fuse protruding. Stanley Williams had an idea – stimulated, it is to be supposed, by the knowledge that his mother's landlord did not approve of Stanley's digging holes in his garden.

'Look at this,' said Stanley.

He led me to where a brand new clothes line post stood at the end of the garden. The careful tenant had dug a beautiful socket for it, a foot deep or so, lined with wood, into which the base of the post fitted most accurately. A combined effort on our part heaved the post out of the socket, and we examined that beautiful hole with admiring care, our heads first on one side and then on the other. It was an ideal mine, and the tall post would constitute ideal 'tamping' – that was the word the Encyclopaedia used. We poured the gunpowder into the hole. We inserted one end of the fuse into it, left the other end trailing on the ground, and then with a vast effort we upended the clothes post again and set it into the hole on top of the powder. I bent to light the fuse, and then remembered we were not treating the occasion with the solemnity it deserved.

'You must go and hide,' I said to Stanley. 'Hide behind the corner of the house in case of the explosion.'

Stanley went. He was a biddable soul, and although he did not think there was the least chance of an explosion he was willing to enter into the spirit of the game. Then I lit the end of the fuse, and stood admiring the spark for a moment or two, as it crept along the string, spluttering valiantly and smelling

27

adorably. Then some instinct (or it may merely have been the same spirit of make-believe as had influenced Stanley) sent me running to the side of the house to where Stanley was peering round the corner. I reached his side and had just turned to look back when the crash came. Underneath that clothes line post was about as much powder as was used to charge a thirty-two pounder in Nelson's day. There was a deafening crash and a cloud of smoke. That solid clothes line post shot solemnly into the air, turning over and over as it did so, and then fell with a clatter into a garden two doors away. Bits of stone rained all round us, and as we stood paralysed we heard the tinkle of broken glass from various windows near by which had been blown in.

'Coo!' said Stanley. 'Coo! Coo! Coo!'

But other voices than that of the turtle were to be heard in the land. Quite a crowd assembled with miraculous haste. I still stood fixed and marvelling; Stanley still said 'Coo!' for some seconds after the first arrivals. Stanley's widowed mother arrived, frantic, and caught him up to her bosom where he instantly dissolved into tears. The owners of the broken window panes arrived. A policeman – terrifying spectacle! – hastened up with his notebook and his pencil.

And that is where my memory breaks down, drawing a dramatic curtain before the scene at its climax. Who took me home, what was said and done there, I simply cannot remember, students of Freud may perhaps advance an explanation. I can remember that for two or three days afterwards I crept about labouring under a heavy conviction of guilt, which nagged at me and sapped my vitality just as an aching tooth might do. But my family, impressed though they might be by the indignation my action had aroused, never really thought I was to blame. They could not bring themselves to believe that an undersized spectacled little boy of studious and solitary habits could, on his own initiative, make fuses and mines in the way Stanley Williams said I did. They did not make enough allowance for the effect of a close study of innumerable books of adventure, backed up with all the illuminating information the Encyclopaedia can give.

Chapter Five

THE adventure of the big bang had no prolonged effect. The memory of it soon became much less acute even among my awestruck contemporaries. Life soon settled down again with its old routine of school work and home work; of Sunday afternoon battles with ships or armies on the playroom floor; of holidays, and of journeys to the library with both arms full of books to change.

There were the periodical great occasions of my father's returns from Egypt on leave, when every day one woke with the delicious feeling that anything, simply anything, might happen. For my all-powerful father had only to say the word for wonderful things to take place. He said it so casually and frequently; he was never in the least impressed by the fact that he had merely to decide on a course of action to carry it out. The Tower of London and South Kensington Museum, Westminster Abbey and St Paul's, the Zoo and Mme Tussaud's, the portals of each flew open at his words in a manner most impressive. Big brothers could never convey that impression of effortless omnipotence when they took small ones to the Changing of the Guard or to the Oval.

Besides, I had read in some novel or other of a mother being charged ten shillings a week for the support of her child. There were five of us, there were my father and mother, and there was the maid. On a moderate estimate, then, with these data, that made three pounds ten shillings a week for our mere keep. To travel from Egypt to England cost my father (as he told me in reply to my questions) 'a whole handful of sovereigns'. I heard vaguely of the monstrous sums it cost to pay my brother's expenses at the hospital where he was a student. The total sum which my father must earn in a year must be simply colossal –

hundreds of pounds every year; no small boy to whom sixpence was comfortable wealth could possibly visualise such an amount. For one brief period of my life my father received my unstinted admiration solely on that account, solely because he was able to do something whose magnitude was beyond my imagination – not many things were.

Yet with all that there was in the air of those nineteen-hundreds a hint of rapid and unstable change which even a small sensitive boy could feel. When first my mother and I went to meet my father home from leave we used to drive home the three of us together in a hansom cab. Later came the time when the whole vast echoing station could not produce a hansom cab and we had to use a taxicab – delightful in its way, but not in accordance with long-standing custom, and therefore not to the taste of a small boy. The system of horse trams along Peckham Road suddenly was changed in favour of the electric conduit system; there was a grand ceremonial opening, when the Prince of Wales (the present King) drove along the whole route, taking off his hat to the cheering crowds, on the top deck of a special white painted tramcar, while the little princes sat in the front in white sailor suits, and the massed elementary schools (myself among them) sang 'God Bless the Prince of Wales' most discordantly.

Motor cars made their appearance; I cannot remember the first I saw, but I remember most distinctly seeing my first motor bus thundering down Peckham Road, past the horse buses clip-clopping sedately along. There was a railway strike in England, and another in France which caused us much more excitement (presumably because my father was on his way home from Marseilles). All gave some impression of instability, or at least of changing conditions, peculiarly stimulating to a child's mind.

For it never occurred to me in the least to doubt the possibility of my own success in life. Success was such an easy thing to come by; my family had enjoyed it in huge quantities. There was my father – but no one could dream of thinking that he might sometimes be unsuccessful; my elder brother went through examination after examination in the course of his medical studies with flying colours, eventually qualifying at the age of twenty; the other brother had climbed to the dizzy heights of cricket and football colours at Christ's Hospital before he made an abdication of his own free will (comparable in my mind with the abdications of Charles V and Diocletian and Sulla) and, turning his back on a possibly brilliant future, retired to the comfort of a City position and a commission in the Territorial Army. I fully believed – I never had the least doubt – that I should combine the successes of these two. I looked upon it as certain that I should win a scholarship to Christ's Hospital, win every sort of colour and prize imaginable there, go on to Cambridge, get my blue for cricket, and my degree in medicine at twenty along with the gold medal of the Royal College of Surgeons, and so enter into a more hazy but none the less positive world of scientific success.

And scholarship examination time came round. I went to the school where the examination was to be held, read and began the papers with never a quickening of the pulse, completed them with philosophic calm, and returned home quite unmoved. Anxious teachers at school next day went through the papers with us to find out how we had succeeded; as far as I was concerned they were bitterly disappointed. There was one nasty sum about a monkey climbing a greasy pole which had tricked me entirely; it was more than doubtful whether I had done various others correctly. I read in their faces their anticipation of my failure, and still I was unmoved. It was not that I remembered having done well in the other papers – an essay and a general knowledge examination; it was solely that I was full of the beliefs first that I could not possibly fail, and second that no member of my family could possibly fail.

Then, long weeks later, results began to drift in. These half dozen boys had won elementary scholarships; that one a scholarship on the foundation of a grammar school; this other a trade scholarship; someone else a scholarship to Bancroft School (we were a good vintage year in that class, as I have said). But still no news that I had won a Christ's Hospital scholarship. At school the opinion was openly expressed that I had failed; even at home the countenances of the Family began to express doubt. My form master gave up asking me every morning on parade in the playground whether any good news had come – he had asked me every morning for weeks.

The summer term must have been approaching its end when

messages began to fly round the school one morning. The sliding partition which divided the largest classroom into two rolled up so that there were two classes sitting together in one big room – my own and another. Other forms began to file in, ushered by their masters, and were ranged round the walls and the back of the room, class after class until two or three hundred small boys were crammed into the limited space, and half a dozen masters were assembled in front of them. Not one of us boys knew what all these elaborate arrangements portended. Then entered the headmaster.

'Well, boys,' he began, 'I have some very good news for you. One of the boys of this school has won a Christ's Hospital scholarship. You all know how difficult that is to do, and I want you to give this boy a good hearty clap and three cheers for having brought so much honour to this school. No, wait until I give the word. It is eight years since the last scholarship to Christ's Hospital was won by a boy from this school, and then it was won by the brother of this year's winner. Now you know who it is – Cecil Forester! Hip, hip, hip—' Three hundred boys yelled and stamped and hammered on their desks. Half a dozen masters, smiling happily, clapped their hands. Six hundred eyes were turned towards me, the spectacled shrimp in the front row on the right. The business did not embarrass me in the least, the news did not elate me, me, the select of twenty thousand entrants. It was something which I had always known was going to happen, which had been expected of me for ten years, ever since the day of my birth, and by me ever since I had expected anything. I sat in my desk and wished that the distressing noise would end, and when it showed no sign of doing so I withdrew into my favourite mental occupation of keeping the Toulon fleet from uniting with the Brest fleet by the manoeuvres of an English fleet weaker than the two in combination. It was no more startling or pleasing to win a scholarship (twenty among twenty thousand) than to find that there was bread and butter for tea, or that the school was at the end of the road. And applause was positively unpleasant when it harassed my eardrums.

So the close of that term marked the end of my stay at an elementary school. Without a doubt it did me a great deal of good, and beyond the damage to my eyesight I did not think that it did me any harm. I had a magnificent grounding in elementary subjects, and thanks to the unsparing use of the cane I had acquired a habit of exactness of work and carefulness of thought which I could not cast off for years afterwards. My morals had no more been corrupted by association with the children of the poor than they had been by the reading of Suetonius. There were many things which I had learned there which I could not possibly have learned at a preparatory. I knew that when the big local engineering works which employed the fathers of most of my school-fellows closed down those school-fellows went short of food and clothing; I had a vicarious introduction, in short, to hunger and cold. Casual conversations had revealed to me the amazing fact (it would never have occurred to me otherwise) that most of the children in London slept two or three in a bed. Observation had shown me that trivial things like nibs and pencils, of which there were dozens to be obtained for the asking at home, were to some people well worth stealing and certainly worth lying for.

In one respect the school may have affected me profoundly, in encouraging me to think of myself as a unique and extraordinary specimen. Because that is exactly what I was at that school – a boy born in Egypt, the son of a father distinguished in his profession, noticeable for the goodness of his clothes and accent, precociously brilliant at school-work, a walking reference library to whom even the oldest boys turned for information on recondite subjects such as fortification and secret inks and sexual development.

Not that this last had any prolonged interest for me. By the time I was ten I knew all that Suetonius and the Encyclopaedia between them could tell me; there was a brief period when the matter bulked largely in my thoughts, but as soon as I had grasped the main facts I lost my interest in the subject almost completely, and I was firmly convinced that I would never be interested in it again. I am quite sure that I was far more sexually minded between the ages of three and seven than I was from seven to twelve.

There were plenty of things which I found far more interesting – things which I never think about now. Such as why some pavements are flagged and some asphalted; why some horses in tradesmen's carts wear a coloured band round their forehead instead of a strap joining their blinkers – they still do, although it is only with a fearful effort that I can bring myself to notice it. Why some telegraph wire insulators are black and some white. Why some boys played one game of marbles and some another.

During the marble season in those days there were all sorts of ways of gambling for marbles. For ten minutes or so before school and during the ten-minute breaks (I can never forget how long those breaks seemed, and what an enormous amount we did during them) about two dozen boys would take up pitches in the playground sitting with their backs to the fence beside the railway. Between their legs they would each set up a screw on its head or else an 'alley' – a glass marble. The screw merchants would shout ' 'It 'im two' or ' 'It 'im three' or even ' 'It 'im four.' That meant that anyone could come along and roll marbles at their screw from some mark decided upon by the screw owner; a couple of yards away perhaps for ' 'It 'im two' and half a dozen for ' 'It 'im four.' All the marbles one threw became the property of the screw owner, unless you hit the screw, whereupon you were given two, three or four marbles as the case might be. Rolling the marble was always the rule; I never came across 'knuckle down' until twenty years later in France and in the North of England.

People who put down 'alleys' (how does one spell that word?) worked on another principle. They shouted ' 'It 'im 'ave 'im' – if you hit the alley it was yours. But then you had to stand a long way away, twenty yards or so, for alleys were very precious, and ' 'It 'im 'ave 'im' was only practised by people very hard up for marbles.

And wandering through the crowd of people patronising the marble-ranges (I cannot think of a better name for that patch of playground) went boys shouting 'Two a dip'. You always asked them 'What's your highest?' and they would reply 'Five' or possibly 'ten'. If you deemed the answer satisfactory you handed over two marbles, and the receiver would turn sideways so as to present his trouser pocket to you, and from that you would extract one out of several pieces of paper. It might be a blank, but it might have a figure on it – the highest possible was the number you had been told in reply to your question – and you became entitled to receive from the dip merchant that number of marbles. Those boys were a simple crowd. I fancy I was the only one ever to wonder about the proportion of blanks and prizes.

The most passionate devotees of marbles played a game called 'sticks' because you struck at it. One side would put down an alley and the other would throw at it, losing every unsuccessful marble, until he hit it. Then the roles would be reversed, and so on for days perhaps, until one side was completely cleaned out of marbles, ruined, exhausted, out of the game for the season unless the fortunate possession of reserve capital in the form of alleys and some luck at ' 'It 'im 'ave 'im' re-established him.

For no one, as far as I remember, ever *bought* any marbles except myself. I used to, every season, and I used to give them away, too (and was thought insane for it) when I wearied of ' 'It 'im two'. But I never ceased to wonder why some people played one game and some another, and where, after the first five minutes, the attraction lay. My reading had, of course, brought to my notice a craze called a passion for gambling, but it never occurred to me that actually it was that which was activating the marble players. Monte Carlo and the racecourses can boast no superiority over that patch of asphalt beside the fence against the railway.

Some time after the marble season died away all these games would revive again with cherry stones instead of marbles – cherry-oggs (possibly cherry-hogs) was the word always used. Marbles and cherry-oggs and tops were seasonal games, more definitely seasonal even than cricket and football. Others were played all the year round – Jum-jimmy-knacker (I should like to know the etymology of that name) which was a kind of cumulative leapfrog; widdy, which bears the same relation to touch as Contract does to Nap, and whose most glorious feature was the periodical flogging of those who were caught by the uncaught with their rolled up caps; 'R.White's', where two boys linked arms as horses, while another behind them, stooping, ran behind holding their wrists and representing a cart, and a fourth mounted on the cart's back and tried not to be thrown off however much the horses galloped and wheeled the cart round. R. White's is the name of a firm which brews gingerbeer – I still wonder what incident it was which led that school to adopt that particular name for this game.

And besides all these peaceful pursuits there were periodical wars – war was endemic in the playground like the plague in India. It only needed a trifle to wake old feuds to life; without more than a minute's warning the whole playground would suddenly be turned into a battleground, where old scores were paid out literally with tooth and nail, where noses bled and clothes tore and the unlucky ones who fell in the press were tramped and kicked with hobnailed boots until some master noticed the disturbance and broke up the mob, sending all he could recognise inside to be caned. It was in these battles that I was first acquainted with the mad joy of fighting 'all out', deliberately flinging away my sanity (and trebling my strength thereby) and plunging into the mass, using head and fists and boots with such a reckless disregard for the consequences that boys twice my size shrank away from before me appalled.

Nowadays, as far as I can ascertain, elementary schools are much more civilised places. In London, at any rate, it is much more unusual to see barefooted children, and the standard of clothing and feeding and cleanliness is very much higher. Children are not so brutal, I fancy – possibly as a result. From what I hear, the standard of knowledge is rather lower – although of course, as I have pointed out before, the school which I attended was very much of a freak school even for that time in the matter of cramming. But nowadays they use 'intelligence tests' and similar subtleties, and – most epoch-making change of all – they have tried to minimise the use of the cane. To cane an elementary schoolboy nowadays, I believe, calls for all sorts of formalities and consultations with head-masters and entries in books, which must bring about a state of affairs which I cannot visualise at all. Twenty executions in a lesson was not an unreasonably high figure in my time, and all disciplinary offences were immediately punished with one smack hand. At the present time masters must either endure more, or maintain discipline by sheer force of personality, or else the boys must be more amenable. I shall never know which is the correct explanation.

Chapter Six

So it was settled that I was to go to Christ's Hospital. For seven years I was to be fed and clothed and taught for nothing, and by the end of that time I would have the other advantages of having attended a good-class public school in addition. My father, returning on leave, rewarded my success with a golden half sovereign, more money than I had ever possessed before, which I lavished away during the weeks of the summer holidays in luxurious living. Those August days are memorable to me because during them I had only to put my hand in my pocket to find money there – a glorious state of affairs when a penny would buy a quarter of a pound of good sweets, and halfpennies and even farthings were capable of buying things.

There was neither exultation nor depression at the thought of going away to school, and wearing the long blue coat and white bands and yellow stockings. It was my destiny, settled years back. I no more thought of questioning it than a French girl thinks of questioning the desirability of the marriage her parents arrange for her. The regulation amount of under-clothing and football gear was bought (the school provided neither of those) and packed up in the regulation wicker basket. September came, and with my father and mother I went up to the offices somewhere near Holborn for the final formalities. There was an additional medical examination to go through, and papers to sign, and various other minor formalities to complete before we went to catch the school train in the afternoon.

The medical examination was soon finished, but the other formalities seemed to take an extraordinary long time. I sat with my mother in the waiting room while my father was interviewing governors or whoever it was had to be interviewed. The other mothers had long ago drifted away with their offspring – my schoolfellows to be, presumably – and still we sat and waited. The room was overheated, I remember, and had a clock with a noisy tick.

At last, when my mother was really beginning to be anxious as to whether we should have time to catch the train, my father came into the room. His entry is one of my clearest memories, for he was furiously angry and his face was as white as his military moustache.

'It's closed,' he said. 'The scholarship's closed.'

It took some time for us to realise that at this very moment, five minutes before we were to leave to catch the train to school, the governors had made up their minds not to allow me a scholarship.

Their decision (though not the time they chose to announce it) was perfectly justified. By the terms of Edward VI's foundation the school was dedicated to the education of the poorer boys of London, and anyone knowing the size of my father's income could instantly deduce the fact that I was not to be included in that class; my father was considerably wealthier than he had been eight years before when my second brother won a similar scholarship. It was anomalous, all the same (as I believe my father had pointed out with some heat) that by the system of 'presentations' and 'nominations' the children of friends of the governors should be admitted with no strict inquiry into either education of circumstances while I, selected from twenty thousand candidates, should be discarded.

I think I bore the blow far more calmly than my parents. Presumably I believed that my own extreme importance in the world's affairs would see to it that I came out all right whatever happened. I left them struggling with their disappointment while I went off to the Oval to watch the last two hours of the last match of the season. It was the champion county versus England, particularly to be remembered because it was the only time when I saw G. L. Jessop bat. He came in about seventh wicket down and made twenty or so by terrific hitting before he was caught in the long field at the foot of the sight screen.

By the time I reached home my father had decided what to do with me – it was an awkward moment for him because he had only one day's more leave in England, and during that time he had to find a school for me and settle me in it. Naturally it was agreed that if there was room for me I should go to the extremely good secondary school (nominally now a public school) at which my other brother had been educated, and thither I went with my father next morning.

The headmaster received us affably. He would be glad to have me in the school – had not my brother that very year qualified in medicine at the phenomenal age of twenty, and was I not the winner of a Christ's Hospital scholarship which marked me as one of the cleverest children in London? But – and this was a very grave but, as I gathered from the serious way in which my father and the headmaster discussed the matter – there was only one vacancy in the whole school; the term had begun several days before. This vacancy was in the fourth form, among boys of thirteen and fourteen. Was I equal, in the first place, to the standard of work of the fourth, and, secondly, would I be able to hold my own among the big boys? The headmaster looked at my stunted figure and pale spectacled face with doubts which were obvious even to me. I was consulted in the matter, I remember, and expressed no apprehensions – my egoism was of that kind. The form master of 4A was called in – that was my first encounter with the dear kindly man – and took me off for a lightning examination. Naturally I passed that with flying colours – thanks to the elementary school I could do that sort of algebra and arithmetic without stopping to think. Then I was taken off to the French master (the Englishman who taught French, not the sweet incompetent Belgian who also taught there, and who was to die of a broken heart when he heard of the destruction of Louvain) and that individual, confronted in the middle of a class with the demand that he should ascertain immediately whether my French was of Fourth Form standard, asked the inevitable question.

'Parlez vous Français?' he demanded. That was a favourite gambit of the old lady who talked French to us at the elementary school.

'Oui, monsieur, un peu,' I replied.

'Quel âge avez-vous?'

'J'ai dix ans – I mean onze,' I said – my birthday had come two or three days before.

'He'll do. Take him away,' said the French master.

So then and there I was flung into the middle of things at a big boys' school, dropped, when the term had just got well under way, into a form where practically everybody was three years older than me and about a foot taller, the only new boy among thirty veterans. Scholarship boys from elementary schools (there were not many of them in those days) were usually put into the Thirds, and had time there to make friends and learn the ways of the school; I was a form higher and a year younger than these holders of junior scholarships.

To this day I still feel qualms when I look back on that first year at school, even though a selective memory has mercifully blurred most of the details. The way of an infant phenomenon at a boys' school is hard. There was one popular torture known as 'racking'; Guy Fawkes was racked, although in a different way, but I doubt if he were more hurt. At school the first step when racking anyone is to take off the subject's necktie – to rack anyone, be it understood, calls for the combined efforts of several bigger boys. Then you take the subject to the railings which divide the asphalt from the playing field, set his back against them, and pass his arms behind him over the rail which is of the most suitable height. Then you take hold of his wrists and bring his arms forward and upward, straining his shoulders back over the railings until his shoulder joints are at the point of dislocation – a little more or less is not of much importance. Then you tie his wrists together behind the back of his neck with his necktie and also to the top rail of the railings, so that he is held fast in this extremely uncomfortable position. Some practitioners (although it is not really essential nor universal) now try poking the subject's stomach, which protrudes in a most tempting and amusing way as a result of this tying back of his shoulders. Finally (and this is most important) you must undo every single button on the subject's clothing, pull up or down every garment which is freed by this process, and then leave the subject writhing against the railings and surrounded by an hysterical mob weak with laughing until some prefect responsible for order comes and sets him free.

That is only one way of dealing with an infant phenomenon; there are lots of others. If you sit behind him in class you can do a good deal with pins. You can chew your penholder until it becomes conveniently brushlike, and then use this instrument for painting pictures in ink on the back of his neck. You can smack his head steadily and monotonously with a book, and when his skull becomes inured to this treatment you can use the edge of a ruler instead. Care should be taken that the infant phenomenon not only has someone sitting behind him who dislikes infant phenomena, but people on each side and in front as well of the same way of thinking. Then by an easy rotation of duty monotony can be avoided, and pressure continuously applied to make the infant phenomenon wish not merely that he was not an infant phenomenon but that he had never been born, or that he was a condemned slave in the Siberian saltmines, or that he was roasting in Hell.

One very amusing thing to do in the fleeting minute between lessons is to take off the infant phenomenon's shoes and drop them out of the window. He has no chance at all, of course, of retrieving them at once. They are picked up by a puzzled porter or gardener and conveyed to the lost property office, whither, at the break, the child must make his way down flights of stairs and along crowded corridors in his stockinged feet to the infinite amusement of all beholders; or with great good fortune he may be called out before the break comes to show up work at the master's desk or to write something on the blackboard, when, his shoeless condition becoming apparent, everyone enjoys a hearty laugh, and a tedious lesson is shortened by a welcome interval while the puzzled master asks questions. Not even the kindliest master can resist cracking a joke or two in those circumstances.

Looking back on those days I can appreciate the fact that most of the things which were done to me were only done in search of amusement and to relieve the tedium of an otherwise monotonous existence. Of cruelty for cruelty's sake there was very little. Pain was hardly ever inflicted solely for the sake of inflicting pain. There was nearly always some more human motive at the back of it, even if it were only a scientific interest in the furious rages which could be induced in an inky and tear-stained little boy. At the time, however, I would have found small comfort in this even if I had realised it. There was a black period months long during which I felt more miserable than I have ever done since; during which I debated the idea of suicide quite seriously, and when I would willingly have exchanged my mode of existence for any other the world could offer.

One source of comfort remained – I could usually manage to shut myself up within myself and, heedless of the outer practical world, indulge in the most gratifying fantasies as to what I would do to Anderson and Melville and company if I had them in my power. My mind in those days accepted easily notions which I can only compel myself with an effort to think about now – buckets of flaming coals scientifically applied; the deft insertion of long thin iron spikes; the thoughtful application of melted lead.

Anderson and Melville bulked enormous to my mind. If ever I had been called upon to make life-size models of them I should certainly have made them eight feet tall. I do not think I should have given them horns and tails, but most certainly they would have had cruel hands and mocking laughs. I suppose if I could see them now as they were then they would appear to me to be very ordinary and uninteresting small boys – rather loutish, perhaps, with a precocious tendency to hair oil and creased trousers, but I should certainly not give a second thought to them. Yet in those days they were easily the most important inhabitants of my world, whose whims and fancies were of the most excruciating importance to me.

In one respect I was lucky. That school was remarkably clean in tone. It was perfectly possible – I knew several examples of it – for a boy to pass right through the school and emerge as innocent as when he entered it. Only once can I remember an Assistant Tormentor suggesting the introduction of a sexual motive into my course of treatment, and he was instantly overruled. If that kind of thing had intruded itself into my life at that point I might have suffered a good deal of harm; I might have learned to 'suck up' to my biggers and betters, and coquette with them in the way which I saw frequently, a year or two later, employed by small boys at other schools, or I might have suffered various moral lesions which it would have taken years to cure.

As it was, a year of bullying did me no harm at all, as far as I can tell, and I honestly believe it did me a great deal of good. I learned a number of lessons of extreme value to a pert small boy. I learned not to use the repartee which came to my lips; I learned to make myself quite inconspicuous continuously as well as on occasions; I learned not to show any emotion of any kind, and especially not to lose my temper – a boy who loses his temper is always more liable to bullying; I learned not to cry out when I was hurt, but to bear it with an absolutely unmoved expression in the certainty that the tormentor would the sooner cease from troubling. I learned that when a small boy plots revenge, and secretly achieves it, the pleasure to be obtained from announcing one's authorship later is not to be compared with the inevitable pain which follows – and, incidentally, there is a more acute pleasure still in hugging one's secret to one's breast and revelling in amused isolation at the black fury of one's victim. The most valuable lesson, perhaps, was that I learned I was not, to put it mildly, a person of great importance in the affairs of the world.

The effect of those lessons may have worn off by now, perhaps (I fear they have) but while it lasted it was of the greatest advantage to me. Incidentally, it never once occurred to me during that black year to admit to anyone in authority at home or at school that I was in the least unhappy. The school authorities may have guessed it; probably they did (I have reason to think so) but with infinite tact refrained from interference which could only have made things far worse. At home I suppose it was pride; I would never admit to my family that the great, the wonderful, the clever, the inexpressibly marvellous Cecil was thought so little of at school that he was kicked whenever a kickable portion of him came in range of anyone's boot.

When I say that I believe this year of bullying did me good, I do not wish it to be understood that I am in favour of bullying. Far from it; in the majority of cases I believe it does a great deal of harm, to the bully as well as to the bullied. I have been in close personal touch with two different clever boys who have been reduced to mental impotence, and who have had promising careers ruined in consequence, by intensive bullying – not at the school where I was bullied, though. And I can remember the expression of inane cruelty on the faces of the boys who did the bullying in one of those cases. The bullying to which I was subjected approached much nearer to the ideal of Gilbert's

Mikado; it was humorous as well as lingering; it provided a running river of harmless merriment; it was not blind cruelty – and without a shadow of doubt I deserved a good deal of what I got, for I must have been a most objectionable little boy.

What saved me from the fate of the over-bullied was, first, that I learned to camouflage my objectionableness, and, secondly, that the bullying only lasted a year. For at the end of my first year I stayed down in the Fourth for another year, while Anderson and Melville and the others passed up into the Fifths where they tended to forget about me and where it was not so easy to lay hands on me – the day school bully has far fewer opportunities than has the boarding school bully. It is the fact that the school authorities permitted me to stay two years in one form which makes me think that they were aware of my hard lot, for I was always quite high up in the form order, and it was the most certain cure for the ills to which I had been subjected.

The school work, indeed, gave me no trouble at all. In several subjects I was in advance of the syllabus on my arrival, and it was some time before I threw off the careful habits of work which the elementary school cane had instilled into me. I was in the habit of presenting homework done absolutely right – six sums out of six; French translation with every word looked up in the dictionary and every irregular verb checked; it was long before I could reconcile myself to my natural carelessness and laziness, and to presenting work with the bare fifty per cent or so of exactitude which kept one just out of trouble in the new school. And we were well and sympathetically taught by men (and not by fanatics) who had between them somehow evolved a system – or created an atmosphere – in which we absorbed knowledge without any conscious effort on our part, and, I believe, without very much effort on the part of our masters; the standard of teaching must have been very high indeed; every year some forty boys or so used to enter for London University Matriculation, and only two or three of them used to fail – and this without any exasperated goading or prodding or cramming by the masters and most certainly without any really hard work on the part of the boys. The most usual punishment was to be kept in for half an hour after school; an exceptionally severe one was to be kept in for three hours on

Saturday mornings; canings (by the Head Master) were very rare indeed and were never made public. It was with these punishments, extraordinarily mild to a boy who came from the sort of council school where I had spent seven years of my life, that quite good discipline and an extremely high standard of education were maintained.

Chapter Seven

ONE of the most important things about the new school was that it was two miles away from my home in a direction which made it necessary to walk to get there. Every day I walked two miles to school and two miles back again, and when a small boy walks four miles a day with unfailing regularity he is getting a fair part of the exercise he needs; compulsory games and incidental games will see to it that he gets the rest. As a result of this exercise – the cessation of overwork must have had something to do with it too – I began to grow. How I grew! The first words any relative ever addressed to me at that period was 'How you've grown!' Between the ages of twelve (which was when I really began) and sixteen (which was when I left off) I grew from four feet four to six feet – five inches a year on the average for four years. I still have my annual medical inspection slips to prove it.

It made a profound difference to me – as a little boy I was always quarrelsome and violent and ready to fight at the drop of a hat, and I took it for granted that anything anyone told me must be wrong; as a tall boy I grew quite tolerant of other people's opinions and did not think fighting necessary to my dignity. For some odd reason a boy (as well as lots of men) is far more ready to admit that another is his equal – or even his better if necessary – when the former's head is on a level with the latter's head – not with the middle button of his waistcoat.

I gradually came to discard the old ideal one to which I had been striving to attain – a flamboyant, irascible individual on whom everyone's attention must necessarily be fixed – in favour of a new ideal, tall and elegant and idle, who did things supremely well when he felt he wanted to, but always nonchalantly, unobtrusively, and without troubling in the least about his audience or whether he received his due reward for his efforts, and not caring particularly whether he succeeded or failed. The worst faults I could ever find in myself were sincerity and ambition.

But it was a long time, of course, before this ideal crystallised in my mind. The first year at the secondary school I had small leisure for introspection. There was always too much happening.

One of the happiest institutions at the school was the dinner hour football. Immemorial dinner hour tradition divided the school (or rather, the larger proportion of it which stayed at school and brought its dinner with it) into four quarters, the big boys of three houses, the big boys of the other three, and the two corresponding sections of small boys. Each quarter had a football and a football pitch (association football) and played massed games of forty or so a side. Every boy had his dinner in his hand (wrapped, like the one talent in a napkin, for school rules did not allow of paper which might be scattered on the playing fields) and with this in one hand and a sandwich in the other we all raced up and down the field, kicking the ball, charging into each other, and generally letting off steam. Sometimes a well aimed kick or a vigorous charge would send a small shower of sandwiches over the pitch, for which reason we always ate our meal as rapidly as the game would admit, and when we had eaten and our small insides were as full as they could possibly be we would run about all the harder. We must have had magnificent digestions.

Looking back, I am surprised to realise that we eighty or so small boys would play like this quite happily for an hour without disputes or arguments – rules were of course a little elastic, but such as they were they were adhered to without dissension despite the fact that not a soul on the pitch was over fourteen. They were very happy jolly games; but at first their special attraction for me lay in the fact that on the days when rain or the condition of the turf prohibited play my tormentors, with an hour idle on their hands, would proceed to make my life a burden to me. They could not have been true bullies because they would always far rather play football than bully me – which led me at first to scan the weather every morning with intense anxiety.

There is little need for a detailed study of my life at that school. It was the normal ordinary life of a moderately clever boy at a normal ordinary school; the years after the first one were sincerely happy. It is a stock joke, of course, that men always say that their schooldays were the happiest time of their lives, without really meaning it; I would not say so myself, but I can truthfully say that those later years were really happy, with the additional advantage that I was conscious of the fact that I was happy.

Boxing had something to do with it. The school was not specially attentive to boxing, and it was not one of the compulsory games, but a minority of enthusiasts practised assiduously under the nominal supervision of the boozy old sergeant-major (late of the Coldstream). It was a game which appealed emphatically to my temperament; and the heroes of most of my favourite books had been boxers; and the best book Jack London ever wrote was a long description of a prize fight –*The Game*. I can remember even now the little thrill of pleased surprise when I first discovered that the straight left properly used did all that the books and the sergeant-major claimed for it, and left helpless the rushing ugly fighter with a bad style. It was one of that sort whom I first encountered in the ring, with my heart going pit-a-pat with excitement. I do not think I was frightened, but I had no confidence in myself at all; most of my life (save for the one great occasion of the slow-match and the mine) I had found that however great my book knowledge I had never been able to put it effectively into practice. I was sure that I was going to be badly knocked about, and was resigned to it in a hopeless sort of fashion. I shut my eyes when he made his first rush, but instinct of training brought my left hand out in the way it ought to go, straight for his nose. There was a most satisfactory thump, and when I opened my eyes the rush had been nipped in the bud and my opponent was clearly very surprised indeed – more surprised than I was, even. After three or four rushes had been brought to the same sudden end I gave up shutting my eyes; by the end of the round I was leading off with that feeling of superb confidence which comes when one knows that one's opponent is an inferior boxer – a new, magnificent sensation to me. There is joy in hitting a screaming drive down the fairway, and more joy still in coming out one step to a fast bowler and sending the ball, a yard out of reach of cover point's right hand, slipping along to the boundary. There is pleasure in hitting the top of the offstump with a good length ball sent down with just the right amount of break to beat a good batsman. But there is only one joy to compare with the well timed straight left, and that is the mad perverse pleasure of standing up to a better boxer and taking his punches and struggling on despite pain and weakness to the very end.

I won that first bout, of course, and it was a very elated and garrulous small boy who emerged from the ring flushed with the very first victory he had ever won with his own hand and brain; but the next evening I came to know defeat, at the hands of a two-handed boxer, as quick as lightning, who could draw and slip my elementary left hand and could then sail in hitting ferociously with both hands until I wilted away, punched into stupidity – a small boy of the under five stone class cannot knock another out.

Yet I had won a clear, decisive victory in the boxing ring, and it did wonders for me in the way of restoring the self respect which Anderson and company had rather damaged. The new respect with which I was regarded by other small boys (only a small percentage of boys at that school boxed) was grateful, but much more noticeable was the effect upon me. The knowledge that one has proved his worth, and the certainty that one can look after oneself against any reasonable odds is extraordinarily comforting. In later life you can argue with a fighting-drunk man amicably and without qualms and much more effectively when reassured by the solid knowledge that you can always stop him from becoming dangerous, and you feel much more at home when encountering angry crowds or men who meditate robbery with violence. I know this too well, now that I have left thirty behind and am oppressed by the knowledge that my punch has lost its speed and my eye some of its quickness, and that soon I will be shirking such encounters, and selecting with care the railway carriage in which I go home from the races, and going a little out of my way to avoid drunken men.

The boxer's genuine freedom from nerves is a curious phenomenon. The same man who goes into a drawing-room with limbs of water and a heart of lead will climb into the ring, into the glare of the lights and the gabble of the ringside, with as little concern as he would get into his bath. He can win or lose; he can stand up to a ferocious attack, wear down his man while vigilantly ready for a surprise punch, and then knock his man silly, and turn and lift an inquiring eyebrow at the referee without ever feeling in the least out of his element. It is the memory of that peculiarly comfortable state of mind as much as the memory of past victories which gives the boxer a certain desirable poise in unpleasant situations.

Another very powerful influence at school was friendship. I was never accepted without reserve as a perfectly sane individual, perhaps, but there were a dozen or so good fellows who welcomed me wholeheartedly into their circle after my first year. Those friendships have endured to this day, and from their very beginning they were simply delicious to a child who had felt like a fish out of water – like a white blackbird would be a better simile – during eight or nine years of school life. It was glorious to have friends who would back you up through any trouble you might encounter, and with whom one might gossip and argue during the summer days. Very serious our conversations were – on our side of the school the subjects of study were largely scientific, and so were the subjects we discussed; God, and the reasons for and against believing in His existence; what it is which lies outside everything (those were days before Einstein's work had become a popular study and we used to talk ourselves weak over the terrifying question of where space ends); the distinction between dead and living matter and the possible existence of a vital element; the evolution of the *Dreadnought* and the likely course of the European war which we accepted as inevitable. Rather priggish were those conversations, but by the necessity of finding support for our arguments we were driven into odd studies for thirteen year olds – Haeckel and Nietzsche and the rather outmoded people like Max Müller whom we could hunt up in the public libraries.

Our hobbies were grave and scientific too – we made a half inch spark coil one year, an operation calling for the careful and accurate winding of about three miles of wire, and we designed and built a model electric motorboat which unfortunately sank on its trial trip before it could demonstrate to the world its unutterable superiority over all other existing boats. We rather ran to electricity for some reason or other – we were always having accumulators charged, fifteen years before the popularisation of wireless telephony made the charging of accumulators commonplace.

Yet we had some redeeming characteristics. In those days Green Lane, Dulwich, really was a lane – we walked along it twice a day to and from school – and down one side ran a little stream, brown with iron, one of the mineral springs which once nearly made the district a popular watering place. To dam that ditch was a usual pastime; as the water banked up behind the dam, and threatened to turn its flank, we would extend it feverishly at each end, scrabbling up mud with our hands to fill the interstices between the stones, and growing magnificently wet and muddy in the process. We were all of us boxers, mostly champions of the school at various weights, and we carried side enough in consequence to have outfitted an international team. I can remember how we used to elbow our way with superb insolence through the crowds of lesser fry at school, caps on one side, hands in our pockets, and none dared say us nay. We exploited our exalted position with all the overbearing haughtiness of medieval potentates. We bullied ruthlessly when we considered our prestige demanded it – the self-same railings which saw me 'racked' as a pitiful small boy were now often adorned by my own writhing victims.

We discovered a sensuous pleasure in smacking boys' heads with thin exercise books. It had to be the right kind of head – a rounded one, rather close cropped; I was as fussy then about the shape of the head I smacked as I am nowadays about the temperature of my Burgundy. The half dozen individuals in our class whose heads conformed nearest to the ideal had a harassing time while the craze lasted. Their heads were slapped with exercise books every possible moment; not a particularly painful ordeal, but an annoying one when maintained for weeks on end. The finest head in the whole collection occupied the desk in front of mine, a beautiful spherical head with cropped fair hair – Maynard, its owner's name was; he was a bovine, overgrown individual – and during the tedium of lessons I would feel the old itch in my fingers just as a dramdrinker feels the old thirst in his throat, and I would surreptitiously take hold of my Blue English Essay Book, or my Mottled Physics

51

Note Book, and brace myself ready for an opportunity until the master's attention was distracted, and then – slam! Instantly putting down the book I would be as innocent in appearance as the rest of the form, my craving temporarily satisfied. No one, save of course masters (who were not consulted) dared dispute our right to slap any head we chose even at a time when we were very junior members of the school, and we swaggered along the primrose path with an arrogance which would have suited half a dozen Charlemagnes or Kings of Dahomey.

Our precious dignity was liable all the same to nasty shocks occasionally. When all was said and done, masters and prefects when sufficiently roused could call up a weight of authority which no one could withstand. We were always in some disciplinary trouble or other, which is hardly surprising. Those days when the state of the weather prohibited dinner-time football were usually fatal. Half a dozen high-stomached louts with a whole hour idle on their hands are absolutely certain to get into mischief. There was the day when we discovered that an inconspicuous manhole in a secluded corner of the playing fields led by a long iron ladder down to a most amazing sewer some forty feet below; further, that sewer, when one had the courage (and strength of stomach) to brave its noisome dark-ness led for a long way underground (bent double, we could just proceed along it with one foot on each side of the channel) to another manhole in a street far from the school. The police stopped our exploitation of this highly convenient back door, and the school authorities backed them up. For our benefit a new punishment was invented. Every dinner-time we had to sally forth to the playing fields carrying each a wastepaper basket as a badge of shame, under orders not to return until we had filled them with the paper which even the strictest of school rules could not prevent being scattered in small quantity over the playing fields. It was an effective punishment until some ingenious mind realised that a small boy's pockets could be crammed with paper in the morning before leaving home, and that paper, well fluffed out, sufficed to fill a wastepaper basket in two minutes, leaving a precious remainder of fifty-eight minutes of leisure for good or evil – usually evil of course.

The sin of which we were most usually guilty was that of libel. To my doubtless distorted memory we were always starting unofficial school magazines, hectographically reproduced, which sold like hot cakes as long as they lasted. To fill their pages recourse was had, inevitably, to personalities of a pungent kind, which was all very well as long as only schoolboys were mentioned, but caused no end of trouble when we began to refer to masters. Inevitably a copy would reach our arch-enemies' hands. More than once boys who ate the school dinner in the dining-hall would emerge with the joyous news that they had seen a copy of the last number passed from master to master at the high table – not reaching those masters whom we had more grossly libelled until the end. Then there would be half an hour of suspense before afternoon school began, and then, in first period, the school porter would arrive with the expected summons to the head master, or an infuriated committee of the libelled staff would descend upon us showering punishments like rain, and extorting reluctant apologies and promises of reform from us under threat of otherwise insisting on our expulsion.

But somehow crises of that sort were welcome in a perverse sort of way. I verily believe that as we progressed up the school and wearied of our placid existence we went out of our way to make trouble for ourselves. The unassailability of our united strength tended towards peace – no one would willingly make war on us – and peace bored us inexpressibly. We made horrid nuisances of ourselves. Suggestions were taken up with alacrity. We soon found that a little ferrous sulphide dropped into inkwells, and just a drop or two of hydrochloric acid poured on top, roused such a stench of sulphuretted hydrogen as to make any classroom uninhabitable, and to cause indignant messages to be sent (usually by the mouth of one of those responsible) to the chemistry laboratories asking whether the master there would be kind enough to limit the enthusiasm of his class – usually to the complete bewilderment of that individual, who was probably supervising a series of perfectly odourless experiments in Titration or the Proportionate Loss in Weight of Mercuric Oxide when Heated.

It was amusing, though not specially dangerous, to smear the merest trace of cycle oil on the blackboard so that writing upon it became impossible; it was always a good joke to conceal a parcel of fish far within the desk of some boy who was absent through illness – we had the floorboards taken up on one occasion before the origin of the stench was discovered; it was splendid fun to get at every single French text book the form possessed and tear out of each the page we were to study in our next lesson. Notions of this sort came as a welcome change from the minor trivial round of annoying masters with musical instruments made from pen-nibs, and sticking boys to their seats with liquid glue, or passing round notes saying 'At 3.15 *exactly* everyone blow their noses' – the latter is an idea quite to be recommended, as puzzling to the master in charge and quite spectacular in execution. The ideas I personally contributed were usually the more involved ones which called for some expenditure of money – the fish idea was mine. One term, with remarkable pertinacity, we managed to smear the classroom door handle with liquid glue immediately before every entrance of one particular master we disliked; it was during that term that he acquired the mannerism (which I believe he still displays) of continually wiping his hands with his handkerchief. The brute had sworn that he would teach me tidiness and good handwriting, and kept me in every blessed evening for a quarter of an hour for months to do copy book writing, so that on matchdays I had to put on my games clothes under my others and rush down to the playing fields peeling off my outer garments as I ran, for matches began a quarter of an hour after afternoon school.

The money for these pastimes of ours – for the purchase of fish and liquid glue and accumulators – we used for the most part to obtain at the expense of our stomachs. Most of us found it easy to compound with our parents to be given money (sixpence a day was my allowance) in lieu of sandwiches. Nominally the money was to be spent in the Buttery – the school tuckshop – and we would always solemnly assure our credulous parents that we would not buy useless things like chocolate cream or ginger beer. Nor did we, save when our grosser appetites overcame us – we rarely spent very much in the Buttery, having much more important things to do with our money. Often and often I (and others too) have left home at eight fifteen in the morning, walked two miles to school, done something resembling a day's work there, played a dinner hour football game, and a serious match in the evening, and then walked home again long after six without having eaten anything at all since breakfast at seven-thirty. But it never did me any harm at all – my physical development was remarkably rapid.

School work occupied as small a part in our interests as it had done in these last few pages. We learned a good deal, being well taught, but we worked as little as we possibly could. I think that our attitude towards work was that any fool could do it, but it took a clever chap to avoid it. Not to do any homework at all – we had three moderate portions set us every evening – meant living dangerously in the way which was our ideal; besides, it had the advantage of leaving us our evenings free for other amusements. It was an ideal hard of attainment, for the well-worn lies about having left one's book at home or about being prevented from working by a sudden attack of illness which left no trace next day and was not accounted for by a parental note could not be repeated week in, week out, for a period of years, and they were best reserved for the more desperate emergencies. But the ideal to which we could attain was never to do any work in time which could be devoted to more interesting pursuits, and to maintain things even on that level meant a continuous excitement sufficient to satisfy the most fire-eating schoolboy. Twenty lines of Shakespeare to learn by heart was nothing – you could do that while walking to school. A page of Virgil or Ovid to prepare for construing was also easily managed; you got that up while standing about in the bustle of the cloakrooms during the five minutes before school, and could apply the finishing touches during prayers, holding the book as though it were a hymn book.

It was the writing subjects which offered a difficulty. If an essay had to be handed in at second lesson it meant much excitement to have to write it during first lesson, which might be Trigonometry or Physics; and during the second lesson, while the essays were being debated, or the difference between a simile and a metaphor explained, it would be necessary to draw ready for the third lesson an Isothermal map of Asia in colours, or something – a most horribly difficult achievement, however cunning one might be at piling the front of the desk up with books to conceal exactly what you were up to. Some masters had the pleasing habit of working through last night's home-work on the blackboard before collecting up the books. That was perfectly splendid, because you could simply write it up as he did it, and hand in perfectly magnificent work for that subject as a counter balance for the scamped, untidy work handed in for the others. It made no difference if the master told everyone to change books with his neighbour before starting – the master does not live who can see that every boy in a class of thirty really does exchange books.

Every master's habits and whims were studied with an attention which would have surprised him if he knew of it. Those of a garrulous habit or possessed with enthusiasm for their subject could sometimes be led astray by a tactful question or two just at the moment when he was intending to ask for the homework so that this last vital matter would slip from his memory. The class team work in this respect was astonishing; the instant the master stopped to sniff at the trail of the red herring everyone would join in to halloo him on with an apparent interest which was obviously and pathetically gratifying to him.

I really do not think that it was sheer laziness which inspired us to go to all this trouble. It was much more likely that we looked on avoiding work as a game, masters versus boys, so to speak. You scored a point if you only did your homework when it suited you; the master scored a point if he caught you out. A run of luck might enable you to go for weeks without ever opening a school book out of school hours, and take you to the top of the averages, in a manner of speaking; on the other hand, you might experience a run of bad luck which would land you in hot water for weeks together – I can remember a period when for half a term I was never out of punishment school.

The year I was in the Fifths was marked by a succession of pleasing interludes which was a great help in keeping me out of this sort of trouble. For a couple of terms I was periodically absent for a day or two every fortnight or so, which meant that after each absence I could turn up at school with no homework done and no excuse needed and a resultant clean sheet which it would take a week or two to dirty again. What I was doing was hunting scholarships at the larger public schools. I realise now that it was rather a hopeless task, for those scholarships are tried for by the very pick and cream of the preparatory schools, trained all their young lives solely for this purpose. For the past two or three years I had been spending most of my time on subjects which, while destined to be ultimately useful, were no more good to me than a sick headache at Public School scholarship examination – things like Chemistry, and Electricity, and Mechanics, while on the other hand the examinations most needed a scholar's knowledge of Latin. The prep school competitors had of course been taught Latin for the last seven years or so, and had been coached by masters who had devoted a lifetime to the study and dissection of examination papers.

Yet I had a few scholarships offered me – Rossall offered me forty pounds a year, Charterhouse twenty, and so on; I was never successful however in obtaining one of the big scholarships which I would have accepted – my father's means were never sufficiently in advance of his expenses at that time to justify his laying out two hundred a year or so on his youngest child. My Latin was only good enough to enable me to struggle through an examination paper with difficulty; my Greek – not part of the school curriculum and only taught me in spasms after school by a kindly master – was not of that standard. My strong suits were the ability to write a competent essay and an extensive knowledge of classical history and mythology derived from a diligent study of Gibbon and Lemprière and Bury and Mommsen and such-like favourite reading at that time. Examinations which included a paper on ancient history were the ones which offered me most chance of success; and I remember that one of the essays was on 'Your Favourite Character in History', and I chose Hamilcar Barca in all sincerity. He was the father of the much more famous Hannibal, but it would puzzle me now to write a dozen lines about him; in those days I covered two pages of foolscap with ease. What I cannot picture is the feelings of the examiner, who after reading essays (I suppose) about General Gordon or King Harold or Nelson suddenly had his eyes gladdened by the sight of an essay on Hamilcar. I cannot help thinking that I am the only scholarship candidate who ever wrote an essay on Hamilcar Barca of his own free will.

The end of all this scholarship hunting was curious, and dates from prize day that year at school. I had already been up to the dais for my prizes, and shaken hands with whatever major general or viscount was presenting them, and bowed to the assembled parents in the hall, and had returned to the side of my own gang tucked away in an obscure corner. Then, just when I had burrowed comfortably in among them to doze through the concluding speeches, my name was read out again – in what connection I did not catch, but the Major General was clearly waiting for me. I struggled out through the press (the mischievous blighters hung on to my coat tails and held out legs for me to trip over) and scuttled up to the platform again, recalling my prize drill as well as I might – shake hands, turn and bow, walk off right. It was an envelope addressed to my father which the Major General gave me, and I took it home rather puzzled and quite ignorant of the contents. My father opened it – he had reached home on leave only half an hour before my return – and was amazingly pleased. The school was offering me a spontaneous sort of scholarship, free tuition for two years more if only I would stay there.

I must apologise for having devoted such length to such a trivial subject, but the incident looms large in my mind because it was the very last scholastic achievement of which I could ever boast. Beyond scraping through a few examinations I have never since accomplished anything in the least noteworthy. Incidentally, it may be worth mentioning that the next four termly reports which arrived contained the threat that 'If his conduct and work do not improve it may be found necessary to terminate his scholarship.' The school seemed to regret having made its generous offer within three months of making it – and remembering my behaviour I am not in the least surprised.

Chapter Eight

WHILE all this was going on there was another side of me developing. It is inevitable that I should have to mention it, but it is not going to be too easy. After a very retarded physical development as a child I suddenly began to change with startling rapidity. I have already mentioned my rapid growth in physique; my sexual development was much more rapid than that. In six months (I can date it quite accurately) just before I reached fourteen everything happened to me at once. My voice broke and I began to part my hair carefully, and I grew fussy about my appearance, and I began to admit that feminine society was at any rate desirable, and my day dreams took on a new complexion. At thirteen I looked an undeveloped eleven; at fourteen people who did not know me took me for eighteen.

It is agonisingly painful to look back at that period, not because it was painful at the time (on the contrary, I was very happy) but because I realise now how very fourteenish I must have been. The girls who condescended to notice my existence were by my untamed imagination instantly regarded as paragons of beauty and perfection. I could spend hours debating with myself whether half a dozen chance words addressed to me meant this or that or the other thing. To receive a voluntary kiss from a girl would be the grandest, most superb experience any mortal could ever hope for – something wonderful happened when a girl kissed you; you were both of you filled with a new divine flame and the world was not the same place afterwards – I can remember the dull disappointment which followed the first dozen experiments or so when I gradually came to realise that my belief was unfounded; I cannot think how I ever came to form the theory.

Nowadays there was much more motive not to do homework in the evenings; evenings were much too important for anything so trifling. No sooner had I reached home from school than the most meticulous preparations had to be made. The new suit had to be brushed, and the trousers extracted from under the mattress. My hair had to be lovingly oiled, and my reflection anxiously scrutinised to see if the handsome good looks I awaited had arrived. I had to choose which of various horrible ties I would wear, and which coloured handkerchief would most fittingly protrude from my breast pocket, and which pair of socks would best complete the ensemble. Then, dressed in as outrageous a parody of prevailing fashion as a fourteen year old mind can conceive, I would sally forth flourishing my walking stick in search of women.

But this horrifying picture must be modified a little; I was not quite the completely hateful little boy one might believe. The funny little streak of idealism which had made itself apparent can be pleaded in my favour. I did not flaunt my ties and handkerchiefs in the park to attract the notice of fast little schoolgirls or of vulgar minded little shop assistants. My geese were all swans. The girls whose acquaintance I made were all of them queens of beauty and refinement. Blotchy complexions and doubtful fingernails went quite unnoticed; so even did Cockney accents and dropped H's. I honestly believed that the girls with whom I walked in park or street were quite as lovely and desirable as Diana of the Crossways, and it was an adorable trait in their characters that they could not understand what I was talking about when I made the comparison.

The plainest, vulgarest, most uneducated little wench who ever made eyes at a boy by the bandstand was to my mind the personification of everything beautiful and good, and, what is more, I treated her as though she was. Time and time again I have sent girls into shouts of laughter by my formal way of treating them and by my courtly manners towards them. They were nearly all of them of the type who considers it very funny when a young man offers her his arm for assistance in dismounting from a tram. I missed the point of a good many conversations, because I was most blandly ignorant of the argot of sexual relations – I did not even know there was such an argot and if anyone had told me so I would have refused to believe that people of opposite sexes could speak like that to each other. I had an encyclopaedic knowledge of what Caligula said and did to his mistresses, but I had not the least notion of what male shop assistants said and did to female shop assistants in dark alleyways. And I had such formal, courtly, stand-offish manners that it was a long time before anyone tried to show me, either. It was only rarely that I got as far as kisses, even, and they were such clumsy, unpractised, shy, botched, bungled affairs that they left unmarred the serene surface of my innocence.

I wrote poetry for them, too, high falutin bits of verse full of extravagant flights of metaphor far exceeding the worst excesses of the Caroline school, and I would quote Ovid to them, and Swinburne. Sometimes they would laugh, and sometimes they would lapse into astonished silence, but it never stimulated them into making the replies, full of lofty sentiment, in the interchange of which I firmly believed the 'love' I yearned for to consist. For I thought that two people 'in love' spent their time in telling each other in the most far-fetched language what magnificent thoughts and emotions they experienced. I knew, and had known for years, that they did other things as well, but I did not believe it when it came to a pinch. I suppose I spent a couple of years looking unsuccessfully for a love of this kind; there was a feeling of dull disappointment noticeable occasionally, but I continually resumed the quest with new hope. The mental picture which it hurts me most to recall shows me, a spectacled fourteen year old in some dark back street kissing tenderly just once the hand of some astonished shop girl (who had believed me to be eighteen at least) and quoting passionately 'Nothing is better, I well think, than love. The hidden well-water—' Even nowadays I feel an uncomfortable, guilty sensation when I read about the love of Don Quixote for Dulcinea del Toboso – it reflects with such excruciating exactitude my feelings of seventeen years ago.

The bloom wore off in course of time, as is only to be expected and regretted. To begin with, the tall, elegant, languid, unexpectedly efficient ideal me who grew up in my mind's eye could not be expected to maintain such wild flights of idealism. A weary satiated cynicism was all that he could possibly rise to, and therefore, all I could allow myself to rise to, either. My experience (is it a usual one? I cannot think of any proverb which bears me out, although I feel there must be one) was that a man who adopts a cynical outlook on life soon finds plenty enough to be cynical about. It was not very long before I formulated a new theory, which my embittered restlessness drove me to try and confirm on every possible occasion, that every woman's virtue is suspect, and that no woman can withstand indefinitely a properly conducted siege. For a time it was a new hobby, a new sort of game which one played, and in which it was only natural that one should do one's best to succeed, but when in the end that aspect of it lost its freshness there was only bitterness and unhappiness left. But by the time that period was reached, which joined with many other circumstances to make one period of my life the most acutely unhappy I can ever remember, so many other things had happened that I must go back again and try to bring up to date all the other influences which were at work.

Chapter Nine

THE school at that time had no officers' training corps; that was
to come later. In those days we used to do military drill, all the
same. The six houses of eighty boys each used to form six
companies of the old fashioned small size; the rank and file
doubled with wooden guns; the Captain of each house and his
two assistant prefects were *ex officio* officers with single sticks
instead of swords, and we would drill weekly on the playing
fields under the tuition of the sergeant major, working up
gradually from simple company movements to all the refine-
ments of open order and tactical formations as understood in
those days, a dozen years after the close of the South African
War. Yearly there would be a grand review and inspection
under the eye of the headmaster, who invariably deputised for
someone who came to be known among us as 'The-Man-from-
the-War-Office-who-never-turns-up'. There was an extremely
well managed miniature rifle range, and the school record for
shooting stood rather high. Every summer there was an annual
camp for a week or so at Bisley, open to all over fourteen, at
which I suppose the boys had a little more discipline rubbed
into them and where they had a chance of shooting with service
rifles over long ranges and in events like the Ashburton Shield.
I cannot describe those annual camps, because I never attended
one for a reason apparent in the next paragraph.

The year I became fourteen I sent in my name, my kitbag
was packed, and early on the first Saturday in August I went
up to parade with the others at Waterloo Station. I met my
friend; we stood about; and then suddenly arrived the master
(Reserve of Officers) who was to take charge of us. He showed
us the telegram he had just received. 'Mobilisation ordered.
Bisley Camp cancelled.' And that was that; there was nothing

to do save to take my kitbag home again to where my family were presumably heaving sighs of relief at being quit of me for ten days.

Things happened with a rush. The brother who was a Territorial officer suddenly turned up from the camp whither he had just gone with his regiment. All the glittering trappings of pre-1914 war were put away; the wonderful uniforms, all fur and feathers and braid; the gleaming cross belt with its dangling silver chains and silver lions' heads; the tight trousers, with the strap under the foot, to emerge from which (especially after an evening in the mess) called for the assistance of a young brother; the plumed busby and the high patent leather boots were all thrust away to moulder in their tin cases the while we combed the local shops for things of new importance such as pocket knives with a tin opener attached, and whistles and field glasses, which had all become extraordinarily rare and which were needed urgently to complete mobilisation equipment. Those hours of violent rushing about saw my brother properly outfitted, and he was off with his Regiment to defend the East Coast against the invasion which people so unreasonably expected. We – the family – expected no such thing. We had worked out too many strategical problems between us, and had conducted too many paper campaigns, to expect Germany to throw good troops away in an invasion without holding the command of the sea; we had always hooted in derision at such books as William le Queux's *The Invasion*, and Childers' *Riddle of the Sands* because of the unnatural way in which the authors dodged the all important impediment of the British Fleet. And I, who had read naval histories in dozens, was one of the few who felt no surprise when it was discovered that the German Navy had no intention of coming out to meet destruction, and that the hardest naval problem to solve would be how to induce it to do so. I had always experienced a sense of amused superiority when reading the grotesque naval strategy outlined in the opening chapters of H. G. Wells' *In the Days of the Comet*.

All the pleasurable bustle of excitement was severely chilled when my father, in reply to my statement that 'people are fighting for newspapers in the streets', threw out the suggestion that 'Perhaps they'll be fighting there for bread soon, son.'

Then came the expected telegram cancelling my father's leave and ordering him to resume his duties in Egypt at once. My mother wept; my father, whose gear had been packed ready hours before, went off within half an hour, and I was left behind to be the man of the house, with a mother and two sisters and a maid to look after – not that any of them needed much looking after except possibly the maid, and I did not look on that as any part of my business.

For a year the war did not make much difference. Life at school went on the same old way. The doctor-brother turned up from the tropics for a few fleeting days before receiving his commission and being promptly sent out to the tropics again. At other schools, I believe the boys used to vie with each other in the matter of relations on active service; nothing of the sort happened in my set at least – if it had I suppose I would have taken high rank with a father who was a Bimbashi (a lovely title that) and two brothers who were Captains and innumerable cousins who were all soldiers, many of them since before the war. There were a few gaps in the staff at school, soon to be filled up with medically unfit and over age. But on the whole things were surprisingly little changed. No one doubted that victory was certain, in three months at first, and later, grudgingly 'next year anyway'. No one thought it at all possible that boys of fourteen when the war broke out would be in the ranks before it ended. No one doubted the justice of England's cause, and no one was in the least surprised that the war should have come. The course of military operations became obscure but remained, in everyone's opinion, quite promising. At first things had been easy. The more intelligent were able to guess from newspaper reports the main features of the German strategic deployment and the march on Paris, and reconstruct the position at the Marne and even at first Ypres. After that it was more difficult. The hypocritical among us found it hard to form a working idea of battles like St Eloi, and Festubert, and (some time later) Loos. We honestly believed the newspapers which spoke of these battles with a string of superlatives as great victories and as we could not reconcile those superlatives with any obvious results we most of us, at that time, came to think that there was something lacking in our mental capacity and military education and went on believing the newspapers and doubting ourselves. We remained happy and confident, and proceeded along our allotted ways without misgivings.

At the end of that school year we all took in our stride the examination which was the climax, to most of us, of our school careers – the Matriculation Examination of the University of London. I passed it, of course, with high distinction; it would have been astonishing if I had not, seeing how excellently I had been educated all my life. People were not expected to fail Matriculation from that school, and did not, either. At that time I took it perfectly for granted that I should never fail an examination, and to pass gave me no pleasurable thrill at all. That I should gain distinctions in such widely assorted subjects as chemistry and Latin and English and Mechanics was to me something just as inevitable as the arrival of next Christmas.

But at the same time Matriculation was the signal for a general upheaval. We moved at last from the little street in Camberwell where I had spent all my life in England. It had been a street of the highest respectability when we arrived there, but it was only a little better than a slum when we left. Ours was the only house which still contained only one family – the neighbourhood had 'gone down' as people said – and for years we had been on the point of moving, only postponing the inevitable from year to year because it had been decided that my mother and sisters were to join my father in Egypt, where the sisters were, presumably, to catch husbands, as soon as the sisters' schooldays were completed and I could be left in a bachelor flat with my brother. The war had definitely ended that scheme, however; no one would deliberately take women to Egypt, and the brother I was to share a flat with was now inhabiting a dugout in France; so we shook the dust of Camberwell from our feet and went off to a much more pleasant suburb, a district of open spaces and masses of trees, where the streets did not consist of long blocks of little houses each like its neighbour.

That was the first upheaval; secondly, I left the school. It was a bit of a wrench, for I was fond of the place, fond of my friends, fond of the pleasant routine of it all, and were I to stay on I would enjoy many more of the school dignities which were just beginning to come my way. They have made a Public

School of it now, with compulsory Greek and corporal punishment and all the rest of it, and I am sorry – but there I am over thirty now, and naturally among the ranks of those to whom any change from the conditions prevailing when I was young is complete anathema.

Instead, I was to go to a Public School, a Real school. It was most unusual that such a school should admit a new scholar who was nearly sixteen, and who had already matriculated, but it was agreed upon as the result of a special arrangement – most of my education was the subject of special arrangement, it appeared to me. It was a very complete change of conditions to me – to move a boy from a secondary school to a public school makes quite as great a change as to move an adult from England to France, let us say. My father appreciated the fact, but his canny idea (an extremely good one too) was that having had the best education to be found in England (which is at a good secondary school, beyond any doubt) I should have the further advantages given to me which only a Public School could provide.

I had a new language to learn, and new conventions, just as if I were in a foreign country. At the new school boys did not take off their caps at the threshold (as I had always seen done) but wore them inside and in the classrooms, only taking them off when a master came into the room. Although bicycles were tolerated, *faute de mieux* (motor bicycles had just been banned) convention decreed that they must be tall, heavy, inefficient machines with raised handlebars – a convention which exists to this day, one of the few which I cannot understand or sympathise with. I was the only boy out of eight hundred or so who used a light bicycle at school, although there were two or three daring spirits who kept similar ones concealed at home for use on holidays and other occasions when the school could not know of it. Paper and books, and lavatories and science and masters and money and trousers and girls all were known by names quite new to me. There were new conventions regarding singing hymns at morning prayers, and addressing or encountering 'bloods' and the tieing of one's necktie, and the mention of one's parents, and one's attitude towards coloured boys. Many of the school rules were enforced not by Authority, but by the boys themselves, and it was the boys who decided

67

whether other rules should be observed at all. Soon after my arrival the Master (that was his title, not 'Headmaster') issued a decree, that in future boys might wear soft collars – mounting laundry costs and a shortage of starch had done their work. But in all the time I was there I never saw a soft collar worn. Public opinion decided against soft collars, and public opinion saw to it that they were not worn. It would have needed the example of a blood of the deepest dye, a man with at least cricket and football colours, before anyone there dared to make a move in the matter.

Boys shrank from doing certain things for fear of being deemed 'brickies' (I do not know how it is spelt, but it means someone who does things which other people do not) while they shrank from doing others for fear of being thought 'sidey'. It was utterly taboo to discuss whether one's parents were wealthy or not, but it was quite permissible to discuss their profession or rank in society. To have a father who was a peer or a general or even a J.P. was an advantage one made the most of (it was very nice for me that I could display a photograph of my father in a tunic adorned with a crown and two stars and the ribbons of various orders) while the sons of tradespeople (large shop-keepers' sons and wholesalers' sons were fairly common) were made to feel sorry for it even at the time when they were being envied for their athletic prowess; but contrariwise the absence of social eminence could be compensated for, oddly enough, by the possession of the right kind of motor-car. To own a Rolls-Royce put a boy's father on the footing, of, say, a Rear Admiral even if he were only a linendraper; one Daimler was worth two doctors, so to speak, especially if you could prove that you were allowed to drive yourself. It was better to disclaim all ownership of a motor-car than admit the existence of a family Ford – a very 'bricky' one that, if ever there was one. I do not know whether nowadays, with ten times as many motor-cars in use, the same subtle grading persists. I expect it does.

Allied to the very desirable convention that money affairs should not be discussed (I wonder whether that still endures?) went an extensive use of credit and a sublime disregard for expense. As in all boarding schools, the school shop existed for the purpose of supplying the boys with whatever they might happen to need – foolscap paper, and text books, and flannel trousers, and chemistry apparatus, and colours caps, and neckties, and pencils, and so on. One had only to visit the shop to obtain what one needed, and at the end of the term the bill came in to one's father.

A single term's experience horrified me; by that time I was living on an allowance from my father which was destined to cover in one sum all my fees and expenses and pocket money, and the bigger the expenses the less the pocket money, and vice versa. The arrival of the first bill brought bankruptcy horribly near – it is amazing how much a boy can spend when he never asks the price, is charged school shop prices, and buys every single thing it occurs to him he may possibly need. After that I decided to do my shopping where cut prices were to be found, and I developed a habit (which everyone else found odd) of asking how much things cost whenever special circumstances demanded a visit to the school shop, and of making a note of how much I was spending. For I was very dependent on my own exertions at the time, with my father and brothers all overseas and inaccessible; I had had to enter myself at that school, and pay my own fees, and budget for my own holidays, which, for some curious reason which I cannot understand but with which I fully sympathised even at the time was held vaguely to my discredit. It was unusual, and therefore suspect.

But there were a few glorious occasions when it was neither 'sidey' nor 'bricky' to be unusual; when the fortunate privileged ones did their level best to be as unusual as possible. A school rule permitted boys playing for the Fifteen or the Eleven to appear at school on the morning of an away match in clothing other than the regulation black coat and grey trousers. Those who could take advantage of this rule did so to the utmost limit. I had a marvellous silver grey suit with a mauve stripe for these occasions; the team slogger, I remember, used to appear in an adorable creation of pale purple, and with bowler hats and canes and yellow gloves and fiery socks we all used to make sure that no one could possibly miss the fact that we were *not* in school clothing, and we could parade the courtyard before morning school with the pomp and circumstance of so many Rajahs.

Privileges of this class were sought after most intently.

Everyone yearned to wear the insignias of rank. There was a different kind of tie and hatband for each of the three Elevens and the three Fifteens; for Prefects and for the Sixth; for the First Shooting Eight, and the Second Shooting Eight; for the Gymnasium Six and the Boxing Team; the Fives Team and, I suppose (but I will not vouch for it), for the Class Eight. Wherever the bloods assembled were to be seen the most bewildering assortment of striped ties and barred caps – it took a year or two to learn the significance of every combination of stripes and bars. It was not done to wear one distinctive hatband with another sort of tie – the fortunate possessor of two different 'colours' had to plan out his attire on rising in the morning to ensure uniformity. Yet at the same time the man who had been given his colours had to wear the appropriate tie; to wear a plain tie when another sort was at one's disposal was either 'bricky' or 'sidey' (I forget which) just as in the army a man who neither moves nor speaks when told off by a sergeant can be caught out as guilty of 'dumb insolence'.

In the 'buttery' (the same blessed word was in use here as in my previous school) at the eleven o'clock break the lordly ones would lounge against the counter admired of all beholders – I was a lonely one for weeks without knowing it. The ideal refreshment at eleven o'clock (but sometimes even lordly ones could not afford it) was a hot bun, fresh from the oven, into which were stuck two sticks of milk chocolate. The fiery interior of the bun reduced the chocolate to a desirable viscosity, and then this delectable combination of warm new bun and melting chocolate was washed down with a lemonade with a strawberry ice in it. But it called for ample pocket money to stand the strain of this slight refreshment every morning of the term; our funds always used to give way before our digestions did.

Violence ruled in a way which astonished me on my arrival. I was quite used to seeing small boys dragged away from the buttery counter by big ones anxious to be served, and to seeing small boys kicked or their heads smacked merely because they happened to be within kicking or smacking distance. I did that sort of thing myself. But I was frankly startled to see a small boy dragged out of a lavatory before he had finished using it because a big boy was in a hurry and all the others were engaged. And the thing that amazed me more than anything else was to find that the boys beat each other, and with what frequency. Everyone seemed to be beaten at some time or other; one kind of offence called for the use of a cane, another kind for an O.T.C. swagger stick. Small boys beat each other, big boys beat small boys, and big boys beat each other as well, and the masters joined in when necessary. Any offence, from cutting football practice to acting in a sidey manner, called for this form of punishment. What I found hardest to understand about it was the casual way in which it was regarded. Boys put up with the indignity of this kind of punishment without any misgivings at all, would put themselves into grotesque attitudes for the purpose at the word of command, and would joke about it afterwards. They never thought it humiliating; I used to believe in those days that if ever I had been deemed liable to punishment in that way I would never have endured it, and would have fought to my last breath against it. But I do not think now that I would have done. I would have submitted as a child in the way the other children did, and thought as lightly of it. Whether it would have done me any good (or any harm) is more than I can say; and I am more doubtful as to whether it did the wielders of the cane any good at all. There always used to run in my mind when witnessing an execution the famous words no less a man than Wellington used to a Royal Commission, to the effect that he doubted whether any soldier in the British army could be made to do his duty save by the fear of immediate corporal punishment. Wellington was wrong; it is at least possible that the advocates of corporal punishment in our public schools are just as wrong, and that a hundred years hence small boys will remain ignorant of the appearance and sensation of a bleeding posterior, and big boys will not vie with each other for the reputation of inflicting the most pain per unit of six strokes.

I was a rather detached spectator of the customs and habits of the school, for I arrived there so late, and was placed, on my arrival, in the serene Olympics of the Sixth – and the Sixth (Science), a most select body, at that – from which I could look down on the troubles of lesser mortals with a coolness and a disinterestedness not particularly usual. The first month after my arrival was marked by the explosion of a frightful scandal;

71

two day-girls at a neighbouring school were suddenly found to be pregnant and were being put through a ferocious cross-examination by parents and mistresses and clergymen and police. I believe they maintained silence very pluckily indeed for a few days, but remorseless questioning broke them down by degrees. Every day or so some fresh name would be dragged from them. Then more girls would hurriedly be called from their classes and put through the same ordeal, and the circle widened steadily, so that every morning a fresh bulletin arrived at my school, and the school porter would appear in the form rooms with a message to the effect that the Master would like to see Mr So-and-so and Mr So-and-so at once in his study. They would go, without alacrity, stuffing caps into the seats of their trousers in case it might be of some avail; some of them we never saw again – they were expelled. It was a time of dreadful agony of mind for a good many of the older boys, who moped about all day long wondering whether or not their names would appear in the affair, and what their lot would be if they did. The business was one of those scandals which crop up regularly in schools and apparently shake them to their foundations, and are marked by half a dozen expulsions, much wild gossip, a guarded paragraph or two in the newspapers, and then silence and oblivion.

For me, speaking coldbloodedly, it was an interesting experience, if only for the fact that for once I was witnessing a first class school row without being in any way involved – a most unusual occurrence. I was able to some extent to find interest in the reactions of the guilty ones – both the convicted ones and the others – but I missed the full savour of it because as a newcomer I did not realise the almost godlike divinity of the boys involved, captains of this and captains of that (what girl with any knowledge of the school hierarchy would give her favours to anyone below the Second Fifteen?) so that I was unaware that the excitement in the school could only be compared with the extent of the public interest if half a dozen royal dukes were suddenly prosecuted for high treason.

I kept out of trouble at that school with very little difficulty, partly because of the ample privileges attached to my position therein, and partly because this was the period of the fine flowering of my languid-cynical phase. It was not merely too

72

much trouble but it was too undignified to make oneself actively unpleasant to anyone. The boys with whom I mixed received me guardedly enough at first. I was a newcomer from a secondary school, and as usual I was clearly to be suspected of all sorts of brickyishness (a clumsy sort of noun, but the best I can contrive to convey my meaning) and the fact that I had matriculated at fifteen while most of them had failed at sixteen or seventeen was positively insulting. But a variety of circumstances conspired to make it obviously difficult for them to show their disapproval actively, so that I was left alone. Then it appeared that, without affectation, I had no objection to being left alone. Further observation tended to show that I would not in the least consider it condescension on their part to take notice of me. And I bore none of the more definite marks of the beast – I did no more work than they, and I did not suck up to masters, and my father was not a linen draper.

Perhaps in the first place it was curiosity, or perhaps it was sheer English hospitality, but it was not long before they were prepared to talk to me as if I were one of themselves, and they were prepared in addition to admit that if I were not, there were extenuating circumstances – I was regarded as older men might regard someone who had spent a lifetime in Central Africa, as a person who as a result of unfortunate experiences might not be quite right in his head, or might be a little warped in his outlook, but who was not to be condemned on that account. The curious fact that I found it hard to agree with them as to the right place of bloods in the social scale only excited amusement now, and not annoyance, particularly as circumstances made me a blood myself. No one thought of assaulting me when I declared that although to write on both sides of a sheet of foolscap might be inconvenient to the man who had to mark it, and might possibly cause trouble if the sheet had to be filed, it was not a social lapse worthy of the uttermost ostracism. They could find tolerant smiles for me when it was discovered that I thought the recent decree permitting the wearing of soft collars an eminently sensible one. They would never listen when I suggested that perhaps it was unwise to give small boys the privilege of hitting other small boys with sticks, but they never tried to prove me wrong by freezing my chest with ether (their playful habit among themselves) or the use of other

73

violent methods. My eccentricities in time were looked upon almost as amiable eccentricities.

But I nearly betrayed myself once, one day in June 1916, when half a dozen colleagues found me hooting with bitter amusement over a paragraph in the *Times*. That worthy paper was trying to clothe the bare bones of the Jutland communiqués with the warm flush of the human touch, and published an extraordinary tale of how the *Warspite*, seeing the *Warrior* crippled and in danger, had dashed out of the English line, sunk two German ships with successive salvoes, and escorted the battered cruiser out of the action. If anyone doubts my word they can look up the back files of the *Times* and see this preposterous lie in imperishable print; if they care also to scan the mass of literature about Jutland they will read of how, at the same time as the armoured cruisers came under the German fire, the *Warspite* helm jammed hard over so that she made two circles under heavy fire and was badly knocked about and forced to leave the battle. The *Times* version was too strong for my stomach; there was not a clause in it with the ring of truth. But when I said as much I was met by an ominous silence. To doubt the veracity of the *Times* was worse than doubting the soundness of the British Constitution; to do so in wartime was something verging on high treason; add to this the fact that the exploit was one redounding to the valour of the British arms, so that to doubt its occurrence savoured of pacifism, defeatism, and worse, then one can estimate the indecency of which I was guilty. Had I persisted in it I should certainly have found myself classed with those dreadful intelligentsia of whom, thank God, not a single example was to be found in the school. With this warning to influence me I was extremely careful, a month or two later, not to deplore the bloody butchery of the Somme. I kept my mouth shut with a hypocrisy I am not ashamed to own. I was not of the stuff of which martyrs are made, and I was beset by too many troubles to go out hunting for any more.

At the school the war had settled down into a permanent institution. When the Somme was reluctantly conceded not to be a decisive victory, everyone came to the conclusion that it was perfectly possible that the war would go on for much longer, certainly until we were of military age. Already, of course, many old boys had been killed – some of them of legendary greatness – and now the casualty lists included names of men my friends had known well, and names of men I had been intimate with at my other school. We, too, we all assumed, would go the same way when our time came. We would, inevitably, be subalterns, and we all had heard about the short expectation of life among subalterns. Most of us would not last three months; some of us, we hoped, might climb to captain's rank, and might even attain to the splendour of the D.S.O. or the M.C., but after that our names would appear on the Roll of Honour, and our bones would fester in Flanders mud. No one minded in the least. No one ever devoted the least thought towards avoiding duty. Everyone prepared for the inevitable and with a stolid stoicism which I admire more the more I remember it; and it still hurts me to think that most of those boys did, in the end, meet the fate they expected – most of them were commissioned just in time for the horrible slaughter of Passchendaele, and the ones who survived that did not have the same good fortune in 1918. Probably my generation of schoolboys (I was always below average age) suffered more during the war than any other. But there was always hope for an army with such a perennial fount of splendid stuff to draw upon for officers, filled with a solid immutable patriotism which cannot fail to excite admiration. The cynic who says that those boys were only doing, as always, the 'done thing', is lying with a more unpleasant appearance of truth than usual.

In a goofing sort of way I realised this, the more acutely because the realisation was much more a matter of sympathy and understanding than of calculation; all this notwithstanding the fact that I was filled with a comforting and blasé sense of my own superiority to everybody, which was not due to wane for some time. Those boys were grossly uneducated. Even on the vaunted Science side not one in ten was equal to any job beyond that of vanboy or lift-attendant. They had the morals of the Stone Age, and were blindly obedient to taboos more absurd than any to be found in Polynesia. With few exceptions they were insensitive to beauty, and would have hated to be otherwise. Their general knowledge was incredibly small, their outlook incredibly limited, and they never had an original thought in all their short lives – nor wanted one. But with all that they were good specimens in a manner hard to define.

Either because of or in spite of the system in which they had been reared they led one to think that mankind was a good deal nearer to the angels than the catalogue of their faults and deficiencies would lead one to believe. The knotty point to decide is between 'because of' and 'in spite of'. If you decide on the one, you will be a sturdy defender of the public school system; if on the other, you will oppose it. I cannot give my own opinion because try as I may I have never been able to make up my mind about it.

There were irritating details about the school; there were boys who had been bullied into semi-idiocy; there was a good deal of unimaginative filth, and occasional sexual perversities which really scandalised me; there was wanton cruelty; there was a fool of a chaplain who was positively imbecile – on one occasion when my guard had been pierced and my late opponent was assisting me groaning from the ring after hitting me severely in the stomach he came up and clapped him on the shoulder and said, 'That's right, always help your enemies' which I think is quite the most idiotic remark I have heard from human lips; there was slovenly teaching; there was some (quite honest) inculcation of faulty historical and political and economic facts; there was a long list, in fact, of things which cried out for reform. But so interdependent are all the various parts of the system that reform cannot be attempted without altering everything from the foundations, and, as I have said, I cannot make up my mind as to whether this is desirable. I wish I could.

Chapter Ten

At one time at school I was playing in a cricket match. We started with three bowlers, but one of them immediately split his hand fielding a hot return, and I was one of the remaining two. I bowled for two continuous hours in a blazing sun, taking my usual twenty yard run and slamming them down in a vain effort to maintain the rip and devil without which a fast bowler becomes a highly expensive luxury. At the end of that time, in the pavilion, I felt oddly ill; I found I could wring trickles of sweat from the bottoms of my trousers in a way I had never noticed before, and I had hardly made the discovery before the world faded out and I did not return to it for some time.

The incident is mentioned (it made only a small impression on me at the time) as a possible explanation of what happened not very long after, when the army doctors rejected me for service with an alarming unanimity of decision. I could not understand it; I had played games desperately hard all my life and my heart had only given out once and I had not been ill since infancy. Possibly the fact that I grew five inches a year for four years may help to explain my rejection – I was as thin as a lath.

I had gone to the recruiting office some time before I was old enough for service in order to get things decently settled up and arranged, for one could 'attest' and have one's medical examination at the age of seventeen, so that on reaching military age all that had to be done was to travel direct to the depot. Premature attestation of this sort gave one the privilege of selecting one's unit, and also earned one some small fee – three and fourpence, I think, although I am not sure. Presumably that three and fourpence had something to do with my voluntary enlistment; seeing that I was going to join the army anyway, I might as well have three and fourpence for doing something I should otherwise have to do for nothing later on, while the knowledge that everything was arranged would be something solid to hang on to during the next few months. The recruiting office was very hot and stuffy; it had been a public swimming bath and the sun beat down through the glass roof until the interior was like an oven. But the harassed staff received me with a politeness I was not expecting; the oath was read over to me with courtesy, my form filled in, my three and fourpence handed over, and my request for immediate medical examination and completion of all the formalities received with a matter of fact kindliness. The one-armed officer in charge led me through in person to the hall where the doctors were at work. There was a horrible mixture of humanity inside – louts of eighteen; worried fathers of families up for re-examination and wondering how best to deceive the doctors; men with diseases, whom the recruiting routine called up periodically to see if they were fit yet or if the medical regulations were by now sufficiently relaxed to include them; newly caught men who had been avoiding conscription; ruptured men; 'debadged' men cursing their luck; in fact a typical series of samples of the riff raff which was being swept into the army in this, the last and most desperate year of the war – the sort of men, I grimly thought as I stripped along with them, whom I would have to lead into action in five or six months' time. Naked, we awaited our turns. Most of us were unwashed and dirty, and our skins were pimply and grey and odorous. Some of the men were rehearsing under their breath the replies they wanted to have ready for the doctors' questions. Others were talking filth worse even than the filth talked at public schools. All of us were ill at ease for one reason or another; it was a relief to me when my name was called.

The army medical examination, I had always understood, was sketchy, and I had nothing the matter with me that I knew of except defective eyesight. I expected the whole business to be over in five minutes like the attestation. But the doctor who applied a stethoscope to my heart (that was a surprise to me; I had not expected such refinement) was not satisfied. He called his colleague over, who listened as well. They telephoned through to a senior doctor, who turned up after I had strolled naked about the building for ten minutes or so. He too, listened to my heart, and tapped round it with his fingers, and asked me questions. Nobody announced his conclusion in hearing. Instead I was told to get my clothes on and that I would find my papers with the clerk in the outer hall. And when I found the clerk he was busily writing in red ink all over my attestation form and registration card and all the rest of it the information that I was medically rejected.

Probably I was more surprised at that than I have ever been at anything in my life. I asked for details; the clerk lifted surprised eyebrows and said he hadn't got any. I persuaded the sergeant on duty to let me back into the doctors' hall and there I questioned the men who had examined me. They were overworked and tired, and hurried, but they managed to find time between two recruits to tell me that there was no chance of my being accepted for service and that really I should be surprised to be still alive. So that I left the building in the shadow of death, and it took me a long time to grow accustomed to it – as a matter of fact no sooner had I grown accustomed to it than my heart and physique had righted themselves, and the specialists who were easily accessible to me as a medical student and whom I periodically consulted pronounced me fit again.

But this I could not foresee at the time, and it was quite a severe shock for a boy of seventeen to be told that he was in imminent danger of sudden death – although, as I bitterly realise, it was nothing to compare with the experience of my friends of eighteen who at that time were encountering sudden death in far more horrible forms every moment of their lives.

Chapter Eleven

This was the culminating point of the troubles which beset me then. A great number of circumstances (I started enumerating them a chapter or two back) all combined to make me most desperately unhappy, as unhappy as only a seventeen year old can be – which is as unhappy as anyone can be except an eighteen year old. All the joy and sparkle had been fading out of life for some time back; largely this was my own fault and due to my deliberately adopted pose of weary satiety, but partly it was due to circumstances over which I had no control. There had been recently too many convulsive changes in my life, first from one school to another and then from school to the hospital where I had now entered myself as a medical student. That was unsettling, and somehow the discovery that I was not destined for the army and the death in action to which I had resigned myself was unsettling too. The older friends I had were in the casualty lists now; I met one or two of them, horribly wounded. It was not pleasant to have to confess to them that I was medically unfit for service – and the mutilated ones who said with a gleam of envy 'You don't know how lucky you are' made me feel worse and not better. It was a crowning irony that I should be serving in an Officers' Training Corps, with my sword-belt tapping on my hip and the crowns gleaming on my arms, drilling other people into readiness for their transfer to the war in which I had no part.

And the irony went deeper than that, for although I wanted to serve if there was a war, at the same time there was rising inside me a terrible longing that the whole brutal, wasteful, beastly business should end. The attitude of civilians towards the war maddened me. When a man of fifty spoke complacently of 'heavy casualty lists' I could call up before my mind's eye with terrible realism pictures of men torn open and carried shrieking on stretchers to the regimental aid posts, and of pleasant boys with whom I had been intimate rotting on the barbed wire in No Man's Land. The huge official figures of sunk shipping called up pictures unconnected with a shortened sugar ration – pictures of shivering seamen crouching in little life boats on a wild sea hundreds of miles from land. I was torn with doubt as to whether any ultimate victory would be worth the price that was being paid for it; despite the fact that at the same time I was convinced that victory was desirable.

It was the civilians who angered me most – people who believed that an air raid was comparable with a bombardment in France, or that the privations due to a shortage of taxicabs or of beefsteak were as bad as those the men in the ranks were enduring. (There really were plenty of people who thought like that during the war.) Barrie brought out a horrible play which represented a woman as lamenting the fact that she had no son who could serve in the army. The lack of one made a difference to her social status – she was only an office cleaner, but it made a difference; and anyway she wanted to have a son in danger of death or mutilation, because everyone else had. The wickedness of such an outlook appalled me – to this day I have never forgiven Sir James for that abomination. I suppose he would be very hurt if he knew. The insults which greeted Lord Lansdowne's very sensible suggestion of peace by negotiation hurt me, I suppose, as much as if they had been addressed to myself. The men who wrote them could never have talked with wounded soldiers.

What made all this emotion very bad for me was the fact that it was all secret. There was no single soul in whom I could confide. My intimate friends were all in the army. The few 'peace cranks' and members of the 'No Conscription Fellowship' and conscription-dodgers whom I encountered were far too cranky for me. A boy of eighteen is not likely to make a confidant of a vegetarian with long hair. The fact that such people shared my views made me ashamed of my views and much more loath to divulge them, and my vivid imagination caused me to realise only too well what the hearty middle-class folk I knew would say about them – people who muddled along at some kind of pettifogging war work, and who tried to sympathise with me for not being in the army. I would gladly have gone and risked death as some sort of wild gesture of respect towards the friends of mine who had died (at least, so I thought. I might have turned coward if the choice had been open to me) and I would have made any sacrifice if it would have brought the war to an immediate victorious conclusion, but I did not have the brainless urge to be in the army that those senseless people attributed to me. But I was not going to make public my convictions, partly because as it happened I never came across the people who might have helped me do so, but largely because I knew what would happen if I did. I was not the stuff of which martyrs are made. So I kept my troubles to myself, just as a man will keep secret the fact that he is suffering from a disease, and with just about as unhappy consequences. Until this moment of writing I have never disclosed them to a living soul. Even now the relief of confession is inexpressible.

There were lots of other things bothering me too. My rejection from the army brought me up with a bump against the realisation that I had a future to be got through – previously I had been content to resign my destiny first to the guiding care of the Family and then to that of my King and Country. I was destined for medicine, the profession of my elder brother. Quite unknowingly that extremely nice individual caused me a great deal of inward disturbance. The profession of medicine was not entirely to my taste, but I decided that any other profession would be equally distasteful, and to that extent I was reconciled to it. But my brother had matriculated at fifteen and had gone on to qualify brilliantly at twenty. The brute had actually made a record. When I matriculated at fifteen as well it was open to me to equal it, but I missed that chance by going on to a public school. All the same, comparisons were continually being drawn between us (he had been an infant phenomenon as well) and I came slowly to realise that all my life, if I went in for medicine, I should be compared with him, and inevitably unfavourably, because he was a much better doctor than ever I should be. I saw no charm whatever in going through life as the pale shade of my elder brother. If ever I am blessed with two sons I shall for that very reason endeavour to persuade them not to follow identical professions – probably I shall be wrong there, too. It took me a long time to come to this conclusion about medicine, but even before it was formed it began to rankle slightly and add its mite to my burden of care.

On top of my loneliness, and my horror of the war, and my growing dislike of medicine, there was another burden, not so clearly defined but none the less onerous, and that was the load of trouble set on my shoulders by women. It is much harder to write about. The prejudice against 'kissing and telling' must be rather more than a prejudice; I find it quite impossible to elaborate in detail the themes I have in mind. But the war had continued now for three years, and morals were relaxing, and men were scarce, and I was an attractive young man who looked older than my age. And I had adopted a pose of satiety which demanded satiety of me by way of revenge; and I had a secret trouble that sometimes drove me into ill considered actions out of sheer unease. A young man can get himself into horrible tangles without the aid of any of these circumstances. I landed myself in far more trouble than I care to contemplate nowadays. There was little enough vulgar scandal; I had enough tact and sufficient ingenuity in the matter of lying to keep out of that sort of thing, but there was worry and prickings of conscience, and nauseated distaste enough to compensate for it. Like OttoWeininger, I divided women into two classes, but my two were the fools and the whores – the fools ran after me and I ran after the whores, foolish though I realised such a proceeding to be. And when the whores ceased to afford diversion I would turn back to the fools – with a feeling of contempt for myself both that I should waste my time over them and that I should put my talents to such unworthy uses. Most of them were easy game, even when one kept to the rules, which allowed you to tell a girl you loved her but not that you would marry her, to take her out to dinner but not to give her too much to drink, to promise her constancy only as long as no one else more attractive appeared and so on. Rules or no rules, conventions or no conventions, there was always trouble when the business reached its inevitable end. The women would rarely recognise that inevitableness; if they did they tended to belong to the class other than fools, and their placid acceptance of the end piqued you into trying to postpone it. There was always trouble, and subterfuges, and harassment, to poison the pleasant gratification of an instinct and the rather subtle feeling that you were scoring off a world that was hurting you atrociously. And in the end you felt dreadfully sick at heart, as though you could not bear to drag on this tortured existence a day longer, and would recall the tempting fact that Otto Weininger had had the sense to die by his own hand, without any foolishness like hoping for a war to end or waiting for a weak heart to kill him.

It was a quite unplanned step which saved me from the very worst consequences of this mass of troubles, and probably kept for me the remnants of my reason. The war had taken my friends from me, and I had no one to go a-holiday making with; I had little enough money for a holiday, too, and yet I had the whole of August on my hands. It ended in my packing up my tent and going off by myself for four blessed weeks. The owners of Brookwood Cemetery gave me a site – a wild wood of birch and fir on the banks of the Wey Canal. Perhaps the trees are cut down now, and there are graves and monuments there, but I shall always remember the place as it was then, with the tangle of silver birches and the waterlilies blooming on the canal, where hardly one barge a week came to disturb the solitude. For four weeks I remained there, surrounded by all the camps and barracks of the Aldershot-Woking district, but (thanks to my choice of site) hardly seeing a soul save for the children who sometimes ventured into the wood and who called me the 'Ole Man in the Tent'. At intervals I emerged to buy food and to draw water, but all the rest of the time I was blissfully alone, and climbing back to normality, and realising (what had never occurred to me before) that it was the most foolish thing in the world to worry, and that worry can be controlled if only one sets one's mind on it. I do not think that even I was so priggish as to debate my spiritual troubles with myself in the way the foregoing lines might be taken to indicate; it all worked itself out naturally – fresh air and the cessation of reading two books a day might have had something to do with it too – and I was not conscious of the enormous good that holiday did me until some months later. Four weeks of fresh air, sound sleep, and absence of all contact with the human world made almost a natural young man of me, as was only to be expected, and it was only two months later that the war came to an end and released me from the worst of my troubles and worries.

What those four weeks really did was to give me leisure to sort my thoughts out and distinguish between instinct and reason. The usual interplay of argument with friends does that for most people; thanks to the war I had no friends I could argue with. An hour or two's conversation with and confession to my father might have done as much for me – but my father was lost to sight in the peninsula of Sinai quite as effectively as the Israelites had been, and I had not seen him since I was fourteen. The chasm between fourteen and eighteen is hard to bridge, particularly by a secretive boy always far too preoccupied to write letters.

Chapter Twelve

It came out quite accidentally in the last chapter that I had become a medical student – I was busy writing about something else and could not devote the attention which is due to such an epoch-making change in a boy's affairs. The vast hospital whose medical school I entered – my abominable brother had preceded me there – was one of those comparatively untouched by the war. Only two wards had been commandeered, and those only for the treatment of rather unusual cases. The most obvious indication of wartime conditions was the shortage of students; there were only seventy or eighty in place of the usual four hundred, and of these seventy or eighty a high proportion consisted of Asiatics, Spaniards, and people like that who were revelling in an unusual enjoyment of house appointments and similar coveted distinctions which were generally reserved for Englishmen. The first year students numbered a bare dozen (eighty would be an average year) and these were practically all bright young boys not yet of military age – more stringent wartime conditions were cutting down the influx of Asiatics. For the first time in my life I began to associate with people younger than myself, but the conditions did not last for long, for no sooner had I passed my First than, towards the very end of the war, the government suddenly realised the imminence of a shortage of qualified medical men, and sought out in the ranks of the army the few surviving pre-war medical students and packed them all back to the hospitals to get qualified as quickly as they might. It was from them, in the intimacies of dissection and laboratory work, that I learnt a great deal about the war, it was brought home to me that the soldiers' mental attitude was not always what a Bairnsfather cartoon might indicate, and that the mass of wartime literature was not twenty per cent lies, as I had expected, but eighty per cent.

People were of much more influence on me at this time than work or literature. The course of study for the First Examination for Medical Degrees made no great demands on a boy who had had half a dozen years of education in science. The chemistry and physics hardly went beyond the matriculation syllabus I had ambled through years before; the botany and zoology were never studies (despite the fact that I was supposed to be instructed in them at my last school) but presented no great difficulties of outlook to me, who remembered lots of arguments about the Origin of Species and the bisexual condition of earthworms with my brothers and with friends at school. The people who found difficulty were those who came straight from a classical education. They had to absorb a great deal of science in a single year, starting from the simplest ideas. It was six years since I had had ground into me the basic definitions on which all else depended – 'A molecule is the smallest portion of an element or compound which can exist alone and still retain its own properties' – and so on, and such notions were an intimate part of my thought, ready for use whenever necessary, and I had never laboured under the delusion that it was less important to know of the constitution of washing soda than of where to place a caesura, although I had views of my own on the latter subject as well. The classical people had to acquire an entirely new set of mental values, a new mental horizon, a new method of thought, and it was hard on them. To get through their first year course in a single year meant grind; hard work for them; for me it meant nothing at all, and I had far too many other interests and vastly too many troubles to bother about work. And although I had the fullest sympathy with those people who could be filled with passionate anxiety about science, and medicine in particular, it was not a matter that I could work up any enthusiasm for. I could see its possibilities of beauty, but it had no irresistible beauty for me.

So I went through the formalities of routine. I lounged through chemistry and physics; I resisted the temptation to be bitten with a taste for biology; I peered into the dissecting room to get a glimpse of what awaited me next year; I made tentative visits to the spectators' gallery in the operating theatres; I joined in the very mild idiocies which were all the very limited number of students could devise, recording just enough appearances at lectures and practical work to ensure my being 'signed up' as eligible for the approaching examination. It was all rather unreal to me, for I had three primary interests above my work – my humanitarian worry about the war, my extremely hectic night life, and, for a time (until I got used to it) the knowledge that my heart was weak and my life might be short. And as I was still reading every book (including scientific books) which I could get hold of, it will be understood that there was not time or thought left over for work.

There was a delicious freedom about the new life. Although time tables and rules were not very much relaxed, even the slightest relaxation was apparently stupendous compared with the rigid restrictions of public school life. There was a blessed comfort in the knowledge that you could, occasionally, cut a lecture or a class if you felt you simply could not face it; at school you could only do that by tedious subterfuges, such as getting a girl to telephone the school to say you were wanted at home immediately (during wartime such messages were unfortunately frequent, and a telephone call excused all need for a parental note) which meant spending the evening with the girl when you probably did not want to. There was more comfort still in the fact that if a piece of work took only ten minutes to do, ten minutes was all the time you had to spend over it, instead of, as at school, spending fifty more minutes pretending to do it. Better than anything was the freedom from restriction. Convention was almost absent; you could wear what clothes and what ties you liked; you could put your hands in your trousers pockets beneath the sides of your jacket instead of in front of them if you wanted to; you could indulge in minor eccentricities of deportment without having to fight for the privilege or being conscious of a tense atmosphere of strained toleration.

In a medical school the tolerant attitude of its limited public is startling – it is more kindly than that of a university, where occasionally 'hearties' wage war on 'effeminates', and the artistic look with scorn on the Philistines. Most of the men in a hospital, of course, have similar tastes and similar ambitions, they work together in close contact, and their studies tend to give them similar habits of thought. But apart from that there is a tendency to regard a man's private life as his own private business which at the present day is growing unfortunately rare outside hospitals. Disapproval is not a summons to action, and complete absence of inquisitiveness is the general rule. By far the safest place for freaks labouring under the necessity of qualifying for a profession is in a medical school; particularly (and this is important) as the absence of persecution and the straightening out of one's mental processes by a scientific education are likely to do a great deal to remedy the initial freakishness. There is one further advantage; although the athlete is held in respect the scholar is held in respect as well. The man who can put you right on some terribly important point regarding the Portal Circulation of the frog which you cannot work out for yourself, or who can find your earthworm's ovary and get it on to a microscope slide just when you have given up all hope, is not a man to be despised, when only a month or two hence the dreaded examination awaits you.

Without any doubt the period of my medical studies would have been a very happy one indeed if the other circumstances, on which I have harped so incessantly, had permitted. But I only knew even slight happiness there for a short time, during the months immediately succeeding the war. I passed my First with a stumble, just as a steeplechaser having cleared several obstacles without 'laying an iron on them' may peck badly at some easier jump. I was 'referred' in Biology – told to take that subject again in three months' time – although I passed easily in Chemistry and Physics and was allowed to move on to second year work. When, three months later, I took the examination again I passed without effort, although I had not opened a biology text book in all that time and had steadily forgotten part of what I knew – I had ceased to care even in the least about my work in that last most awful crisis of the war.

Second year work was decidedly different. For the first time in my life I found difficulty in keeping ahead of my contemporaries – which is a moderate way of saying that I fell far behind them. By the time the end of the war had come, and more especially by the time peace was well advanced, I was beginning to have the gravest doubts as to my desire to practise medicine as a profession, and these doubts (I will air them more extensively later) were reacting on the keenness of my studies at the same time as my failure to learn stimulated my doubts – it was a vicious circle.

Physiology was not too bad; my very thorough grounding in chemistry and physics helped me with that, and I might have struggled through the course and through the subsequent examination if it had not been for the fact that Physiology was only a vassal subject, so to speak, to the supreme Anatomy. Anatomy had to be learned with a thoroughness which was disconcerting. No amount of flair or guessing power or tact will help one to answer an anatomy question if one does not know the answer – I have never come across any other examination subject (and my experience has been extensive) to which the same remark can be applied. It is quite impossible to draw a red herring across the trail which an anatomy examiner is pursuing. The student of anatomy must acquire a mass of hard, solid facts, most of them not dependent in the least on any others, and he must store them in his memory so that any one of them is instantly available. Imagine being given a large book. You must learn the contents of that book off by heart – not the meaning (that is Physiology or Morphology) but the word-for-word contents. But that is the least of it. You must also know the position of any word in that book, the number of the page and the line, the position in the line, and what words come before it and after it, and what words lie above it and below it, what word is printed on the back and what word on the opposite page lies on the front of it, and what words occupy corresponding positions on fifty other paragraphs. The pages are not regular; some have more lines than others, some lines are longer than others, and some pages and some lines are not in their correct order. You must know all about these irregularities, in addition to their bearing on the position of individual words. Moreover, there have been two or three editions of the book, each with slight variations, and you must know all about each edition. Lastly, the book has been put together by very eccentric editors and compositors and binders who did their work in a muddled fashion, first this bit and then that, turning this page upside down and reversing the order of that, dropping the whole lot on the floor and then picking it up again; and you must be able to recount the history of each individual word and the adventures it went through during this curious process of arrangement.

A man faced with a task like that might well groan with despair, yet it is a very fair comparison with the task of learning anatomy, which hundreds of medical students approach every year with a comparative equanimity and an astonishing amount of success. I certainly approached the task with equanimity, but I never had any success at it. Usually I found that after half an hour or so's muddled effort it was far better to drop the business and go over to the Students' Club to play bridge.

There was good bridge to be had there, too. It is amazing how carefully a young man will play when, if he loses, he has to go without his lunch, which was the case with most of us. That is the time when the reckless player holds back and resists the temptation to call the extra trick which he has no chance of getting, and when the careless player playing the hand will really stop and think in the effort of winning that one more doubtful trick which makes the difference between game and three. It used to be with a little thrill of interest that I would tear my attention away from my own immediate interest in the game to contemplate the scene with a more impersonal eye – four keen young men sitting round the table, speaking quietly, betraying no hint of hope or despair, and yet, probably, with two of them at least faced with the immediate prospect of having nothing to eat that day as a result of an unlucky lie of the cards. There was another more dramatic scene that I remember, when a fleshy young Bengalee, who had long importuned us for permission to play with us, and who had eventually been granted his request, broke down into sobs over the card table. The picture is still clear in my mind's eye – the tiny sitting-room thick with tobacco smoke, the three coldly inexpressive Englishmen, and the plump spectacled Indian weeping heart-broken in his chair. He had been losing money, he explained between his sobs. Much money. Not merely with us – we played a shilling a hundred when in funds, and his losses to us were not more than twenty pounds – but with another gang of brighter young sharks who knew a good thing when they saw it. Oh, it was dreadful, he said, how much he had lost. All his own pocket money was gone, and not merely that, but he had lost the money his fat Bengalee father had sent him to pay his fees with. He would have to write to that stern parent and confess that seventy pounds were wanting – seventy pounds which he ought to pay into the office of the medical school that very week. He had small sympathy from us; we merely cursed him roundly as a blithering fool who had spoiled sport. So he nearly had, for the irate father in Bengal wrote indignant letters to the hospital, and card playing was promptly barred by authority; but seeing that authority never presumed to interfere with what went on in people's private rooms in the Club there was little enough real difference.

The money question was always with us. After the Armistice, when we all plunged into a sort of nightmare of pleasure seeking, I doubt if there could have been found in all London a dozen young men more desperately hard up than we were. To win money from each other at bridge was as unproductive as reciprocal taking in of one another's washing on a desert island. There was one bright young sport who lived at the Club and who ran himself completely out of funds and out of credit. He had written home for money until his parents were weary of him, and sent him lectures on extravagance instead of cheques. The Club committee suddenly decided to allow him no more credit until he had paid his bills – he ate his meals of course, at the Club. Faced with the prospect of immediate starvation, he did not know which way to turn. He wrote appealingly to his family, but he had written appealingly before, and they were not going to be cozened again; naturally they did not believe a word of the black picture of starvation he drew for them. He scraped together the coppers for a telegram, but his father was a hard-headed Bradford manufacturer who was not to be moved by telegrams. He went on his knees to the committee, but the committee had had too many interviews lately with young men who protested, with extravagant emphasis, that 'they hadn't a bean'. He tried to borrow from us, but we had nothing to lend – already our microscopes and skeletons and spare suits and everything else were at the pawnshop. The poor devil was actually starving; we were lunching on penn'orths of bread and cheese, but he had literally nothing.

It was his completely desperate position which moved us to crime, to larceny, and presumably, housebreaking. A general turning out of pockets – money intended for our fares – among us raised a shilling or so, enough to pay for the hire of a barrow at the old clothes shop near by. That barrow we brought round to a back street on which the Club smoking room windows opened. Carefully timing everything so that neither members nor servants were at hand inside, nor policeman outside, we whipped up a window, passed out an armchair, and with it on the barrow we set off to the Mile End Road where we sold it to an accommodating furniture dealer who winked at us as we chaffered with him. Good furniture – a fine, well upholstered club armchair, for instance – fetched colossal prices shortly after the war, and the supply was in no way equal to the demand and no furniture dealer would ask too many questions about where any good piece came from. The price we got relieved us for the moment of need, even when divided between five of us. The last I saw that evening of the man who had been so hungry was when he was just applying himself to his third go of steak and chips.

Those months following the Armistice were mad ones. People came pouring into the hospital; some came from the army, but more still from the public schools. Everyone seemed to have decided together to become doctors. The number of students trebled itself overnight, as it were. Where formerly in the dissecting room you had a whole limb to yourself, you now had to work with a partner and might consider yourself lucky not to have two more men thrust upon you to watch your dissection going on. It was by favour now that you were granted a new 'part' when you had finished your old one, and canny young men put their names early on the waiting lists.

The traditionally riotous medical student life arose again like magic. Men who had commanded batteries and companies in battles which decided the history of the world now managed somehow (I cannot guess how) to raise enthusiasm over Hospital Rugby Football Cup ties. The dusty club gymnasium was reopened, and boxing began again in which I joyfully joined, damning my weak heart into oblivion, and not caring very much if it struck work or not. For that matter, I was past caring what happened to me – but to explain why calls for a long digression on Art and Inspiration for which I apologise beforehand.

There is, I think, an undoubted instinct for story-telling

present in the human race; it is noticeable enough in children, and it is the mainspring of the obscure motives which inspire the needless lying so amusing in a few adults. Generally it dies away, or is repressed by modern conditions. No one ever imagines that the children who start school magazines or write stories are going to be authors later on – it is not a significant symptom. There is the classic case of the authoress of the *Young Visiters*, who, after writing quite a carefully constructed story in her teens (or was it earlier? I forget) never wrote another publishable word. But sometimes the instinct persists, just a pure, barbaric yearning to tell a story, possibly even to a non-existent audience. When the urge becomes unbearable, it is justifiable to call it 'inspiration'; whether the result is the 'Ode to a Grecian Urn' or Bill Brown's account to his friends in the public bar of an incident which never happened. It is the quality of the mind of the inspired one which determines the quality of the product – not the inspiration. A very good example of a man who was alway conscious of this urge, whose ambition always was to gratify it, and who devoted much care to selecting his medium and to training himself to achieve what he wanted, is Joseph Conrad. And I knew inspiration, too, just as Keats and Conrad did – just as Bill Brown did, too, which must be pleaded in my favour after comparing myself with Keats.

I do not think the desire for an audience came into it at all, really. When I wrote school magazines, and contributed humorous articles (God forgive me!) to the hospital gazette it was only to please myself, not to please other people. Certainly when I wrote verse about my light loves I never dreamed (after one or two experiences) of an audience. I kept that poetry pretty secret. Probably if my life had been untroubled and if I had entered a profession which satisfied me the story-telling instinct might have evaporated (have become sublimated, I believe the psychoanalysts call it) painlessly, so that now if I were to be confronted with my early efforts I would wonder how on earth I came to do such things. But a turbulent life, a life of uncertainty and worry and disappointment, wakes the story-telling instinct up. I put the suggestion timidly forward as a possible explanation of the greater upheavals in literature – after the Persian wars, for instance, and in the Renaissance. The nagging of an unsatisfied want pursued me during my later teens and when I reached the twenties; to make matters worse I was perfectly well aware of what it was that I wanted. I knew the feeling of exhausted satisfaction after writing a sonnet which rhymed and scanned correctly, and I had made botched attempts at writing short stories, and had written a good deal of matter for school and hospital magazines, official and unofficial. But it was a long time before I would admit my need to myself.

Somewhere within me there is a cautious, canny, long-sighted guardian angel who does his level best to keep me from making a fool of myself. He does not succeed, but he does sometimes contrive to put a brake on my more reckless actions. I can picture at this period a conversation between me and my guardian angel – nothing like it ever happened, of course, but it makes a fair diagrammatic representation of what was going on in my unhappy soul.

GUARDIAN ANGEL: You don't know what it is you want.

ME (*sullenly*): Yes, I do.

G.A.: Don't be a fool. It's a delusion. You don't know when you're well off. Here you are, on the threshold of a good profession, and you want to muck it all up for nothing at all.

ME: On the threshold? Don't you believe it.

G.A.: Yes, you are. Just knuckle to and do a spot of work and get yourself through your Second. You'll be all right then.

ME: I'll eat my hat if ever I get through my Second.

G.A.: It only needs an effort.

ME: That's all the other thing needs.

G.A.: Does it? How many people who write for a living make a living at it? They starve, most of them, and so would you. You know perfectly well that you've never written *anything* worth reading.

ME: But those bits of verse. You said yourself—

G.A.: Yes, perhaps I did. But three bits of verse won't keep you in bread and butter, nor three hundred. You might as well think of being a professional novelist as of being a poet.

ME: That's just what I *was* thinking about.

G.A.: *What?* You're a bigger fool than I thought you were. You've never tried to write a novel. You don't know if you could. You're like the man who didn't know if he could play the violin because he'd never tried.

ME: You've never let me try to write a novel.

and though it might be cowardly to evade difficulties in that fashion – like falling in boxing, without being punched off one's feet, to avoid further punishment – at least it was one possible end, a comforting reality to which I could cling.

That thought was, however, only the last thing to weave into my day dreams, when my more sensible half refused to allow the other half to continue any further with fantasies of a literary life or of some freakish success in the Second Examination. Meanwhile, there were other ways still of escape from a harassing present and an ominous future. Women could help me usually to forget about these things. Not, of course, that they had the least inkling of my troubles – to them I was a medical student with a brilliant scholastic past and a probably brilliant professional future. But in running after – or away from – women there was some sort of oblivion, eagerly to be sought, and very precious. The muddles and tangles and tragedies such indulgence brought with it were valuable in themselves as giving me something to think about.

Looking back on those days the one thing that amazes me and causes me pride is the knowledge that at no time did I ever yield to the temptation to find more complete oblivion in drink or drugs. The opportunity and the example were always at hand. Most of the social circle in which I was moving drank very hard indeed, and one of the men at the hospital with whom I was more friendly was fool enough to smoke laudanum poured on his tobacco. I knew by experiment what relief I should find in either practice, and the temptation was often pressing, but I somehow always retained enough sense and willpower to resist it. I cannot help feeling proud of that. The one glimmer of rational behaviour I displayed in this mad period was when – after two experimental opium bouts and one of hard drinking – I resolved not to drink until my difficulties were settled one way or the other, and never to touch drugs again in my life; and my one bit of decent conduct at that time was my unwavering adherence to these resolutions. As I say, I am proud of it to this day; there must have been a streak of good stuff somewhere in my composition.

But without either drink or drugs my preoccupied self could still vie in utter lunacy and recklessness with my companions. No one in my set could compete with me in insane disregard for consequences, whether it was flirting with the wife of a man who had sworn to poison her next lover or merely standing dinner for four at the Savoy without a penny in my pocket and no reasonable excuse to offer the irate management at the time of the presentation of the bill. We were all of us utterly irresponsible, and I feel sure, even now when cynicism has modified my estimation of motives, that we were not consciously irresponsible in the way which bright young people often are. I can remember a holiday in France which ended with a visit to a French seaport, which ended in its turn in a visit to the vilest of the harbour-side resorts. There was a quarrel and an immediate fight. Razors came out, and knives. It flashed across my mind at the time that for once I was seeing those instruments being used as the best textbooks advised – the razors bent back edge outwards across the knuckles of the negro coal trimmers, so that a swinging punch carried with it a long slash, and the knives, in the dirty hands of the Spanish fishermen, held with the thumb along the blade for an upward jab, hard to guard against, into the abdomen or between the ribs – the human ribs (I had learned this much in anatomy) are arranged in Venetian blind fashion so that a downward stab is likely merely to scrape harmlessly down them without penetrating between. Both razors and knives were directed against us English intruders; in the scurry of the fight no one shouted, the women did not even scream, but drew hissing breaths of rapt attention. For two or three seconds, I suppose (I cannot believe it was the half hour which my memory insists upon) we opposed solid punches to razor cuts and knife stabs as we circled fantastically round the stricken man on the floor, and then a blowzy Englishwoman among the drabs in that place turned out the lights and shrieked to us to get away. We found ourselves in the street, and it was there that our recklessness slowed up. For we shrieked with laughter (I at least was not drunk, and I do not think the others were) and, still laughing, we turned back into the place in a hysterical offensive. It was our pleasant intention to clean the place up, to turn it inside out, and I think we went a fair way towards it with bottles and chairs. Another mental note streaked across my mind at that time, while I still hooted with laughter, to the effect that neither a negro with a razor nor a Spaniard with a knife is half as formidable an opponent if you go for him all out as if you wait for him to attack you. There were shouts and screams enough now, as the furniture crashed to splinters and the bottles smashed against skulls, and then at the front door came the imperious voices of the police. We did not stop to interview them; we went out of the back windows like an avalanche, hotly pursued over walls and down alleyways, but we all of us escaped by the grace of God to meet again an hour or two later at our hotel. No one had worse injuries than slight cuts and bruises save I, who had smashed a knuckle, and my waistcoat and shirt were ripped clean up – presumably by a jab from a knife which had come just too short to go up in among my heart and lungs.

The chances are that any man I meet in the street went through much more exciting and dangerous experiences than that in the war, but it is not the danger which constitutes the point of that incident. All I want to emphasise is the absurd recklessness which took us back into that place after we had got clean away. I cannot think that it could have been merely pose – it must have been constitutional, at least temporarily. Nowadays I would not walk along that waterfront at night, let alone go into that horrible place, and as for starting a fight—! And yet, possibly – I cannot ever be certain – that old absurd recklessness may show up at some inconvenient moment, all the same. I am consumed with doubts that I am not the staid and extremely sensible man that I think I am now.

That complete carelessness about anything showed up in another way in London; in a way which I cannot recall with so much equanimity. I have to force myself to write about it, but I suppose it might amuse others, little as the memory of it amuses me nowadays. The initial impetus was given by the need for money – money was always short with me, as was only to be expected when I tried to live the life of a man about town on the allowance of a medical student. A dinner and a dance on the correct scale would consume not merely a week's pocket money, but conceivably the pocket money of a month. No amount of hard-headed audacity at bridge or economy on lunches could keep pace with expenditure on that sort of scale, and soon so much had been pawned that further pawning would result in positive inconvenience. It was sometimes possible to order a new suit from a long-suffering tailor and go straight away and pawn it, but it was not possible to do that twice a week. Theft was impracticable; I had so much to do with my time that I could not spare a moment for housebreaking. To earn money was a solution of the difficulty which did not readily occur to me, and anyway it is practically impossible for a nineteen year old medical student to earn any reasonable amount of money while still maintaining the fiction that he is a medical student.

With borrowing and stealing and earning all ruled out, there was only one thing left to do, and that was to beg. The need for money was one day so peculiarly urgent that this last possibility had to be seriously considered. The lady of the moment was a première danseuse, and that kind of lady is very expensive to take about. But I had pledged myself to her service for that evening, and I was at my wits' ends to think where I could possibly raise even a matter of shillings to struggle through the evening with. The wrong headed pride in my nineteen year old makeup decided that no degradation could be as great as the degradation of admitting to the lady that I could not afford to entertain her; even though she was ten years older than me I knew that I did not stand so high in her favour because of the little I could give her, but because, fantastically, she liked me – and that made me all the more desperately, overwhelmingly anxious to spend money on her. Had she not been fond of me, and had she been mercenary, I should probably have delighted in telling her what my allowance was and how much it was overdrawn. As it was, the need for money to conceal my poverty was overwhelming, utterly irresistible.

So there was nothing for it but to beg and the only way of begging of which I was capable was to sing in the streets, and I sang in the streets. The long headed half of me refused to see anything undesirable about it; it would not do me any harm and I needed the money. The other, more absurd half of me, disliked the notion from motives of pride, but was forced to give way under pressure of circumstances. And both halves felt that it would be a new and original experience, which might be told with much éclat later in some drawing-room – that was a mistake, for up to the time of writing I have never told a soul about it.

It was the beginning which was the hardest. It was easy enough to plan the scheme, to select my field of operations, the older Hampstead streets where there was plenty of money and not much chance of meeting friends. It was easy enough to go there, filled with determination. But it was most infernally hard to drop my comfortable privacy, to leave off being a respectable citizen, and to step off the kerb into the roadway, and to lift up my voice in song in the full gaze of the passersby. To do so called for a frightful effort of will, much stronger than that needed to take the most nauseating medicine, or to step into the coldest bath. I managed it in the end when pride came to my rescue – pride which forbade me to draw back from a scheme planned and taken in hand. I admit that I chose a moment when there was no one about at all in the quiet street in which I found myself. Then I pulled myself together, stepped off the kerb, and began to blare ballads in my tuneless baritone. It was an odd sensation, quite as odd as that which many people know in nightmares when they find themselves at a levée or in a court of justice with no clothes on. It felt stranger still when someone appeared at an upper window, and my first copper came tinkling into the roadway.

Since that date I have become acquainted with people living in that road in Hampstead, either at the house of the first copper or the one next door – I did not notice the house exactly – so that it may have been the lady who now is nice to me at the dinner table who threw that penny; on the other hand, it may have been her housemaid. I have never asked either of them about it. And I am quite unable to date this adventure accurately. It must have been quite early in 1919, I think, because it must have an unusual spectacle to see a well dressed young man of refined appearance singing in the streets; the public had not grown accustomed to the sight of masked men in officers' uniforms with medals playing barrel organs in the street, and of ex-servicemen's bands at every corner, so that, as I say, I must have made this essay in the early months of 1919 before gratuities were all spent and before the great slump recruited thousands to begging.

Certainly I attracted a good deal of attention, and it was not the beauty of my voice which was responsible, because I am constitutionally unable to range more than about three tones.

People gave me money and received my gratitude in return; other people stopped me and spoke to me, much to my annoyance. It was money I wanted, not sympathy, or attention, or charity organisation cards. I found that the best reply to make to these impertinent inquirers who wanted to know why I was doing this was a simple smiling 'Because I am in need of money'; that simple enunciation of the self-evident usually stopped the conversation and sometimes brought silver in return as well. A great many people gave me coppers, and here and there I received a sixpence, and twice I received a shilling. The pockets both of my trousers and my jacket grew, after a time, quite uncomfortably heavy.

But it was not pleasant; nor did custom stale the unpleasantness. I might tell myself that it was a joke to receive this money from housewives and retired majors, but I could not convince myself of it. The argument that it was a new sensation, and that I was collecting new sensations, was not at all consoling. And there were one or two slight clashes with the police which were fundamentally disturbing. Accustomed, as is everyone in my position in society, to deference from policemen, it was eminently distasteful to find them condescending towards me. I would have preferred to find them actually hostile. The feeling of dislike for the whole business grew greater as the day went on. Where at first it merely called for a certain amount of resolution, now it demanded the exertion of all my will to keep at it, and my nerves were jangled and I felt sick. And I began to feel a most unbearable distaste for the ballads I was singing, 'The Devout Lover' and 'Parted and 'Two Eyes of Grey'. Already I had found that my repertoire was limited; one may fancy one knows many songs, but as soon as one starts singing them in the street one soon discovers that only the very familiar ones remain clear in one's memory. To try to sing a song when one does not know the words at the same time as one cannot sing the tune gives a certain formlessness to one's efforts not likely to produce many coppers. The three songs I could sing right through I had never liked (I had mostly learned them as a result of the amusement their sentiments aroused) and after about the hundredth repetition I simply hated them. To finish 'worshipping her with distant reverence' and then, after a dozen silent paces, to strike up 'Dearest, our day is over' became, in the end, acutely painful – like shifting from one blister to another towards the end of a long march.

Eventually I brought the obstinate side of me to see reason. I broke off 'Two Eyes of Grey' in the middle of a bar – just as their sadness was breaking my heart – and left the purgatory of the roadway for the heavenly privacy of the pavement. Now I was seized with a sort of panic, and dashed away round corners in a hurried effort to get away from the scene of my labours. The memory of it, even at that short distance, was revolting to me. I felt hot under my collar. The coppers jingling in my pockets seemed to betray me to the passers-by even though I was positive they had not seen me singing in the streets. I felt as if I could not turn enough corners away from the scene of my secret labours, just as no amount of washing will seem to rid one of the scene of contamination after accidental contact with filth.

I suppose that an appropriate gesture following this change of heart would have been to throw the mass of money I had acquired down the drain, but I did not. I changed the coppers at a couple of tobacconists' shops – they were glad to do it for me – and found rather to my surprise that the total takings amounted to only a few pence less than a pound. That meant an average of nearly a penny a minute during five hours' singing – far more than quite highly skilled labour is paid. But it must have been a lucky day and I must have taken all the cream off the market. Later in 1919, and, as far as I know, from that day to this, it was impossible to gain a pound by half a day's street singing. But that pound served its purpose; it paid cab fares and things during a very enjoyable evening. I must have been more ingenious then than now – for the life of me I could not nowadays entertain a première danseuse (even supposing I was familiar enough with one to try to) for a whole evening on a single sovereign. Of course, that evening I was the victim of a certain hoarseness and soreness of throat which elicited the sympathy of the lady in question, and that may have helped.

Chapter Thirteen

TIME seemed to fly by in those mad months; there seemed hardly time to draw breath between the beginning and the end of a term; vacations passed in a flash. The passage of every one of those flying days saw me left farther behind in my work in the hospital. Already I was no longer a student of brilliant promise; I had dropped back into the ranks of the lower average ones – one of those who would presumably just scrape through their examinations after a failure or two, and would never be given the better hospital appointments, and who would subside in the end into the poorest of general practices. A little more waste of time, and ridiculous behaviour at the hospital, and I would sink still lower, and be numbered among the few thoroughly unsuccessful ones, the ones who became legendary figures, pottering about round the dissecting room and the laboratories, spoken of by their old contemporaries with a tolerant smile, and finally falling away (it is to be presumed) into the ranks of casual labour, or of the down-and-outs, until pneumonia and bronchitis did their work and their bodies, as those of unclaimed paupers, made their appearance on the dissecting room tables to complete the cycle. Every detail of that picture was clear to me, and I was so far sunk in distressed apathy that it could not stimulate me to exertion.

Something else did, however – the arrival home of my father. With old age close upon him, and looking forward to a well earned and honourable retirement, he was shocked to find how little his scapegrace son had progressed towards independence. It must be borne in mind that we did not set eyes on each other from the time I was fourteen until the time I was twenty; he had left me in England with every grounds for expecting me to achieve success, and he was accustomed, thanks to the achievements of my inconvenient brothers and sisters, to expect success of his children. He was horrified, genuinely horrified, to find that his youngest child was already a comparative failure – and I suppose there were not wanting hints and indications that I was a loose liver; there was a vague but unmistakable aura of scandal gathering round me. He was far more worried about me than I was.

No one had ever worried about me before (which was largely my fault, because I secretly kept the details of my life to myself) and I fancy it was the shock of that discovery which started me working again. I began to reappear in the dissecting room; I arranged to have a 'part' allotted to me; I even took part, with ultimate success, in various 'signups'. I found that by transferring my allegiance from the University of London to the Royal College of Surgeons I could proceed to take Part II of the Second Examination before passing Part I – the latter including that impossible test, the Anatomy Examination. Part II dealt with pharmacology – drugs, medicines, British Pharmacopeia – and I made a lightning rush through the course and passed the examination with absurd ease at the end of it. That was comforting, in a vague way. It showed that I was not the complete idiot most people had come to believe me, but it still left me with the anatomy examination to face. I could not nibble round that much longer. And as my new anxiety to get on died away, and as the longing within me for another career grew more unbearable, the old scenes in the dissecting room came to life again – the old ludicrous 'signups', the old amusement among my fellows, the old feeling of lacerated nerves, the old sick disgust with the whole abominable business.

There was an atrocity in the dissecting room which periodically lifted up its frightful head – the School Examination in Bones. That title probably sounds amusing to the lay mind, but to a medical student it carries a more sinister significance than any frightfulness of the Inquisition. It was incumbent upon everyone to pass the School Examination in Bones before taking Part I of the Second, and periodically the Professor of Anatomy would chalk up on the slate walls of the dissecting room the announcement that there would be an Examination in Bones on such and such a date, and all men were to remember that they must pass this as early as possible. Everybody did pass it except

106

me – I honestly cannot understand how they did. The human body, especially the human skull, contains a bewildering number of bones of the most fantastic shapes and sizes, and muscles are attached to their prominences and their 'rough surface' and their grooves, in the most arbitrary fashion; they articulate with each other in a manner which always struck me as being entirely senseless; and arteries and veins and nerves dash in and out of the holes (foramina, the student calls them) in them in a far more perplexing muddle than a kitten can make of a ball of wool. I would far sooner start to learn the features, tastes, habits and past history of every one of the seven million inhabitants of London than all the intricate details of the four hundred bones of the human skeleton. For those who can achieve this latter task I have the very utmost and most genuine admiration. But at the time I hated everyone who passed the Examination in Bones with a most bitter and envious hatred. I believe that to this day they still smile at that hospital when they discuss reminiscently my attempts at passing that examination. I myself would no more dream of laughing at those attempts than I would dream of laughing at the amusing contortions of a man poisoned with strychnine.

The one thing I cannot decide in my mind is whether, if I had really wanted to qualify in medicine, if I had never wanted to write books, and if I had never had an infernal elder brother who made records, whether, in that case, I could ever have passed that wretched examination. I cannot bring myself to believe that I could, but of this I am certain, that I shall never, while life endures, go back there again and try. The feeling of unretrieved failure is not particularly pleasant, but the alternative would be a great deal worse.

It is very difficult to remember exactly what eventually turned the balance and decided me to break out of this hopeless impasse. Various stimulating things happened in one way and another. I had drifted into the artistic and literary set which was in those days to be found in Chelsea – the première danseuse before mentioned was a member of it, and about the only one who ever did any honest work. Work was already at a discount in Chelsea; within a very few years painters and sculptors (not literary men so much) who had any ambition to work, and who had the queer notion that it was better to produce work than to talk about it in a weary string of epigrams, have all migrated to unatmospheric places like Golders Green and Chelsea studio rents have mounted to a colossal height, and the studios are tenanted largely, I believe – but I do not lay it down as a positive fact – by people who believe a studio is the right place to give parties in and further that parties should be the only activity noticeable in a studio. In those years this movement was only just beginning. There were people with unearned incomes who took studios in Chelsea, in the hope that Augustus John might one day come visiting, but the majority of folk there still at least talked of work, even if they had ceased to do any. At first I was dazzled by all the talk of the pictures and the books and the plays and the poems which were just going to be painted or written, and I was a little awed by the independent manner in which artistic reputations were blasted with a breath, but that effect wore off after a time. Probably what influenced me most was the fact that these world weary poets and about-to-be-creative artists all had a remarkable tendency to borrowing money and never paying it back; the large salaries which theatrical companies paid to the première danseuse were quite largely absorbed, I discovered, by these untidy-haired people.

I might have borne with that, despite the indignation it aroused, if it had not slowly become apparent that all their talk was merely talk; those people who spoke so glibly of pictures and poems and novels had never had anything whatever exhibited or published – at any rate, had never finished anything. One or two of them had had unfinished poems published in little magazines (one could hardly spend one evening with them without hearing about that) but not one of them could show me a bit of solid work which they had ever completed. Even the plays which I heard about on every hand, which were just going to be produced by an artistic company at an artistic theatre, never seemed to reach even the scenario stage of development. Why, I myself, with my humorous articles in the hospital *Gazette*, had published more than they had, and the poems which I kept locked away in my desk were far better than the maundering fragments I heard bleated forth at alcoholic pyjama parties. That tended to set me thinking.

But there was another incident which may have been the deciding factor, and that had nothing to do with art or literature in the least. It was the breaking off of Puggy's engagement – I do not think either Puggy or his wife (who is not the girl he was engaged to) will mind if the story is told. Puggy was, and is, one of my friends – not a Chelsea acquaintance, but a friend – and he one evening told an assemblage of my friends and me that he was engaged to be married. Puggy was easily the best catch among us – he was a year or two older than the rest of us, he was comfortably stupid, he had a wealthy father, he had a City position with a good salary, and he was comparatively free from vice. Certainly he was the one among my friends who was the most likely to become betrothed, but there was something about his manner when he made the announcement which exalted our interest. He was not sufficiently brazen about it, and not sufficiently embarrassed, to convince us that he particularly wanted to be promised in marriage, nor even that he was prepared to give up his freedom in exchange for those privileges of marriage which he could not get otherwise and wanted badly. The story came out bit by bit as we questioned him.

From first to last Puggy refused to believe that he had fallen into a trap, and I am inclined to agree with him. It was about the next best thing to a trap, all the same. He had been caressing the not unwilling daughter of the house where he was visiting when her mother entered. The mother instantly assumed that he wished to marry her daughter, and Puggy, for the sake of peace, agreed. The father, arriving shortly after from his office, gave the pair his blessing, and the matter was settled. Puggy told us all this dolefully, while we tried hard not to laugh. It was the complications which made matters so much worse. Puggy's future father-in-law, a Mincing Lane merchant, or a Leadenhall merchant, or something, was a strict Nonconformist, who went to Chapel three times on Sunday, and who made his family go too, and who now expected Puggy to accompany them – it may sound incredible but it is perfectly true. And Puggy's father did not approve at all – it was not specially the Chapel-going which excited his antagonism, for he did not care two hoots about that – of his son's engagement, although he had not vetoed it.

It was not to be expected that Puggy told us about this all at once; he was not that kind. It only came out bit by bit, as we sat round my bedroom drinking the whisky I kept for visitors. I can see his puzzled honest face now, contorted with dismay, as he blurted out some fresh horrible complication in the affair which had just occurred to him. Somewhere towards one o'clock on Sunday morning – the session had begun on Saturday night – a brilliant idea came up into my mind. The two things which suggested it were probably the sight of Puggy drinking whisky with a hand trembling with emotion, and the knowledge that in my wardrobe lay a reserve bottle of whisky, quite full.

'And I don't like the girl, I tell you,' wailed Puggy. 'I don't like her.'

'What did you want to kiss her for, then, you fool?' asked someone.

'I don't know. You know how it is. And she wanted me to.'

I got out the fresh bottle and filled another glass for Puggy. At the same time I flickered an eyelid at the other two. There was no need to do anything more definite; those men had fought shoulder to shoulder with me in faction fights innumerable at school, had backed me up in complicated lies at the smallest cue, had planned all sorts of irregularities with me. It only needed the merest ghost of a wink to let them know that some scheme was in the air, and that anything I put forward would need their unfailing tactful support.

'Go easy,' said Puggy, regarding the depth of colour of the fresh tumbler.

'Oh, you can manage that all right,' I said. 'Of course you can. What about you blokes?'

The others accepted similar drinks, and kept them by their sides. They had already reached their modest limit.

'Come on, tell us some more about it,' I said to Puggy. 'You say she wanted you to kiss her?'

Puggy reasserted the fact, with emphasis. It seemed such an unlikely thing even to him that he could not help speaking of it. He sipped generously at his tumbler with the force of his emotion, and no sooner had he put it down than one of the full ones was dexterously substituted – a distinct improvement on my original idea.

From that point matters progressed like clockwork. There was no need to coax Puggy into further drinking; he had drunk sufficient to make him disregard the refilling of his glass, and his burden of trouble and our sympathetic reception of his plaints made him thirsty. He waxed talkative; he spoke more and more wildly; there even came a time when in a maudlin moment he began to speak with enthusiasm about his fiancée. The fact that she had come unsolicited into his arms seemed now a virtue in his eyes. No one else in the world loved him, except Margery. That was the time to say 'I don't believe you' – somewhere about two-thirty a.m.

Puggy blinked at us across the room. The others took up the cue enthusiastically – as tactfully as ever they had helped to set a talkative master on his hobby horse.

'She does, I tell you,' said Puggy.

'Go on,' said we.

Even with seven whiskies inside him it was not easy to coax Puggy to the point of accepting a challenge, but we did it in the end.

'You just show us,' I said.

'Hear hear,' said the others, the plan of campaign now obvious to them. Puggy's muddled brain resented our doubts.

'Come along and show us,' I said.

Puggy agreed, stupidly.

The cold night air outside was as effective as a blow from a club in depriving him of the small remainder of his wits. We had the utmost difficulty in preventing him from bawling out songs as we hurried him along the quiet streets, and our opposition had the effect of arousing his belligerent mood. He was fighting drunk when we reached the house. He never had the least hesitation in leading us up the path and into the porch. All he wanted to do was to find his Margery, and anyone who opposed him would be asking for trouble. He banged at the knocker; someone else leaned against the bell-push. We managed to raise a volume of sound in the silent house quite surprising for three in the morning. The absence of instant response roused Puggy's ire, and he thundered at that knocker until the street re-echoed with the sound.

At last a light appeared within, and someone opened the door with much fumbling – Puggy's future father-in-law in dressing-gown and pyjamas.

'Who's there!' he asked; looking up across the hall we could see his future mother-in-law and his fiancée and the two maids all peering over the balustrade to see the cause of all this commotion.

'It's me,' said Puggy. 'I want to see my girl. I want these gentlemen to see my girl.'

'Why, you're drunk,' said Puggy's future father-in-law in disgusted surprise.

That is about the most tactless thing anyone can say to a drunken man.

'I'm not drunk. Who the devil are you to say I am?' demanded Puggy, trying to push his way in.

'Get out,' said his future father-in-law. Someone was still leaning against the bell push.

There were all the makings of a magnificent row already, but a beautiful coincidence cropped up at this very moment. Someone else came striding up the garden path.

'Why, it's George!' said the old gentleman, still more surprised. George was the son of the house, evidently returning from some secret nocturnal ramble, and not at all pleased at being discovered by his father at three in the morning. 'What are you doing out at this time – on the Sabbath, too?'

The interruption gave Puggy his chance, and he staggered into the hall, yowling 'Margery!' at the top of his voice.

'Hi! Come back!' said his future father-in-law, running hastily after him. 'George! turn these fellows out.'

That started the real commotion. It was not my hand which knocked out the irritated George. It was not my hand which pulled the string of the old man's pyjama trousers and shamed him before the maids and his wife and daughter. That was all Puggy's doing, while we stood outside helpless with laughing. I do not think I had any part in the scuffle which started a huge valuable vase rolling across the hall, remorseless as death, to where stairs led down to the kitchen and where it flew to pieces like a shell. I remember that throughout the whole business someone was still pressing on the bell push – it may have been me. Windows were opening along the whole street; public interest was growing intense. It could only have been a matter of a few seconds before the arrival of the police that we dragged Puggy out of the hall and down the path.

The betrothal was terminated from that day – Puggy's father even saw fit to laugh at the indignant expostulations of the outraged family and to declare that he was glad to find that his son had so much vice in him. Puggy was grateful to us later, but he soon showed how little he deserved his freedom by getting himself engaged all over again to someone else almost as soon as the scandal died down – he was a born married man. And his wife has never ceased to regard us with the very gravest suspicion.

I cannot help thinking that an existence of harassing uncertainty punctuated by incidents of this sort – most of them it is true, not in the best of taste just like this example – was peculiarly stimulating to my mind. I knew that the time had drawn near when I might find myself a down and out without visible means of support. The prospect worried me very considerably, sufficient even to interfere with my sleep and to sow the seeds of the insomnia which troubles me to this day, but it was not sufficiently worrying to goad me into the acceptance of medicine (and general practice) as a career – certainly not to goad me into doing enough honest though tedious work to get me through the Second Examination. The strain and stress of this tormented existence, backed up by a series of adventures of all sorts (most of them unusual for a boy of nineteen or twenty) reacted violently on me. My mind was a torrent of ideas, mostly fantastic, occasionally practical.

To my great regret, I cannot remember what it was which gave me my final impetus to adopt the career at which I have since earned my living. It was some adventure or other, and probably it was a disreputable one, but which disreputable adventure out of many is more than I can say. Long ago I had reluctantly allowed the possibility of my becoming a novelist to be included among the permitted subjects of my internal debates. I wanted to be a novelist, without any doubt. But practical common sense still held me back. As I pointed out to myself over and over again, there was no shadow of an indication that I would be any good as a novelist. I knew no one who had ever published a novel. I knew no genuine literary people – only Chelsea caricatures. I did not know if it were possible for a literary beginner to live on his beginnings – and I very strongly doubted it. And I realised that there would be lots of things about a literary life as lived in the present century which would irritate me profoundly. I would never be able to describe myself as a novelist or as an author either by word of mouth or on a document without a sense of absurd shyness (that is still the case); I would simply hate to do things which (I supposed) would be forced on me, like reading proofs and studying press cuttings (proofs, I regret to say, are still part of my existence, but I have never paid a press-cuttings subscription); I would meet people at parties who would consider any author as necessarily a more valuable product than any doctor or brick-layer, which would annoy me intensely; and even if by a miracle I succeeded in overriding all these difficulties and established myself as an author I would still be harassed by the fear of a waning inventive power. It was only after a very dreadful struggle that the uncalculating half of myself won the victory over the calculating. But the victory was won in the end. I can remember very clearly indeed the afternoon when I threw my cautious self overboard; when I left my childhood behind and stepped blindly into what was as near adult life as I shall ever attain.

Chapter Fourteen

EVEN then it was not too easy to take the next step. Perhaps it can be pictured how a highly successful professional middle class family received the announcement that the absurd youngest child, who was already well on the way to wrecking his life, had decided to 'be an author'. The practice of literature was a quite unknown profession to the Family, despite the fact that every member of it was a voracious reader. By a strange chance no one in the Family knew any authors, or publishers, or reviewers – how it was I cannot imagine, for nowadays they seem to grow on every bush – and that made the respectability of the profession of literature extremely suspect, more so even than it would have been to most middle class families. Moreover, it made my new choice seem the more undesirable, because they all thought that people could only succeed in literature with plenty of influence and friends behind them (were they right?). The Family could wield a good deal of influence in my favour were I to choose any profession other than literature, and they were fully accustomed to pulling strings and seeing strings pulled – I was cutting myself off from all the advantages of being my father's son and my brothers' brother and my uncles' nephew. And I was letting down the Family too; any member of it would be pleased to meet an author, perhaps, to have a drink with one, or sit at his table on the P. & O. boat, or even possibly to entertain one to dinner, but to have an author as a son or brother or nephew was asking too much of their forbearance, it would incarcerate a skeleton in the family cupboard, and family cupboards are flimsy places of concealment.

Moreover, there is something intrinsically absurd about wanting to be an author. If only I had expressed an overwhelming desire to leave off being a doctor to become an accountant, or an architect, or an average adjuster, which (if only I would do a little solid work) might still be respectable and might possibly be brilliant. They did not like the idea of my starving; naturally they would not feel any sympathy for my determination that I would far rather starve and try to write than live in plenty and not write. Danger and doubt and difficulty had been part of the air I breathed for years past. For at least a year I had been reconciling myself to a future of failure and possible starvation, and the prospect now held no horror for me. Only a year or two back various doctors had expressed the opinion that I was likely to die quite soon, so that death was a familiar thought. I had nibbled so long at the idea of suicide that it had come to be regarded by me as a pleasant and quite desirable end if all else failed. There is no doing anything with a man who has reached that condition of mind. No arguments that can be produced can be more cogent than the ones he has already thought of, and no consequences can possibly be worse than the ones he is prepared to face.

As a last possible resort compromises were suggested. The first and feeblest was that I should get myself qualified and then turn my energies to writing, after the example of Mr Somerset Maugham and Mr Warwick Deeping and various other very distinguished men. That called for no consideration before refusal. I had not faced all this commotion merely to start again. It was more tempting when it was suggested that I might abandon medicine and find some less exacting profession wherein I could indulge my queer whim for writing. As Louis XIV was once 'almost obliged to wait' so I almost began to hesitate. But I knew that in my heart of hearts it was no good; the canny side of me realised that the slump of 1920 was not a good time to start trying a commercial career, and the artistic side of me having got a firm grip of the possibility of my actually beginning to write there and then refused to leave go. I would not permit myself to be dragged away from the sanctuary I had reached. My worried family saw this temporary madness of mine develop before their eyes into permanent mania.

It was a bad time for them, as I am glad to acknowledge. My father, who, as responsible for my coming on earth, chose to feel responsible for my welfare on my reaching adult life, was terribly worried. I can feel for him now, because nowadays my chief source of anxiety is fear that my small son (who at the moment is scrabbling in the wastepaper basket beside me and making inarticulate noises of wonder at the marvels contained therein) should choose to try to be an author when he grows up. I shall be alarmed and terribly disappointed if he does, although with my own example before me I know that it is possible for a young man without influence or any apparent talent in boyhood to achieve a competency in literature. What my father felt about it without even that one example before him to cheer him I can well imagine.

And as everybody pitifully pointed out (it was so obvious that the remark maddened me – it was obvious enough for me to have noticed the point unaided) I had never given proof that I could write. It was only a surmise on my part. Humorous articles in the hospital *Gazette* were no proof that I could write novels, and I had declared that it was novels to which I should devote my energies. To their mind my decision was simple, sheer lunacy – and I do not blame them in the least. But I had the bit between my teeth now, and I broke away rejoicing in my hard-won freedom. They let me go, rather sadly. And if their sadness was somewhat relieved by the thought that inevitable failure would soon bring me back under control, submissive to rein and spur, that is nothing against them. They could not be expected to realise that I would genuinely much sooner prefer to die than to admit failure now that I had won my point.

Chapter Fifteen

So childhood and irresponsibility and careless disregard of the future were left behind now. I had taken my career into my own hands now. I was much more my own master than at least ninety-nine men out of a hundred. Any exertion I might make would solely be for my own benefit and the result of a genuine desire on my part. Even at that time I formed the resolution (to which I have clung ever since) never to write a word I did not want to write; to think only of my own tastes and ideals, without a thought for those of editors or publishers or even of the general public – a perfectly splendid resolution to make when no single editor or publisher or member of the general public was in the least aware of my existence.

I did not form that resolution in words (I have only in all my life kept one 'good resolution' in that form) and I certainly did not frame it like a text and hang it over my desk; it is only now with leisure to think about it that I realise that there was any such resolve. But it was there all the same. It is hard for me to associate literary and artistic ideals with myself. I jeer at them when other people state any. That is probably the result of early association with people in Chelsea who never left off proclaiming their ideals and yet never put them into practice. But I suppose I have some, and I think they have profound influence on my work. Unstated though they were, I pursued them hotly, madly, during those early wild months when I began to write.

Apologetically, I must call attention again to the fact that I knew nothing about the technical side of writing at all. I had never met an author or a publisher in my life. I had a vague idea that the length of a novel was measured in thousands of words, and also that when it was finished you chose your publisher, sent in your manuscript to him with your name and address, and awaited results; it might be better to obtain an introduction to him first, but it was not strictly necessary. This was all true, as it happened, but not of a great deal of use. I had to count words on a page of the various books I had at hand, and multiply the answer by the number of pages, before I had the least idea what was the usual length of a novel. Publishers at this moment were people quite indistinguishable – it had never before been of any importance to me to know of the subtle distinction between Herbert Jenkins and William Heinemann, between Jarrolds and the Fanfrolico Press. No one need ever bother about publishers as long as he never intends to write.

It soon became a matter of importance to know the permissible limits of the length of a novel, and even as to the individual taste of various publishers, for my first novel was finished in a wild explosion of energy in a fortnight. Presumably for years the canny half of me and my family as well had been sitting on the safety valve of my desire for artistic self expression. The pressure accumulated had become enormous, and now that it had found a vent it blew itself off with a terrific crash. I could not stop. I felt I must write at hectic speed without a pause. The fact that there was need for haste for me to get my work done before the pursuing bogey of failure caught me up did not come into consideration. I wrote and I wrote, morning, afternoon and evening, and in the night as well. The material came bubbling up inside me like a geyser or an oil gusher. There was no need to bale it up with a bucket or a pump – it streamed up of its own accord, down my arm and out of my fountain pen in a torrent of six thousand words a day.

It is not easy to convey to the lay mind just what six thousand words a day implies, because the picture is confused by the fact that a man writing original work, when he is fit and his mind is working easily, can write a thousand words in an hour. At that rate six thousand words a day implies only six hours' work a day – less than a civil servant does. But that is quite an inappropriate criterion. What should be borne in mind is that the production of a thousand words a day of creative work is generally the limit of a man's strength when maintained for any length of time. Very few novelists publish that amount – a thousand words a day means four longish novels a year. To write three thousand words a day for more than a day or two means the loss of all taste for enjoyment while the effort lasts – complete inability to obtain any satisfaction from reading or pictures or music or food or conversation or even (in severe cases) from tobacco. Six thousand words a day means utter, delirious exhaustion from the end of the first day onwards. It is like a coal heaver trying to empty a cart by carrying six hundredweights of coal at a time instead of one. During that first insane spasm I kept up that pace for a fortnight.

The work was atrociously bad. I had not the least idea of how to set about writing a novel. For me to take pen and paper at that time and try to write a novel was comparable with my ordering a truckload of bricks now and trying to build a house without stopping to think. By the time I had finished (if my enthusiasm carried me to a finish) the thing might be recognisable as intended to be a house; it might just possibly keep out rain and wind; if no one in the world had ever tried to build a house before it might even be considered a good house, but actually it would be a very bad house both from the aesthetic and the utilitarian aspects. Similarly this was a very bad book; like human nature, it was neither good nor beautiful. It was (as perhaps one could only expect) a hectic account of the adventures of schoolboys and medical students. It was absolutely crammed with incidents (some of them very like one or two which have appeared in this book) and it included characters by the dozen. All that sounds more like praise than condemnation. In a well written book these characteristics might be desirable, but in a badly written book they were absolutely ruinous. The plot was jerky and episodic; the characters displayed chameleon-like variability to suit each new development; the climax came some way before the end so that the last six chapters were no more necessary than corsets on a statue.

It had never occurred to me that it might be as well, before writing a novel, to stop and let the idea settle itself down; that with patience and a little thought a smoother development of the plot might be obtained so that the characters might not be bewilderingly inconsistent; that a selective taste might decide that every single thought that came into my head might not be worth writing down. That wretched book displayed in every line the fact that it was written by an out of work medical student in the early twenties in a desperate hurry – to that microscopic extent it might be considered a good book. Otherwise it was very bad indeed.

I did not appreciate these weaknesses. I fancy I was conscious of them, far back in my mind, but I had no thought to spare for them, just as a man might notice and yet disregard a twinge of lumbago when kneeling at the altar at his wedding. Perhaps it was optimism, or more probably it was simply a result of the fact that that wretched book had occupied every second's thought for a fortnight, but anyway I regarded the finished achievement with awe. I thought it was very good indeed. Possibly the most difficult task an author ever encounters is to decide upon the merits of work just completed or in progress. In this respect a good secretary earns far more than her salary when an author employs her (or a wife either, for that matter) and even then allowance must be made for the fact that the unfortunate secretary, too, has been living with the thing for some weeks and is likely to be biased one way or the other as well. It is for this reason that I refuse to be ashamed either of that book or of my opinion of it at that time.

A kindly friend saw to the typewriting of the monstrosity for me, and it was wrapped up and dispatched to a publisher (I cannot remember who was the final selection) and I fell into the coma of complete exhaustion while awaiting what I looked upon as its certain acceptance. I honestly could not think it possible that any publisher (although I knew publishers were supposed to be fools) could fail to observe the transcendent merits of the thing. I really and genuinely believed that any publisher would be deliriously pleased to have it offered to him. Meanwhile my head ached, and my insomnia had become unbearable, my right thumb was afflicted with the horrid little pain which is a premonitory symptom of writer's cramp, I could neither sit still nor be active, neither read nor think, neither smoke nor eat as a result of my weariness.

A fortnight of unhappy, lonely inactivity cured me. I was fit again just in time to meet without panic the first of a whole series of smashing blows a rather implacable destiny was about to deal at me. The novel came back from the publishers. There was only a printed slip with it, stating that he regretted he could not 'see his way to publication' – a perfectly horrible phrase. It was a shock to me, there is no denying that. But after the first numbing disappointment it was easy to find comfort. The publisher's reader was probably a fool or a knave; conceivably he had never read the thing at all. The next publisher on the list was chosen as the lucky recipient, and the manuscript was sent to him. At the end of a fortnight he sent it back to me.

I cannot remember whether my faith in the merits of the book began to be shaken as early as this. I believe it was, but it might not have been until after one or two more rejections. What I can remember very distinctly is thrusting my disappointment aside, along with the opened parcel, setting my teeth, reaching for pen and paper, and starting another novel.

The motives influencing me are easily analysed. Desire for publication, just as publication, was not a very powerful one. The longing to write books was far greater than the longing to have them read. The imminent pressing fear of hunger and cold was a powerful stimulant, but I think it is true that starvation was more unpleasant in prospect because it would put an end to my writing of books than because it would put an end to my life. There was somewhere within me a desire for flamboyant success on account of the way such success would wipe the eye of my Family. They all, I knew, were confidently awaiting my failure and the collapse of my obstinacy and the knowledge irritated me in a way which I cannot well appreciate now. I wanted very urgently to be able to flaunt a resounding success in their faces. I was even prepared, when success came, to wear long hair and an astrakhan collar and to talk to them in a Chelsea manner solely to rub the fact of my success well into them in the way which would hurt most – I somehow have never done it.

The new novel was written in a saner manner than the first one. I must have had a glimmering of sense by now, for I forcibly withheld myself from writing more than two thousand words a day, so that the writing of the book actually consumed as much as six weeks. But I still had not realised that (as far as I am concerned) the better part of the work is done before pen is put to paper; a novel made up as I go along is weak in places, episodic, somewhat incoherent, possibly self-contradictory. To start work upon a book without having a definite end to lead up to (the end is more important than the middle) means slipshod, makeshift work most of the time. If anybody cares to check this statement I can only refer him to the book in question, which was eventually published as *The Paid Piper*. The title will not be found in the list of my books at the beginning of this one, not because this is published by another firm (although that is another reason) but because I think it a very bad book. It is just as painful a memory to me as any other foolishness of mine.

Most of the book was written in Free Libraries; it was more comfortable there than alone in a cheerless, fireless room, although Free Libraries have very distinct disadvantages as places for literary composition. They are always full of shivering out of works who have also come in to get warm, and who scan the 'situations vacant' columns of the newspapers in dull hopelessness. The struggling author looks at them with a shuddering fear that he will be like that too in a week or two, and it is brought home to him that his worn clothes and broken shoes stamp him just as unmistakably as theirs do them. And weeks of enforced inactivity have given those out of works a pitiful interest in the petty things around them – for instance, in the shabby young man who sits at the central table writing away so persistently. For the life of them they cannot help but come and peer over his shoulder to see what he is writing, and he, knowing that the inverted commas and paragraphing will inevitably disclose that he is writing a novel, self-consciously puts his arms round his work (like a little boy who does not want his neighbour to cheat from him at school) and waits, consumed with shyness, for them to go away. And library porters are apt to be officious, too. Begging letter writers often make free libraries their workroom, because the dictionaries are available for use there; the porter has instructions to impede the activities of begging letter writers. Sometimes, in a manner not too polite, he impedes the activities of struggling authors, too. I was used to the deference extended by public servants to a young man of good appearance; the curt camaraderie of a library porter towards my shabbiness (I was suspected of begging letter writing, remember) was maddening to me. It was only a poor satisfaction to turn upon them in fury, making the most use of a refined accent and a fluent vocabulary, and to see them wilt before this unexpected encounter with a 'gentleman' albeit one with fringes to his trousers. Such incidents were always degrading and upsetting.

But that was not so maddening as the arrival of bills – strange reminders of my former life of a few months back but seemingly centuries old. To be pestered for payment of things which I had already come to look upon as unattainable luxuries was savagely ironical. Those bills were numerous, and some of them were of old standing. They reached me in shoals; soon they began to threaten me with all sorts of penalties if I did not pay. They worried me nearly frantic – it must be remembered that I had a good deal to worry me at that time besides overwork. The worry has left its mark; to this day I pay bills now by return of post – not, I think, for fear lest things should go wrong again and lest I should have them to worry me during a new period of abject poverty, but because of the sheer savage pleasure in writing the cheque and getting rid of the horrid thing.

Even bills were not quite as worrying as the infernal shoe question. I believe the most degrading sensation on earth – worse even than the discovery of lice in one's clothes – is the feeling of icy, filthy water leaking in and out of one's shoes at every step. There is nothing so calculated to break a man's spirit. Nowadays, I still find myself, when I receive an unexpected cheque, saying to myself, 'I had better get another pair of shoes.' Yet I used to think in those days that whenever success came to me so that I could afford extravagance I would make up for those shabby clothes and ragged collars by wearing the finest clothes money could buy; I used to look forward to a highly decorative middle age distinguished by the most elaborate dandyism, and nevertheless the clothes I wear nowadays when I can afford better are if anything rather more shabby and battered than the ones I hated then. That is the effect laziness has on my ambition.

Another worry of those days has persisted in a modified form till now, and presumably it will continue until I die, and after that will linger on as a worry to my heirs. That is the influence of the postman. Of all people on earth the author is the one who depends most on the postman. Every single turning point in his career, whether for good or for evil, is preceded by the postman's knock. At any time the postman may bring him an acceptance or a rejection, an offer of a thousand pounds for film rights or a solicitor's letter threatening action for libel, a congratulatory letter from an archbishop or a page of filth from a suburban spinster. He cannot help being interested in what the postman brings, and in whether he has brought anything. Publishers have an engaging habit of promising in their agreements to send cheques and accounts at a specified date, and then of not doing so until a couple of months after that date has lapsed. During all that two months the hungry author who is depending on that cheque to buy himself food spends most of his time waiting for the next post. A man who works in an office can usually be sure that only at specified times and seasons can he receive his dismissal or a rise in salary; an author can receive what is their equivalent by any post. And when his whole well-being, physical and mental and moral, depends on what the postman may bring him (as it does when he is a beginner) his anxiety about the postman is quite excruciating.

I was well aware that I had begun my career from the wrong end. Men who write novels usually only do so as an expansion of some other side of their life, whether they are clerks or newspaper men. They mostly have some sort of dependable living, even if they are only freelance journalists or short story writers on which to rely while they write novels. Most of them, as far as I can see, have been in contact one way or another with the London literary world before they try to publish; quite a fair proportion of them bring to their first novel a fair reputation as magazine writers or as people prominent in the circles in which critics live. I was doing very much the other thing. I was trying to write novels without having seriously attempted any other literary form; I could not write magazine stuff to save my life (although I tried once or twice for that very motive); I had never set eyes on a critic as far as I knew. I do not believe that my lack of a magazine reputation or my unnatural ignorance of writers ever hindered my attaining publication, but I can safely affirm that my lack of a profession on which to live while writing novels very nearly prevented it altogether.

And yet despite all these cares and irritations I was, although not happy, far more comfortable than I had been. I was filled with the pleasurable feeling that I had set myself a task which was worth doing, and worth doing well, and was sufficiently difficult to satisfy the most high falutin of ideals. It was not exactly pleasant to thrust out of one's mind all thoughts of the rejection which arrived last night, and of this morning's headache, and of prying out-of-works, and officious porters, to set one's teeth and to turn doggedly to the completion of the day's two thousand words, but it was a far saner sort of life than being a medical student and a would-be man about town. Not in the darkest hours of those days did the idea of suicide crop up in my mind in the attractive guise it had at one time presented. Even when despair came to be added to misery there was a grim pleasure to be extracted from fighting a losing battle to the last ditch.

The new novel grew in its six weeks of development into a tangled jumble of stories, some long and some short, most of them bad, but one or two of them good, supposed to be told by the three main characters. It was a horribly difficult technical problem; I fancy that if I were to read the book now I should be pleasantly surprised at the ingenuity with which I surmounted those technical difficulties. By the time I had finished it I was not quite as pleased with it as I had been with the first novel when I finished that, but I liked it better than I did the other at the moment. Two more rejections of the first one had set me thinking about it in a more cold-blooded fashion. I tried to criticise it ruthlessly to myself, and eventually found some points about it to criticise. I would even admit to myself that it was possible that one or two odd people might exist who would not like it. The admission came the more easily now that I had a new book to think about.

The new book was an odd production in its way – it was an awful example of what happens when a young man takes pen and paper and lets his imagination loose without stopping very much to think. The hero was let in for the oddest adventures, into which he was led by chance sentences carelessly written and then found too attractive to erase. He fought in the Turkish Army; he languished in a Syrian prison. All sorts of subjects which might be considered taboo at that time were brought in regardless of any possible reader's feelings. The war, for instance, bulked large in it, and in those early nineteen-twenties, before *All Quiet on the Western Front* and *Journey's End* achieved their success, a convention had arisen to ignore the war. There was one whole chapter whose point depended on actual cannibalism, and cannibalism in the first degree, too – the devouring of a very beautiful woman by her lover when the two of them were locked in the ancestral dungeon by the jealous husband. The last seen of the erring wife was in the form of raw joints which the lover was gnawing – a perfectly horrible story. But war, cannibalism and all, *The Paid Piper* was finished and packed off on its rounds, following up the unlucky first one. To have two novels out with publishers meant more interest than ever in the arrival of the postman.

And no sooner had it begun its rounds than I seized pen and paper again and started my third novel. The urge to write it was pressing and overwhelming – the artistic urge, that is to say. There is no need to accentuate the fact that the economic urge could not possibly have been more noticeable. This time I had a skeleton plot to work to, a ready-made one, moreover, for it was a historical novel which I was beginning. Long before, when I was a small boy, my attention had been caught by three remarkable incidents all of the same character in Napoleon's career, which have never been properly explained – occasions when his volcanic energy deserted him and he delayed with fatal results just at the moment when he should have been most active. The first time was in 1812 when he dallied at Moscow at a time when a prompt retreat would have saved much of his army; the second time was in 1813 after the battle of Dresden when he neglected to follow up the retreating Austrians, thereby allowing them the opportunity to make good their retreat and incidentally to overwhelm the twenty thousand French he had sent to cut them off – in this case his dilatoriness deprived him of a victory which would have saved him his throne and cost him a whole army corps. The third occasion was during the Waterloo campaign when he failed to press the Prussians after Ligny – wasting half a day in a most odd manner – and so deprived himself of any chance of victory at Waterloo.

It was easy enough to provide him with a motive for these three delays; I created a mythical mistress for him. At Moscow she is sent in to him by his life-long Corsican enemy, Pozzo di Borgo, and the retreat is delayed by an impromptu honeymoon. She follows the Emperor, and, at Dresden she is wounded while riding with Napoleon's staff (several of the Marshals had feminine *aides de camp*, although Napoleon never did after

Egypt); at Ligny she reappears, after Napoleon has cast her off for supposed treachery, and shoots herself in the Imperial tent, so that during the vital three or four hours Napoleon is delayed by his sorrow and by the necessity for burying her. The general idea was a good one, and the local colour which could be worked in was perfectly gorgeous. The idea had been steadily maturing at the back of my mind during the writing of *The Paid Piper*, and I was all of an itch to start it. But still I had not learned how to use material. I never bothered to stop and think out important details until I had actually reached the point when they arose. When writing a novel, if it is realised at the start that certain characters, for the sake of the plot, must be in a certain place at a certain time half-way through, it is much to be preferred if arrangements for getting them there are devised quite early on; otherwise it may necessary to drag the characters to the rendezvous by the scruff of their necks in a manner likely to strain the credulity of the reader, and at the cost of some inconsistency of character or clumsiness of machinery which may spoil the book entirely and will certainly constitute a blemish. To take an example from a very great writer, Mr H. G. Wells in an early novel *The Island of Doctor Moreau*, has to make use of a shipwreck, an accidental rescue, a drunken captain in the new ship, and a general straining of possibility, all to get his hero safe and sound upon the uncharted island, presumably because he was in such a hurry to write the book that he could not stop to devise a more easy method. I believe (but I cannot remember for certain) that he also goes to the trouble and uncertainty of two successive shipwrecks in order to land his hero on a desert island in a much later book, the one about the megatheriung. I – without a thought of comparing myself with Mr H. G. Wells – found myself in similar tangles all through the new novel (which, by the way, inevitably acquired the title of *A Pawn Among Kings*). The motivisation had not been properly worked out at the start, with the result that I had to make use of various most unlikely changes of heart to provide a reason for various actions of the characters. There were a few good passages – a Napoleonic novel can hardly be imagined without a few good scenes being presented to the writer gratis – and the general idea was interesting, but there were glaring weaknesses.

Fortunately for me, perhaps, those weaknesses were not apparent to me at the time. I was toiling now through my third novel in less than six months. I think I must have been over-worked; certainly I was over-worried. And I was so engrossed in the writing of the thing to the general idea that I was likely to brush away minor details as negligible. Possibly – in fact it is very probable indeed – I was so convinced of my own ability as a writer that I thought that minor blemishes would be unnoticeable in the general splendour of the whole achievement. I was only just beginning to acquire any power of self-criticism which might enable me to guess at the effect of individual passages on the mind of the reader. And I still tended to tell myself that I could put things right in the typescript or in the proofs. I did not know then that I am constitutionally and temperamentally unable to make corrections in any finished work; the typescript of one of my novels has perhaps twenty corrections, the proof perhaps five – apart from those twenty-five all very minor alterations the thing appears in print exactly as it first leaves my pen, and I know now that as a result of this idiosyncrasy I must have the book worked out accurately to the last detail before starting work upon it.

But my theme had carried me away on this occasion. I marched armies to Moscow (just as I had done as a boy) and I sent cavalry regiments charging into the battery smoke; I burned Moscow, just as five hundred novelists from Tolstoi to G. A. Henty had done before me; I sent the shattered regiments trailing back across the snow-clad plains with my mind's eye full of Verestchagin's pictures. I followed up hotly in my anxiety to develop the plot; and I made a lamentable hash of what might have been quite a good book.

I finished it in the state which had now grown familiar to me – a state of feverish, restless weariness, tormented with insomnia and headaches and depression; the only merit about such a condition was that it left me no energy at all to be irritated by all the other troubles which are likely to annoy a harassed young author. Whether now, ten years later, I would survive a repetition of such a period of accumulated horror is more than I like to think about. My daily prayer is that I never shall have to try.

The pranks of a destiny which I had come to look upon as

positively malignant were by no means exhausted as yet. Just as *A Pawn Among Kings* was being finished I received the letter I had long been looking for; for the first time the postman had brought me something worth having. It was a note from a publisher to whom I had sent *The Paid Piper* asking me to call and see him. I told myself that this was the first step out of the valley of the shadow. I was too tired and distraught to feel elated at the knowledge that publication – and royalties – were approaching. I tried to brush my seedy clothes into a resemblance to respectability, and I went up to town to keep the appointment.

When I was a little boy at school we used to walk everywhere that we wanted to go; we had much more important things to spend our money on than bus fares. We used to walk to South Kensington when we went to see the museum there, and we used to walk back. Nowadays I spend idle moments wondering how much an eccentric millionaire would have to pay me to induce me to walk to South Kensington from South London, spend a day in a museum, and walk back. Walking up to London to see a publisher in an interview on which one's life depends is a far worse experience, as far as I can remember.

This was the first publisher's office into which I had ever penetrated. A girl secretary took my name, and ushered me into an inner room where a magnificently handsome young man (all publishers are not young and handsome, I have since discovered) sat at an opulent desk. But for once my photographic mind declined to take in details, and my memory is somewhat wanting too. I suppose we shook hands; I suppose I sat down. I remember we spent some minutes discussing irrelevant details such as the weather, and I remember that I smoked several of his cigarettes, which were peculiarly grateful to me. What I cannot remember positively is how much business we talked. I know that my impression is that I left that office and started on my three mile walk back firm in the conviction (and a little elated at last) that *The Paid Piper* was going to be published on ten-per-cent royalty terms and that the agreement would come by post. I may have been mistaken – I hope I was, for at that rate the curses I later hurled at that publisher's head will do him no damage – but whether I was mistaken or not the postman brought me no agreement. What he did bring me, eventually, was the typescript of *The Paid Piper*, sent back by that publisher without a word of explanation. It was a rather shattering blow.

Presumably (if my memory of the interview is correct) he had changed his mind or been overruled by higher authority (he was not a principal in the firm). Otherwise the only explanation of the incident is that he wanted to see what a man was like who wrote casually about cannibalism. I do not blame him in the least for his curiosity, but he might perhaps have sent me my bus fares before dragging me up to town to gratify it.

Once more there was need to exert my will to thrust aside a very bitter disappointment. It was on that occasion that I noticed another example of the truth of tags of minor fiction; a man confronted by a frightening situation and in need of all his resolution really does set his teeth; his nails really do cut into his palms; his jaw really does come forward. If things had not been so desperate it would have been quite interesting to watch myself reacting to all these blows of fate, but it was not specially interesting to me at that time. I had too many things to interest me already.

But that visit to the publisher's had actually done me a good service; it had shown me what a publisher's office was like. I could see now that it was perfectly possible for an author who had steeled himself against the insolence of office boys to deliver his manuscripts in person. To post the normal sized manuscripts costs sixpence, and the constant drain of sixpences was creating an impossible situation. But to go to town and back by bus only cost fourpence, thanks to the blessed mid-day fare – and it was always possible to walk. Further, now that I had three novels finished I could allow them to accumulate and then take all three to town together, delivering them in a circular walk to three different publishers, and save myself eighteen-pence.

There were disadvantages, I found – there are bound to be serious disadvantages to any course which saves such a colossal sum as eighteen-pence. Publishers' office boys in those days were a most objectionable tribe. They used to smile in pseudo-secrecy when a tattered author came stalking into the outer office and laid a ragged parcel of a manuscript on the counter. Those half-hidden smiles were most exasperating – quite as exasperating as the allusions to me in the old days as 'a budding author'. It was worse still when they failed to realise at once that the parcel did contain manuscript, and instead asked what it was. It was most embarrassing to have to own up verbally that it was a manuscript – usually with two or three typists and perhaps a waiting visitor or two within ear-shot. I was always very conscious of the stale old jokes about penniless authors and stonebroke poets. Why I should object to being thought a penniless author when I actually was one I cannot quite decide, but the thought of all those jokes had much to do with it. I felt even more gaunt and tattered and like something out of a comic than I actually was. To this day the one good suit which hangs in my wardrobe is maintained specially for the benefit of publishers' office boys.

There was very soon a chance of putting into practice my plan of taking all three manuscripts up to town at once, although I had sent *A Pawn Among Kings* out on its travels before I thought of it. One evening I sat in my room listening through my window to the postman on his nine o'clock round, waiting as he came up the street towards the house. As he neared it, I rose and went downstairs and waited by the street door for his possible arrival – there were occasions when I could not wait upstairs until he had knocked before I went down to see if there was anything for me. This evening as I reached the door he knocked a double knock. A parcel? Or a registered letter? The chances were it was a parcel – I was used to the arrival of parcels by now. I opened the door and the postman thrust an armful of packages upon me, or so it seemed to my distorted imagination. I peered at them in the light of the gas-jet. Steady the Buffs! Die hard, Fifty-Seventh! All three of the novels had come back together. By coincidence three different publishers had decided on the same day to reject some of my work. But there was a letter, too, addressed to me, and bearing on the top of the envelope the name of a very distinguished firm of publishers indeed. Perhaps those publishers were only sending back the manuscript for some trifling alteration; perhaps the letter indicated their wishes and held out hope of publication. I tore open the envelope. The letter inside ran something like this.

Dear Sir, We are returning to you under separate cover the manuscript of your novel *The Paid Piper*. We regret that we cannot see our way to publication, while thanking you for having allowed us the opportunity of reading it.

You will note that the return postage amounts to 6d. We shall be much obliged if you will remit this sum to us.

I believe they are the only firm of London publishers guilty of this crowning enormity. I think I must have tried nearly all of them. But it was about the last straw that they should make this demand on the very evening that all three of the immortal works should come home together.

It was not very long after this catastrophe, thank goodness, that the long expected letter arrived. *A Pawn Among Kings* only visited about three publishers before acceptance. The postman brought me one morning an envelope bearing the embossed name of a publishing firm (I came to know those envelopes so well) and in that envelope was an offer of publication; no 'ifs' or 'buts', but a straightforward offer, with royalty scales and everything else laid down, and the suggestion that if I approved of the offer they would send me the agreement to sign. I approved of it; the agreement came, and was signed, and I had nothing more to do than to await the arrival of the proofs, and publication, and certain success, and huge sums in royalties.

Success is an odd thing. In my innocence I believed that having achieved publication of a novel I had achieved success, but it brought little pleasure. For one thing I must have been through too much trouble before attaining it. There was none of the intoxication of delight I had anticipated. It all seemed stale and uninteresting. The fact that in something like a year's time I should be paid a sum of money was too remote to gild the cloud of disillusionment. A year is a long time; I had to wait some months before publication, and payment was only made at regular dates, the first, six months after publication. But that anticipated year's delay was only a minor part of the feeling of dull disappointment. Stevenson (whatever opinion one may hold about the quality of his work) was perfectly right when he said, 'It is better to travel hopefully than to arrive.' Arriving is not at all pleasant until one becomes accustomed to it; at any rate it is not pleasant to an embittered young man half dead with anxiety and overwork.

Something else happened to make of success a Dead Sea fruit which turned to ashes in my mouth. Now that someone

133

else had seen fit to approve of my work, and even to accord it a little temperate praise with true publisher's caution, I could look upon it with a less biased eye.

I could even bring myself to read the things over again in a critical mood, seeking not for perfections to admire but imperfections at which to sneer. I found them in plenty. The discovery was the more devastating in that I had long half-suspected the existence of those imperfections and yet had refused in the blindness of prejudice to admit it. That first novel of mine which once I had read over with awe I now read with shamed derision. The crudity both of its idealism and of its cynicism made me squirm in anguish. The bad taste of its plain speaking (there can be good taste as well as bad taste in indelicacy) set my teeth on edge. It was so obviously a young man's work, and now that I was six months older, and had been through six months of serious anxiety, and had achieved success, I was well qualified to judge of young men's work. I put the thing aside. It would have been a comforting gesture to have thrust it on the fire (if I had had a fire) but I shrank from such melodrama. I kept it as a curiosity – in fact I still have it, locked away where no one can see it. I resolved at that instant never again to attempt to have it published.

The question with regard to *The Paid Piper* was more difficult. Parts of it were good (and even then I thought much more of it was good than I do now) and I was far too tired to think of attempting the difficult re-writing which would be necessary to preserve the good and to eliminate the bad. In the end I came to the conclusion that the proportion of good stuff justified the existence of the bad stuff, and decided that I would consent to its publication – by a fortunate coincidence it had never been submitted to or rejected by the publishers who had accepted *A Pawn Among Kings*.

So now with one novel 'in the press' (a fine expression that) and another ready for the publisher I would take a holiday from literature. I was badly in need of one, for several reasons.

Chapter Sixteen

I HAVE not been to the annual 'Ideal Home Exhibition' at Olympia for the last ten years. I saw far too much of it the last time I was there; I spent thirteen hours a day there for a month, for I was one of the people employed there. During those years of the slump that was the only sort of job a young man of no experience at all could get, but while it lasted that kind of employment was well paid, and there were no bothersome questions asked about references and things which I had no hope of producing.

Of all the casual jobs I drifted into, Olympia is the one I remember clearest. The year I worked there the exhibition was a great success, although I do not think that there was any connection between the two facts. I can call up before my mind's eye without any difficulty at all the picture of the seething crowds which swarmed along the passages between the exhibits, the din and babble of thousands of people talking at once, the accursed band which played the same daily programme, the dust and the heat and the commotion. What I sold mostly was carpets, and the carpets were all fluffy and dusty, like everything else in that unspeakable hades. People would want carpets shown them, and I would pull my stock out, and turn it this way and that, and say the usual polite things, keeping myself in hand despite the feeling of irritation doing this aroused on the numerous occasions when I was approached by people who clearly were not (one soon develops an instinct in the matter) potential buyers. But buyers, especially the opulent ones, were as irritating as the merely inquisitive.

'How much is that?' the wife would say.

'Sixty-five pounds.'

And the husband would instantly ask,
'Would you like it, dear?'
That expression 'Would you like it, dear?' used to madden me. Those husbands had not come to the exhibition expecting to buy sixty-five-pound carpets, but they were quite able to do so; they had bank accounts capable of it. They had to think far less about the expenditure of sixty-five pounds than I had to think about the expenditure of threepence. It was the casual disbursement of these colossal sums which so infuriated me. I might have been prepared to forgive those people if only I could have thought that they had gone through times when threepence was an important sum of money, but I could not. They were well dressed, and well covered; they bore no signs of privation or anxiety, while I was gaunt and shabby and lined. Mostly they were polite, with the politeness of people addressing shop-assistants, and that was not in their favour. Perhaps it was thoughtful of them to say 'Please do not trouble' when overhauling my stock – but it was no comfort, seeing that I had to trouble, and they knew it, and I knew it, and they knew I knew. Sometimes they were rude, and that was more pleasant, because then I could become unhelpful and rude in return in a vague indefinable way so that they would look sharply at me, puzzled, wondering whether they could believe their ears that I could possibly be guilty of such blasphemy as irony addressed to a customer. One or two would recognise and treat me as an equal, and that was more irritating than anything else; I do not think it at all comforting to be recognised as one who has seen better days.

The caste system among the employees at the exhibition was irritating, too. The upper caste was composed of the regular employees of the big firms, to whom this sort of job was an interesting but not very exciting event; they were the well paid organising class mostly. Next came people who were brought down from the shops of the exhibitors to do a turn here instead of behind their usual counter; this was an exciting and pleasant change for them, they enjoyed themselves as much as if they were having a holiday. Lastly came the untouchables, the class to which I belonged, of casual labour brought in at the last moment, who would be dismissed as soon as the show was dismantled, not to be trusted out of anyone's sight, and about whose welfare no one specially cared. Being casual labour (especially at that time, when the slump was only just beginning) necessarily implied that there was something to our discredit; we must have lost our previous jobs either through misbehaviour or incompetence – and most of us had, as a matter of fact. Everyone withdrew the hems of their garments from contamination with us, especially from me, whose manner and accent implied that my fall had been farther than that of the others.

We untouchables clustered together, in the bars and places during off-hours, and tried to explain to each other that we were not really untouchable. One man in particular used to cling to me and tell me over and over again that he was not as the others were; he had once been his own master, owned his own shop, until bankruptcy and the slump in the drapery deprived him of it. Since then a year of unemployment, a year of unsuccessful seeking for a job as an assistant once again, had broken his spirit. He was even glad to associate with me, who must obviously have been in gaol. He could see that the original material of the clothes I was wearing must have been good stuff, and that I must once – long ago – have patronised a good tailor. In those early nineteen-twenties one could only descend from the opulent middle-class to the ranks of casual labour via a prison. I let people believe it of me; it was far less trouble than telling them that I had ambitions to become an author.

Money came from here and from there; never enough of it, of course. I sold a few bits of verse to the magazines and reviews – my first appearance in the general press. That verse was far better than my novels of the same period. I cannot write verse of nearly as good a standard nowadays. There is something about the mental quality of the late teens and early twenties which makes for the writing of good verse, something apart from genius or talent. Certainly the ability to write quite good poetry at that age is the least significant symptom, usually a quite deceptive one, as regards literary ability. I think I must have realised this, for I never had the slightest inclination to regard myself as a poet, despite the attitude of Chelsea. For my acquaintances these were enormously impressed on my now infrequent visits there by the fact that I had verse appearing in the good reviews, and was actually being paid for it; despite the superior attitude they adopted in theory towards the review and towards money payments. They even tried to borrow money from *me*! Presumably they would have been still more impressed had they known that I was writing novels, that I had actually had the energy to finish one, and more than one, and later that I had actually had one accepted by a reputable firm of publishers. I never told them anything about that, however; I had a distaste for discussing my own work with that class of person. And soon I dropped out of that circle altogether. Premières danseuses are not for struggling young authors, especially after a year or two's acquaintance. I have never had the privilege of so much as speaking to one since, and if it should come my way, I doubt if I should find anything to say. I am not as young as I was.

Lack of money did not keep me entirely away from the world where one dines and dances. I made quite regular appearances there, by the obvious arrangement. My expenses were paid by the lady I accompanied. About that I do not feel the shame I might be expected to feel. The lady I escorted was one of the sweetest women I have known, and a sincere personal friend, but she was now old enough to have difficulty in finding male escort – she was a widow. She was extremely wealthy, and the fivers those evenings cost her meant literally nothing to her. The evenings meant a good deal to me, both in consequence of the charm of her society and the contact with luxury which they brought. We were both of us a good deal happier as the result of the arrangement, and no one was at all the worse, so that no one can have a word to say against it.

The word 'gigolo' had not come into common English use at that time – at any rate I never heard it – and I do not think I was a good example of the type. I could not bring myself to take full advantage of my position. Often there was change left over from the evening fiver, and I always gave it back to her. She did not expect it, and I knew she did not. And it was quite easy to argue with myself that I was entitled to payment for my services for the evening in addition to my dinner and supper. But I handed that change over meticulously each night, perhaps not for motives of pride, but because I was going to be an author and I was touchy about my profession, and refused to admit my need even to myself.

Gigolos (is that the correct plural?) are usually distinguished too, by the lavishness with which they disburse their employers' money. I could never bring myself to achieve unnecessary lavishness, presumably because money meant much to my fevered imagination in those times of scarcity. There was an evening at the most important night club in London when a charge of a guinea for flowers appeared on the supper bill. I looked for the flowers; I asked the waiter about them. He pointed to three distressed carnations in the vase on the table. I refused point blank to pay a guinea for the privilege of looking at three pink carnations during supper. The waiter fetched the head waiter, and there was a little scene – my hostess, with true British horror of such situations, would gladly have paid several guineas for the scene never to have happened, but I would not permit it. The item was taken off the bill, with apologies.

But – this is the odd part of the story – there was something strange about that head waiter's manner during the argument. I could almost suspect him of winking at me. In the heat of the moment I thought he was merely being rude and told him so. Now, in cold blood, I begin to suspect that there was more behind that guinea for flowers than met the eye. Possibly the management had guessed at the relationship between me and my hostess – does any young man appear repeatedly at night clubs with a woman old enough to be his mother and still pay all expenses? Possibly if I had paid that guinea, a half-guinea would have been returned to me privately, in the cloakroom or somewhere. And presumably if I had insisted on drinking champagne instead of dry ginger (I was still keeping myself very carefully in hand in those dark days) I might have made a bit of commission. Yet I cannot bring myself to believe it of that particular night-club – of any other night-club, perhaps, but not of that one; everybody knows which one I mean. That head waiter's odd expression must have been accidental, a coincidence.

I was fortunate in my employer – we can call her that and not mince words. She never tried to spoil me. She never gave me gold cigarette cases or pearl studs, – not even a set of waistcoat buttons. More remarkable still, she never raised objections or turned sulky when I was poor company as a result of obsession with my work; if she had tried she might possibly have coaxed or ragged me out of my preoccupied condition on evenings when I was deeply engaged in working out some detail of some plot. She understood things remarkably well and endured wordless evenings with a kindly stoicism which amazes me nowadays. She was a very good friend to me indeed, and I still feel a deep sense of loss now that she is dead.

Had she not been so sincerely my friend I might perhaps have given way in the struggle I was carrying on. I might now belong to the little hopeless army of attractive young men one sees everywhere where women have money to spend; sunburning myself (with a due regard for the market value of a manly complexion) at Hyères; accepting with feigned reluctance platinum wrist-watches from stupid women; closely scanning the women at dances to pick out the wealthy ones; picking up a precarious and dubious living in the fifty more opulent hotels of western Europe, and hoping for a legacy from one of the more aged and stupid women to keep me in my old age. I had that picture before my mind occasionally when I was writing those early novels. It could have become a reality with just a little less fanaticism on my part. It would have been much the easier way. Even with the picture's more unpleasant details vivid to my imagination it seemed a good deal less unpleasant than what I was going through, and sometimes a less hopeless prospect, too.

It was the breakfasts which used most of all to conjure up pictures of attainable luxury – guilty splendour – to my mind. Often I would spend the night at my employer's house, when I had stayed too late in town to get home. I may as well state here and now that my employer was only my dance and dinner partner; I can guess what people may have whispered to each other about us, although no one has dared to whisper it in my hearing. In the morning I would descend to a solitary breakfast – my employer had far too many preparations to make to be able to appear in public before lunch-time. And there would be the butler and the parlour-maid to see that I was comfortable, and a dozen different dishes on hot plates awaiting my choice, and new rolls and real butter, and both the possible breakfast drinks, and half a dozen assorted newspapers to read, and a comfortable fire; it was those breakfasts more than anything else which made it hardest to tear myself away and go back to continue my struggle against the fate which was so very cunning at devising new ways of hitting me below the belt.

Chapter Seventeen

THE first money I earned by my pen apart from the guineas which my poems brought me came unexpectedly from a book I had not yet written. It was during the period after the acceptance of *A Pawn Among Kings* and before the arrival of the proofs. I was trying to keep alive after that highly unpleasant pre-acceptance time when a letter came from my publishers.

The mere sight of the envelope cheered me up; it had seemed such a cold-blooded business to arrange the publication of a novel by a single interchange of letters. I had always imagined that a certain amount of correspondence went on between author and publisher, possibly even correspondence not directly related to agreements and proofs. I had heard vaguely that publishers took authors out to lunch. So far I had received one letter and one agreement only from my publisher, and I had never looked upon his face (or rather upon their corporate faces, for he was a limited company) far less lunched with him. I thought of all this (I distinctly remember doing so) while opening the envelope.

The letter did not invite me to lunch; instead it was an invitation, brief and to the point, to write a book about Napoleon. If I thought I could, would I please let them see a synopsis and ten thousand words or so, and an agreement regarding publication could then be drawn up. Could I write a book about Napoleon? Of course I could. His period had always been one of my favourite studies – anyone who reads any history at all is sure to read largely about Napoleon. I honestly believed that I could find something interesting to write about Napoleon, and that there would be people who would be glad to read my opinions. There was some excuse for me, because the publisher seemed to think the same.

To knock off ten thousand words about Napoleon was mere

child's play; I merely took pen and paper and let my memory do the rest. It roamed about beautifully uncontrolled, collecting up all the odd and interesting things which I had come across in my reading of the period – those early years of mine when I read everything in the public library were bearing fruit at last. Anyone who cares to read those ten thousand words may find them in a book of mine called *Napoleon and His Court*, which also does not attain to the honour of a place in the list of my books which prefaces this one. I do not recommend the book. The style of it was rich; one might almost say gaudy. Macaulay was the main influence, with a dash of William Napier – I was full of the desire at that time to beat Macaulay at his own game. I thought I had done so when I wrote that book.

The synopsis was not so easy. I had not the least idea what was going to be in the rest of the book; I knew that I could produce eighty thousand words on the period without any effort, but it would be just as easy to write the whole thing as to try and work it out in a synopsis. But I managed to scrape some sort of hint about it in a funny little synopsis (I am sure it was funny. I have never seen anyone's synopses besides my own, and I do not know to this day what one ought to look like) and I sent synopsis and opening chapters up to the publisher. Then I went on with the book without waiting to hear the publisher's opinion. I was fascinated with it. The old tag about 'being intoxicated by the exuberance of my own verbosity' was very true in this case. I had a whole lot of mental material left over which I had not included in *A Pawn Among Kings*; there were lots and lots of things I wanted to say about Napoleon, and more still about the fascinating lesser figures of the period Murat and Ney and Davout and so on. I poured it all out in that Neo-Gothic sort of style which sets my teeth on edge nowadays. Even as I wrote I fancied people admiring my wealth of adjectives and fiery paragraphs. I thought it was marvellous stuff.

The publisher apparently thought so too. Very promptly indeed he wrote back that he approved of the opening chapters and of the synopsis, and would I please call and arrange about the agreement. Up to town I went, hoping that my despairing shabbiness would not be noticed. I suppose it was, but I was not so susceptible to the gaze of the office boys as I had been in earlier days. For now I was an accepted author; presumably that office boy had heard about the marvellous book *A Pawn Among Kings* which was soon to be published by the firm, and also was I not an author who had reached the divine state of signing agreements for books not yet completed?

I do not wish to appear to sneer too cruelly about that publishing firm; it is horribly bad manners to be rude about people who have been a help in time of trouble. So that in my allusions to the firm in question I do not want to be considered spiteful; I am only giving as true account as a not-too-exact memory has retained of the relations between me and a kindly but stupid firm of publishers. It was not the Managing Director or any other director who interviewed me in a smart efficient looking office, but a subordinate head of department. The Grand Panjandrum himself was in an inner room; the man I interviewed had every now and then to run inside and obtain authority for each successive clause of the agreement in the oddest sort of fashion.

The first, the vital point to be settled, was about money. I was in the most desperate straits as regards money; it is difficult for me now to picture that state of extreme desperation. I was desperate enough, anyway, to stand up to Mr R. (I am sorry to have to introduce these accursed initials, but to call him 'the head of department' is far too clumsy) and demand money, immediate and ample supplies of money. The book could not be written without money. So urgent was the need that I carried my point. Mr R. emerged from the Grand Panjandrum's office with an apologetic

'Well, Mr Forester, if twenty-five pounds will do—'

Twenty-five pounds! I would sooner see twenty-five pounds in notes than twenty thousand angels of light.

'Oh, that'll do,' I said.

That is one of the achievements of which I am most proud. I was a shabby young man of twenty-two; as far as they knew I had only one book, and that an inferior novel, to my credit, and yet I was able to conjure twenty-five pounds in cash out of a publisher's pocket on account of a work of serious history which was not yet written. The money question was settled; the royalty question was soon disposed of, for I could afford to be generous about minor points of percentages when I was sure that sales would be enormous. The draft agreement appeared, almost ready for signature. I tried to look like a hard-headed business man as I read it through. One point attracted my notice. 'The author will provide material for sixteen illustrations.' Material? I asked what 'material' might imply. Oh, as far as the block, said Mr R. after diving in to consult with the Grand Panjandrum. The block? The photographic block that the printer uses, he said. I could only say 'Umph' in reply and do some mental arithmetic. Apparently I was expected to find the material for illustrations at the British Museum or somewhere, get a firm of photographers to photograph sixteen pictures, and have the photographs worked up into 'blocks'. What I did not know about the economics of photographic reproduction would form the basis of a very full essay on the subject. But at a rough guess each block must in the end cost five pounds or so. Five sixteens make eighty. I should have to find eighty pounds for illustrations before the book could be printed. The miserable twenty-five I had just extracted on account fell away promptly into a minus quantity.

'I can't do that,' I said.

It took a dreadful lot of argument and visits to the Grand Panjandrum to convince them that I could not. I do not think they were dishonest, but merely stupid. The argument was prolonged, and threatened to become heated. As it developed, I came up very forcibly against a rule of that office which must be worth thousands of pounds a year to them. Smoking was not allowed on the premises; that was a rigid cast iron rule not to be relaxed even in favour of necessarily loose-minded authors. No man (except in desperate emergency, or unless he is a non-smoker) can discuss vital points of business without smoking. Lure an author into an office and discuss business with him while forbidding him to smoke, and he will sign anything so as to get outside again where he can. I would have signed that agreement if they had held out much longer for just the same reason. But as it was they ceded the point (about the illustrations, I mean, not about the smoking) and consented to change the wording to 'the Author will indicate to the Publisher where to find material for sixteen illustrations.'

With that clause settled, Mr R. approached the next one with a rather apologetic manner. How long did I think I should take to complete the book? There was some need for haste. Did I think I could possibly finish it, with an effort, by the end of the year? The date then was November 5th. Guy Fawkes' Day. I had done ten thousand words to their knowledge; I had another ten thousand words completed which they knew nothing about. At that rate they were being apologetic for asking me to write seventy thousand words in eight weeks – my first sure indication that my usual rate of work was too fast. As it was there were only sixty thousand words still to be done. I could promise to do that in time without even stopping to consider – to me who had once written over seventy thousand in a fortnight it was mere child's play. Clearly Mr R. was impressed by my offhand way of promising to achieve this feat, and even if he still retained doubts as to my ability to deliver the work to time, a clause governing this arrangement was inserted into the draft agreement. That settled the business. I had extracted hard cash from a publisher and induced him to promise publication of a book as yet unwritten – possibly the best feat of business I had ever performed.

While a fair copy of the agreement was being drawn out, a royal command arrived from the Grand Panjandrum summoning me into the Presence. The attitude of everybody seemed to imply what enormous condescension this was, but somehow by now I failed to be impressed. I was far too tired, and far too hungry, and I wanted to smoke. And if the interview were too prolonged the banks would shut and I would be unable to cash my cheque that day – a matter of huge importance. I was ushered with due solemnity into the great man's room, like a small boy before his headmaster, resenting the atmosphere in which I found myself very bitterly indeed. Somehow the Grand Panjandrum and I took an instant dislike to each other – at least, I can answer for myself and I think I am right about him, although I cannot understand why a man of great and established reputation should take a dislike to a struggling author young enough to be his son. Personally even before that interview I had thought his published work feeble; since that date prejudice has caused me to think it not merely insipid but positively distasteful. Perhaps I was snappy and sulky with hunger and the lack of tobacco; perhaps I did not defer to him as I should have done; perhaps it was merely a case of mutual antipathy as between dog and cat; perhaps my demands for cash payment and the incident of the photographic block had annoyed him. Anyway, the interview was not a success, and an alarmed Mr R. shooed me out of the room just as we began to snap at each other. I have not set eyes on the Grand Panjandrum since that day, although he published half a dozen of my books, but I fancy that the antipathy has never died down – a ridiculous state of affairs to prevail between author and publisher and one which may possibly have done me a little harm.

The one useful purpose the interview served was to clear up the mystery of why I was invited to write this 'book about Napoleon'. It appeared that it had suddenly been realised that there was no 'book about Napoleon' ready for their spring list, and that firm always had a 'book about Napoleon' in their lists. Such was the queer reason – quite typical of that firm – for the invitation to me and the need for haste.

The agreement was ready now, and signed. There was one more little delay and reference to the Grand Panjandrum when I insisted on the crossing of the cheque being cancelled, and then I fled from the office and ran panting through the streets – not even stopping to light a cigarette – to reach the bank before it shut. I was just in time, and then I could return home gloriously, with, in my pockets, four five pound notes, four one pound notes, a ten shilling note and ten shillings in silver. A most glorious sensation. Between town and home I bought a pair of shoes, it called for self restraint not to buy half a dozen.

Chapter Eighteen

I WISH I could explain more clearly what this business of being an author is like, and what 'inspiration' is like, and so on. A chapter or two back I wrote coldly enough about 'an urge to tell stories' which is a true but inadequate description. I can only tell of my own sensations, and supplement it with what I have extracted in conversation with better authors than me about what they feel like. There is this definite urge, which becomes far more marked after a period of stress. A day or two after my life has been in danger, for example, I can feel the old symptoms developing in their old style. The more agonizing the mental pain, if it is not too prolonged, the better eventually for the work that will result. A man may write beautifully soon after the death of his child, or after his loved wife has just caught him with another woman. Possibly this is merely because by reflex action he seeks for a means of escape from his thoughts; a majority of people who write must necessarily be people who indulge in fantasy; if this is true then the more worrying his circumstances the more he will seek escape from them by writing. But this is only partly true. A great many authors lead happy and tranquil lives and yet produce good work and great quantities of it – although no one except the author himself knows for certain whether he has anything to be anxious or excited about. And undoubtedly most books are written during tranquil periods – anything which irritates or causes anxiety is likely to interrupt the work.

Yet this is somehow not quite to the point. The gestation of a book is likely to be a business calling for patience and care, like any other gestation; the conception is a more exciting business, like any other conception. There is a more thrilling mood when books are more usually conceived; most people have perhaps heard of how Arnold Bennett was inspired to write *The Old Wives' Tale* by the fleeting sight of the wrinkled face of an old woman in a Paris crowd. The pulse rate definitely increases, there is a sensation of warmth under the skin, there is a feeling of activity which makes it desirable to walk aimlessly about, there is a consciousness that the brain is working more rapidly. It may all be caused by indigestion for all I know, but there it is. And the moment when consciousness of this condition is realised, it is usually realised simultaneously that the germ of an idea is present. Probably it is only a mere germ; if by chance it could be expressed in words to anyone else who was not an author he could not conceive of a whole complicated novel being built up out of it. But there it is; the author has it. To many people that mood may be dangerous. If they succumb to the temptation to sit down and work at it at once they produce badly planned work bearing the mark of haste and faulty development – nine first novels out of ten are like that. If the mood is allowed to simmer down the germ remains, possibly – probably – forgotten for the moment. Then recurrently it bobs up again, and at every reappearance it is more developed, mainly without conscious effort on the part of the author. He picks it up and looks at it, so to speak, turns it over, and drops it back again, possibly after adding one or two slight improvements. Finally the idea presents itself as fully formed as unconscious work will make it, sometimes quite complete, more usually needing just a little conscious effort on the author's part to finish it off.

It may be necessary for instance to devise some means of enabling two people to meet without coincidence; or if the idea lays it down that someone must grow rich the author must devise the mechanism by which this is brought about. Some authors do this final working out in a draft, some do it mentally, others do not do it at all. In one of John Masefield's novels, I fancy, the hero is pressingly anxious to get through a certain locked door leading out of a street. Someone unknown to him passing by drops a key out of his pocket which the hero finds is the key of the door. I do not think Arnold Bennett would ever have been satisfied with that simple solution of the difficulty; he would have fitted in some logical means of giving that key to the hero. And I think it will be generally admitted that if these necessary steps towards development are endowed with an appearance of inevitability, or at worst of probability, the book will gain – will be a better book – without our having to lapse into a discussion of what constitutes a good book.

And then, when all these developments are complete, it is time to begin work on the thing. The result may seem to have no real connection with the initial germ. The very first little idea may have been a visualisation of a hand coming in from the outer darkness through an open window into a lighted room; the final novel may be a careful study of miserliness or lust and the hand may never come in through the window, that incident being finally discarded. Sometimes it is just possible to guess on reading a novel what was the initial idea. I can offer one example where I am prepared to bet on my judgment. I fancy that in Mr Somerset Maugham's novel *The Painted Veil* the whole first history of an unfaithful wife developed from the original visualisation of the opening incident – the wife and her lover in a locked room together watching the door handle move as someone outside tries the door. The initial germ need not of course be an incident; it may be an appreciation of a state of mind, or of a state of affairs, or of a condition of tension between two minds, or of a trend of affairs.

However it is, the thing has now to be written. Usually the approach to the work is keenly enjoyable; in a way it means the achievement of an ambition, the keying down into words of what so far has only been thoughts. There is a curious and pleasurable sense of mastery in doing it, if one's critical sense decides that it is being done well. It is not too easy, all the same. The translation of thoughts into written words is a delicate matter. To describe anything calls for care; it is not easy to be sure that the words written will affect the mind of the person reading them in the same way as the idea affects the mind of the writer. There is the mechanism – necessary mechanism – of grammar and vocabulary interposed. As an analogy, a golfer on the tee knows that what he wants to do is to belt the ball down the fairway, but to achieve that result he must make use of the mechanism of eye and muscle and golf club. An inexperienced person cannot be relied upon to do it properly. And to continue the analogy a practised golfer may always be expected to get round in good workmanlike fashion, but he nevertheless knows his days when he can do nothing wrong, when his touch is sure and his judgment correct, when at every stroke he achieves exactly what he had planned in his mind's eye. So with an author, he is liable to feel a mood of working inspiration (as contrasted with creative inspiration) when he handles his tools – words and sentences – with perfection of touch, when he knows that every line he writes conveys the desired image, and that that image is a beautiful one – but please do not let us be dragged into a theoretical discussion of beauty. This working mood is just as impossible to force as is the creative mood; its physiological symptoms of accelerated heart beat and so on are much the same; and it is likely to be as short lived. Moreover, a man who waited for that mood before putting pen to paper each day would have many blank days; it is extremely rare to experience it before starting the day's work. It grows upon the author as he proceeds with his task; he finds suddenly that it is upon him, and usually the speed at which he works increases at once. Once it is attained – and it may come with the writing of the second sentence of a novel – it may be recaptured as long as one does not try too hard to do so, even when there has been a break in the work. The reading over of the last few completed lines and the mechanical uncapping of the fountain pen or opening of the typewriter starts the flow again. There are joyous occasions when the whole book is completed under this influence, and the author knows later that, other things being equal, they are his best books – they are further likely to be so because this mood is captured more easily when working on a good scheme than on a weak one. The books written without this inspiration may be competent, interesting, and of a very high class. I would hazard a guess that Mr Bennett's *Strange Vanguard* was written without working inspiration. But on the other hand the books which are written throughout in this indefinable mood usually possess some indefinable quality which marks them out and often makes 'best sellers' of them. I believe that both *If Winter Comes* and *The Green Hat* were written in this fashion. It is worth pointing out, I suppose, that it is not the inspiration (what a hateful word that becomes if discussed too long!) which makes for good literature, leaving best sellers out of the discussion, but the quality of the mind and soul of the author.

It is not presumptuous on the part of the most minor author

to claim that he goes through the same physiological processes as Goethe or Plato; the presumption is if he claims that his physiological processes produce as good results. A stupid man, an unsympathetic man, can write a best seller if the mood seizes him, but he will never write a good book.

Experience in the use of one's tools is almost always necessary, and that has nothing to do with inspiration. To describe a technical process, or the furnishing of a room, or a state of mind, is a difficult task. To do it in interesting fashion and so that it enhances the progress of the story is harder still. An unpractised author fails frequently, he may either not describe effectually or his description breaks the thread, or both. Anyone who troubles to compare *A Man from the North* with *Clayhanger* will appreciate the point immediately, or a more illustrious example still can be found in comparison of Shakespeare's early plays with his later ones.

But all this extremely theoretical discussion seems terribly serious and far-fetched when I realise that all I was trying to do was to work out a better analysis of my own motives and experiences and methods of work. I have never bothered about myself to the extent of half a dozen pages like this before; I do not believe I bothered to work out my motives even in those days, when I took myself far more seriously than I do now. On the happy day I had reached in this story before I interrupted myself with a dissertation on inspiration, all that mattered to me was that I had twenty-five pounds in my pockets – distributed with meticulous care, a bit in each pocket – and work to do which I liked and which I felt capable of doing.

Napoleon and his Court was finished joyously and delivered immediately after Christmas, at least three days before the date I had contracted to deliver it. It would have been finished some time earlier still, except that I was ill; I had a week's influenza – come just too late to cause total disaster – during which even my enthusiastic spirit refused to rouse itself. The thing was done; the pale echoes of Macaulay's lyre sounded through its style in the most ridiculous fashion; it was a haphazard book; it jumped from theme to theme in a tiresome manner; it was full of conscientiously fine writing and deliberate waywardness. It was a better book all the same than any I had written before, and I told myself so – at that time I thought that was praise.

My publisher really liked it too, oddly enough, and it is not anticipating too much to say that the press liked it as well when it appeared. It was treated as a serious contribution to history. I feel positively awkward now when I remember that the *Times Literary Supplement* gave it a column's notice and gravely debated its merits. Some of the other papers gave it columns too, full of gentle praise; in the half dozen reviews which came under my notice there was not a single word of censure. That is some excuse for my continuing to take myself seriously at that time, although somehow I never took myself seriously enough to pay a press cutting subscription.

Things certainly were moving. When I received the proof of *A Pawn Among Kings* – I waited until that was in print, lest perhaps the new development should interfere with its publication. I sent in *The Paid Piper* and that was accepted at once. And when I had read the proof of *Napoleon and his Court* I was commissioned to continue the good work with a life of the Empress Josephine, on the same terms as *Napoleon* – which meant another twenty-five pounds in my pocket at a vital moment. The time came for the publication of my first book, *A Pawn Among Kings*, which appeared shortly before *Napoleon and his Court*. It is very hard to remember how I felt when the day came. I do not think that the mere fact of publication was pleasing. The book had long been written. Now it had been printed, and I could not work up any more excitement over it as a book. There would be a certain amount of interest in reading what other people thought about it in the reviews. What would be exceedingly interesting would be the sales and the consequent money. Money was a matter of colossal importance. Lack of it meant a constant gnawing anxiety; it made life a sequence of undignified and exceedingly painful tricks and subterfuges; lack of money is amusing enough for a month or two, but it becomes tiresome after that, and after a year or so it becomes absolutely maddening. Most of my memories of that period are blurred and telescoped as a result.

So that it will be readily understood that I awaited publication and the subsequent arrival of the six monthly cheque with horrid anxiety. As I cannot repeat too often, I had never had conversation with anybody who had ever published anything before. I had only the vaguest idea how much a first novel might be expected to make. Somewhere I had picked up the fairly correct information that an edition of a first novel was about fifteen hundred copies. Assuming that most of them were sold my royalties would amount to about seventy pounds – I had worked that out often and often. Producing two novels and a biography every year, then, I could rely upon earning something over two hundred a year, with always before me the hope and possibility that I might make a hit at any moment and see my income multiplied a hundred-fold. Two hundred a year was the limit to which the conservative sane half of my mind would allow my imagination to wander – enough to live on in genteel poverty without acute discomfort. But the other half of my mind would not hear of any such limits. It refused to be confined to a single edition. It thought of sales in thousands, with royalties paid on an increasing scale, and of great sums of money pouring in to me. Five thousand – ten thousand was well within the bounds of possibility from that point of view.

I was at this time in fairly close contact with my publishers – the necessity for arranging for the publication of four different books assured that. But I could never bring myself to ask outright what they expected these books to earn for me. After publication I could never demean myself by asking how sales were progressing. There was always an atmosphere of antagonism between me and those publishers, possibly as a result of that unfortunate interview between me and the Grand Panjandrum. On my visits there I confined my conversation strictly to the matter in hand. I would not ask about sales, and they proffered no information.

I had to read the columns of 'literary gossip' in the newspapers, and study the firm's advertisements, in an effort to find out how things were going. The reviews of *Napoleon and his Court* were quite enthusiastic; the reviews of *A Pawn Among Kings* were tepid – the kindly sort of review dealt out to a first novel written by an obviously earnest beginner. But I could not find in the advertisements anywhere the magic words 'Second Edition' or 'Fourth Printing'. No sort of stir was being caused in the book market anywhere. With a little dull feeling of disappointment I resigned myself to a sale of fifteen hundred copies for each book. The resultant cheque, when deductions were made for advances made, would be about a hundred and twenty pounds. That would be a splendid lot of money when I did not possess that number of pence. When at last the date came round which the agreement laid down as the time for the payment of cheques I awaited the postman with anxiety.

Day after day he brought me nothing; I have never yet heard of a publisher who makes his royalty payments on the agreed date. It is an exasperating habit of publishers. Other payments they make with laudable punctuality. Cheques on publication really do arrive on the day of publication; if a stony-broke author writes to his publisher and begs for some payment on account he often receives a cheque by return. But when a publisher promises under his hand and seal to pay royalty accounts at the end of September it is never safe to rely upon his doing it before the beginning of December. I had yet to discover this. Day after day, morning after morning, and evening after evening I waited for the postman to bring me that hundred-odd pounds. My fevered imagination, twice a day when I heard his knock approaching up the street, transmuted that hundred-odd pounds into shoe repairs and comforting meals – trousers with no holes in the seat. And twice a day the postman passed me by. The period of waiting resolved itself into a struggle between me and my pride – and between me and my belly. I could hardly believe it possible that a publisher could be dilatory over such an enormously important matter as royalty cheques. I fancied that as a result of some clerical oversight in the office they had forgotten to send out my cheque with the others. But I would not deign to appear too eager for it. Presumably I did not want to be too obviously the starving struggling author. I told myself that it would be best to wait six months, when the next payment was due. Then either they would notice their error or else it would not be too undignified for me to write and point out that they had never made the payment previously due. The thought of having to hold out for six months in that condition with a hundred pounds only waiting to be asked for sent cold shivers down my spine. I do not know whether I could have held out for that time, because I was not put to the test.

One evening the postman brought a letter for me, with the publisher's name embossed on the back; a fat envelope, clearly containing royalty accounts and a cheque. So it did. The cheque was for something less than forty pounds.

That was rather a facer. The sale of a first novel which did not succeed was not fifteen hundred copies at all, apparently; only five hundred. Instead of an annual income of two hundred pounds, with genteel poverty, irksome but not excruciating, there would only be an income of eighty pounds a year, less than that of an unskilled labourer. That meant filth and anxiety and holes in my trousers all my life, with instant starvation should my invention fail me or a publisher happen to dislike a book. Oh well, I should have to endure it. I had come through worse than that. I could still hold on and hope that if I went down I should go down fighting. There seemed in that black world to be little else to hope for; but hope was for weaklings and fools. There was not much credit to be won in a battle when there was still hope. I must put my disappointment socially on one side and go on with my work.

Chapter Nineteen

THE Empress Josephine is an interesting person to write about. She was only a very average sort of woman – a man like Napoleon could not have thought her marvellous if she really had been so – and she was plunged into extraordinary circumstances. She viewed poverty from all angles, and wealth and high position and decline and agonising uncertainty without learning any lesson from any of them. She was incorrigibly, delightfully ordinary, in wonderful contrast with her background of gaudy Directory and tinsel Empire. I found it a very pleasant employment to write her life.

When I started her biography I knew far less about her than I had known about her second husband. To write her biography meant quite a large amount of exacting work. I penetrated – as does every single English author sooner or later – into the numerous recesses of the British Museum Library. I followed up clues through volume after volume in search of minor details. There were all sorts of odd things to be discovered about her environment, from details of her underclothing to the court etiquette controlling her giving of alms – about Josephine herself there was singularly little to learn. The biography of her which I eventually put together is not a specially bad book. I had contrived to get that Macaulay-cum-Napier style more under control, having learned a little of the gentle art of self-criticism, and I had read my subject very thoroughly indeed. Of all the books written at that period *Josephine* is the only one which still sells; it valiantly struggles along selling a dozen copies a year – goodness knows who buys them. Once or twice I have seen acknowledged quotations from the book in serious histories, and a later biography paid it the compliment of incorporating paragraphs from it word for word without acknowledgment.

There is a soft spot in my heart for that book. It helped me through a long and very dark period in my life. It introduced me to the British Museum Library, where it was always warm and where porters were not officious and where every book which I had ever wanted to read and had been unable to get hold of was available on the mere signing of a form. It gave me plenty to do without making too great demands upon my stamina – it was not the creative work which drains the strength from a man if he keeps it up too long. It taught me a lesson of which I was sadly in need on the importance of methodical work and of stopping to think before starting a new chapter. It brought me in an immediate twenty-five pounds. It taught me to use a typewriter.

I have never had lessons in typewriting; no one who knows how to handle one has ever given me any tips on the subject. The one I got hold of was old, and displayed all the crankiness and perversity to be expected of old age. Its ribbon would not move along of its own accord, and nothing I could do would ever induce it to. Instead I had to jerk it along with my fingers every few words; if in the heat of composition I forgot to do so the type promptly wore a hole in it – that ribbon was full of holes at the end of a week or two. Every page I wrote was covered with mistakes and the inevitable corrections to be made in the course of composition gave an odd appearance to the page – rings and arrows, and transposed sentences, and that sort of thing. My present exemplary secretary turns pale with horror when I tell her of the sort of typewriting I used to send into publishers without a qualm. Still, it was typewriting, and the machine cost actually less than the typing of a single book, so that I was relieved of one standing source of anxiety; incidentally, I was saved from the torments of writer's cramp which had begun to plague me. By the time I had finished the eighty thousand words of *Josephine* I was almost a competent typist – and not the most lunatic behaviour of my typewriter could ruffle my painfully acquired and philosophic calm.

Something else had happened to me during the completion of the book; something which it is not at all easy to write about and of which details are not to be expected. Odd as it may appear, there was room in my life for something beside my work and the unceasing worry about money and the black fear for the future which obsessed me if I did not fight against it. The something beside all this, of course, was a woman. With the very best of intentions and with the utmost purity of motive and with complete angelic idealism we had been lacerating each other's nerves for years on end. It is only young people, I think, who can hurt each other so. She would hurt me and I would hurt her with fastidious cruelty. She could hardly help being hurt, for she had the sensitiveness and pride of a lonely and artistic temperament; and I had enough to worry and to hinder me from making allowances for it, and I was young, and sufficiently worried to be on edge, so that I went through pretty bad times too, and my burden of troubles made me clumsy and irritating. We acted and reacted upon each other in a manner fatal to any hope of happiness at that time.

It is hard for a happily married man to write about a woman who is not his wife and yet meant much to him when he was young. But it was a matter of such desperate importance to me and it influenced me so profoundly that I must allude to it to attain any completeness in the picture of those years. We caused each other the most agonising pain and unhappiness. In this pleasant security of the thirties I can look back at those hurt twenties and tell myself that nothing can do things like that to me again – but I do not stop to think what might. It was not good for my work; whoever else may hold it I am entirely against the view that painful affairs of this sort improve an artist's product. They might do so twenty years later, but I doubt it. At the time they do serious damage. Poverty will not spoil a man's work if he has enough strength to endure, but those thoughtless words spoken to him can take all the beauty from it, if the speaker is chosen with care.

In the end of course the business came to the end one would expect. It was quite as painful as an operation in the pre-anaesthetic days, but it did as much good and brought as much relief as the most successful operation known. Nowadays I can smile about it and say that such things come to youths in their twenties just as measles come to children, and are as little likely to do harm. But when with an effort I can force myself into sympathy with the extravagant demands the young make of life I still can realise the potential unhappiness of youth. Perhaps the day will come when I can do so no longer.

The interval which followed the tearing-apart operation just mentioned, and the completion of *Josephine*, was strange and unnatural at first. *The Paid Piper* proceeded towards publication. If I were to maintain my self-set standard production of two novels a year I should have to start a new novel almost at once. I found I could start one, but not one that pleased me. There was a story about the campaign in the North of Italy in 1848–49 which appealed to me, and for which I read enormously. I finished a couple of chapters, realised it was poor stuff and threw it away. I wrote the greater part of a novel about a young minx of a girl before I gave that up too. They did not satisfy me. All the time I knew what the novel was which I wanted to write, and yet I could not begin it. The theme was so powerful (in my opinion) and would require such a careful handling that my better nature refused to let me start on it until I was certain that I could do it and had devised methods of attacking all the difficulties. That is a high falutin way of expressing it, but it is quite truthful.

I had found an ideal of beauty now to which I wished my work to attain. I do not want to quibble about a definition of 'beauty'; the story of grim horror which resulted from these internal convulsions may not appear in the least beautiful to some people. But I called the standard I set myself 'beauty'. From that time I think that every novel I have written has conformed to that standard; I have acquired, I believe, the ability very nearly to measure my novels against that standard. The defects in those novels are not to be attributed to inexperience, or lack of skill in writing or any other weakness which time will cure; they are to be attributed either to defects in me at the time of writing, or else to the fact that my standard of good work does not coincide with the standard of the critic. The only point in my favour after such an enunciation of opinion is that I do not take myself half as seriously as I do my work.

The idea of the new novel had begun to form a long time before. Now, when I had begun to recover from the affair before alluded to, I had some time and energy and sensitiveness to spare to shape the complete but rough plot into a practicable form. Much of the plot had the highly desirable characteristics of inevitableness. Given the preliminary data, a good deal of the rest simply had to follow. The original germ of the idea was the thought of a man with the body of a murdered victim in his back garden. That settled his station in life immediately; no duke could bury a body in his back garden because dukes either have no back garden or else there are too many butlers and people about to allow of it. The hero (to use the term in a technical sense) must be a small clerk or tradesman in a small suburban house; of a certain station in society above the lowest to ensure that his family alone occupied the house, and of a certain station below the highest to ensure the absence of servants. Then came the consideration of motive. It might be lust or jealousy or avarice or need. Lust was possible, but undesirable; Crippen killed his wife from that sort of motive, and buried her in his cellar, but with everything taken into account the machinery needed to make a man kill for lust in his own small suburban house is too difficult – the Crippen ménage is too strange for fiction. Jealousy would do, except that a murder through jealousy is too wanton a crime to suit the motive of inevitability which is already apparent. Avarice could be ruled out at once – a man who could kill for that reason, like Seddon, would not be an interesting enough person to write about. That left need alone, and need it had to be.

Promptly the plot took a step forward. A small clerk in need of money must be of a certain type. He must hold some small position where financial rectitude is essential – as a clerk in a bank, therefore. To get into such a state as to have to kill for money he must be a drifting sort of character, with a rather helpless wife, and one or two children. The story would open with him worrying over his domestic bills and with the prospect of distraint and of consequent dismissal from his job close upon him. If he is the sort of man to allow his affairs to get into this sort of state it is likely that he is a weak character, with a tendency to drink too much – which last would be cause as well as effect. His wife clearly must be a slack housewife, liable to let things drift; she could drink too, if necessary, but obviously there is a chance to draw a rather lovable and pleasant character – a woman who lives in a sort of indistinct dream, who adores her husband, and is perfectly hopeless as regards practical affairs. The children can be left undefined for the moment.

Next comes the consideration of the victim. He must be a person with fifty pounds or so in cash in his pockets – no bank clerk, however hard pressed, would kill for less. For the dead

161

man to lie unsought in a back garden for some fairly long period (that is obviously going to be the motive of the book) he must be someone in whom no one is going to take much interest, which is difficult to reconcile with the fact that he carries a fair amount of money. However, that is not impossible. An orphaned nephew, newly come home from the colonies, having just realised the fortune left him by his dead parents, will fill the bill admirably. His first step on arrival would be to cash some of his letter of credit; his second would be to call on his only living relative – the hard-pressed and suburban clerk. Conversation would soon make apparent the fact that he was an ideal victim. Certainly it would take a very long time for inquiries after him when he is missing to drift back and forward between England and Australia.

The next point to be settled is the means by which the murder is committed. A man of the type of the hero is not likely to use a revolver readily, nor would he have a revolver in the house. He probably would not use an axe or a knife or a club, partly from fear of bloodstains. There remains poison. But to poison a man rapidly – in a drink of whisky, say – is not an easy matter; the common and domestic poisons such as carbolic acid and spirits of salt are too easily detected even by an unsuspecting man when they are present in a lethal dose in food or drink. There is only one poison which is fairly undetectable, which kills instantly, and which a stray bank clerk might possess, and that is potassium cyanide. He might possibly have that on the premises if he dabbled a great deal in photography. It is necessary, therefore, at the opening of the book, to give him a hobby of photography.

Thus we have the beginning of the book settled – a weak-moraled bank clerk, his hopeless wife and his two children; his hobby of photography, and his accumulation of small debts; his tendency to drink whisky; his badly furnished little suburban house – that sort of couple would never have furnished well. Suddenly arrives the young nephew from Australia; his pockets are full of money; he has done nothing since his arrival in England that very day save to cash his letter of credit and book a room at an hotel. No one knows him in England; his parents in Australia are dead. There is potassium cyanide on the shelf upstairs. It is a combination of the most pressing necessity, the perfect opportunity, and the ideal victim. The bank clerk (at this point I started calling him Mr Marble; that seemed the most fitting name) yields to the temptation and poisons the young man after Mrs Marble and the children have gone to bed, and that same night he buries him in the backyard – it is pouring with rain so that no one is likely to observe him and the traces of the grave will not be too obvious. Then there follow all the consequences – the grinding anxiety lest his secret should be discovered, the puzzled wonder of his wife, the inevitable tendency to drown his anxiety in more whisky.

But something more than this is necessary for a book. There must be an ending. Undramatic ones leap to the mind – Mr Marble might commit suicide under the strain; a forgotten relative from Australia might trace the nephew. Better than that would be if Mrs Marble eventually discovered the murder and disclosed it against her will. Then suddenly I thought of the right ending. Mr Marble's perfect murder must go undetected. He must be hanged for a crime he did not commit. That would be dramatic; it would be satisfactory in the way that a murderer would receive his deserts; it gave a title to the thing (a title is always difficult) which would be perfectly suitable, *Payment Deferred*.

Now it would be only necessary to work out a train of circumstances to compel Mrs Marble to kill herself in such a way that Mr Marble would be proved guilty of the crime. That would be easy; it was going to be a book of cumulative horror; after she had found out that her husband was a murderer, and that there was a corpse in the backyard, and after her son had met with an untimely end and her daughter had quarrelled with them, she would be in such a state that the discovery that Marble did not love her and was unfaithful would be enough to cause her to kill herself. If she were ill, Marble would allow no one to nurse her save himself lest something should be discovered. That would be suspicious; the poison was ready to his hand as well as to hers; his unblessed love affair would be a motive – oh yes, that could be worked out.

With the beginning and the end and the minor characters all settled there was only the middle to elaborate. So far Mr Marble is an unprepossessing creature – a slack drunkard, a murderer, a callous man towards his wife. It would be perfectly horrible to have to write a whole book about him. He must have some redeeming qualities – he must be someone for whom I could feel sympathy. That can be done by picturing him, after the inevitable has forced him into murder, as making a valiant fight against fate. He will have plenty to contend against, with the fear of the gallows always before his eyes. Stimulated by this fear his good qualities can come to the surface for a time before he is engulfed in the inevitable. The surest way for his crime to be discovered is for him to have to leave the house and garden he guards so carefully. If he is given notice to quit he can only protect himself by buying his house. To do that requires money; to make the money – to make great quantities of money – requires nerve and courage and cleverness. He can display these if the compulsion is sufficiently agonising, as it is. So that in the middle of the book he must make a fortune – to find how a bank clerk could do that called for many consultations with bank clerk friends – and that opens up all sorts of possibilities.

There will be the irony of a wealthy man who is compelled by fate to spend his life in a little suburban home guarding the backyard; there will be the irony of queer, weak-minded little Mrs Marble with a fortune at her disposal, compelled to do all the housework because her husband will not risk the presence of a charwoman. The unpleasant fate of the son and the revolt of the daughter will be easier to arrange. The infidelity which is the last straw of Mrs Marble's load of troubles will come more easily to a wealthy man. The excitement of the making of the money – when Mr Marble's life as well as his money is at stake – will be an asset to the book. To work out the development of Marble's psychology under the two potent influences of fear and wealth will be a very interesting thing to do. Best of all will be to study how his fear will grow stronger and stronger the more he has to lose, and to mark his degeneracy from a man of decided possibilities into a weak-kneed victim of circumstances.

To me, in the full flow of putting this plot together, and set upon getting Mr Marble properly in my mind's eye, it mattered nothing that the story was one of grim horror almost unrelieved, that it was not a book which was (to say the least) a certain best seller, that it would probably scare the Grand

Panjandrum out of his wits. All I knew was that I wanted to write it, and that I would not be happy – that I would be decidedly unhappy – until I wrote it. And so once more the old typewriter was brought out, and once more the mystic signs 'Page One. Chapter One' were inscribed at the top of the sheet, and the exhausting task was taken in hand.

For three months the thing lived with me. I will not be so silly as to affirm that the work was not enjoyable. It was undoubtedly enjoyable to build the thing up remorselessly, to work in all the little touches which conveyed atmosphere, to watch Mr Marble fighting a losing campaign against the inevitable despite his occasional tactical successes, to follow poor silly little Mrs Marble slowly being crushed by forces much too strong for her, to work up to the disasters which Mr Marble's crime calls down on his unoffending children. There was a strange, odd sense of familiarity and mastery while writing that book which I have never known before. Yet on the other hand there were disadvantages. It is not good for a young man to live alone in the atmosphere of unredeemed horror which a book of that sort conveys. The black hopeless misery of Mrs Marble's life, and the besotted fears which beset Mr Marble grew so real to me that at times it felt as if I could not bear it any longer. The other troubles which I had to endure – the troubles any young author must expect – became unreal compared with these imaginary ones. I fought against the ending of that book as madly as did Mr Marble himself, and with just the same feeling of ineffective effort.

But the thing came to an end at last. I have a very clear memory of tapping out the last few words on the typewriter and then sitting back in my chair rather dazed. All round me was a muddle of typewritten sheets – top copy and carbon – for as the end came near I had abandoned my rule of not more than a thousand words a day and I had finished the last six thousand words in one wild sitting. On the table beside me lay a massive pile of paper – two copies of the seventy thousand words finished before the last sitting. I looked at it with exhausted pleasure. For the first time in my life I had finished a book which completely satisfied me – a book which came up to my standard of belief as well as my standard of hope (I had learned to differentiate between the two). I am quite prepared to admit that the book is faulty; moreover, if I were to write it now it would probably be a different book in more than matters of detail. But the book as it stands is the very best I could have written at twenty-three and in the circumstances in which I found myself. I knew that the moment I had finished it. And I do not think that many people will contradict me when I say that it was a very remarkable achievement for a young man of twenty-three.

There followed the weary job which is liable to madden a wretched author until he is well enough off to pay a secretary to do it for him – sorting out the mass of typescript, putting it in order, punching and binding the sheets into two volumes, making covers for them, typing out labels and sticking them on. Preparing typescript for the publisher is a business which I find quite as irritating as the study of anatomy, although fortunately it is one in which I grew more adept. Then I sent the thing to my publisher – not with a prayer as Miss Marie Corelli (who was published by the same firm) used to do, but with a feeling of emptiness; the blank friendless feeling, which I have come to know so well since, similar to that which follows influenza, which is always present when a book over which I have toiled with supreme conscientiousness for two or three months is completed.

The publishers sent it back to me with a letter of regret. They could not possibly make themselves responsible for introducing the book to the public. It was not at all their class of literature, and they did not think it would sell. I might have known beforehand – I fancy I did – that they would take up exactly this line. If *A Pawn Among Kings* and *The Paid Piper*, those two bad books, had sold even moderately well they would have published *Payment Deferred*. As it was, they honestly thought *Payment Deferred* was poor stuff; from that they deduced that I was not worth consideration as an author of anything better than hack biographies, and they cautiously decided not to throw any more money away after their original losses over me. It is a curious example of the fallibility of a publisher's judgment, for when *Payment Deferred* was ultimately published it sold notably well, and has sold to this day, and has now attained to the dignity of having a dramatised version of itself presented on the London stage. I have often wondered whether the Grand Panjandrum has since repented of his decision, but I have never bothered to find out.

All the same, I was not to know of all this when the parcel of ill omen returned from the publisher; the rejection of the manuscript was a genuine shock to me. It did not diminish my faith in the book, but it raised a whole series of tiresome problems. The old business of hawking the manuscript round the publishers would recommence, along with the payment of sixpences for postage or the alternative necessity of having to face publishers' office boys. Not merely that, but there was the horrid prospect of having to face a gap in my income. *Payment Deferred* was finished in the late spring. If there was any delay in finding a new publisher it would not appear until the following spring, and my first royalty payment for it would not come in until the autumn after that, nearly eighteen months hence, and a year later than I had counted upon receiving it. My money difficulties were harassing enough as it was without this complication.

In the end I was driven – loath as I am to confess it – to write two more hack biographies for my original publisher. They are the poorest work I have ever done, written about subjects I know nothing about, and the sole motive for writing them was the twenty-five pounds I received on the submission of each synopsis – I was becoming adept by now at the construction of synopses. Those books, as it happened, made a good deal more than twenty-five pounds each for me. They were published in America as well as in England, and apparently there is a class of reader in America who is prepared to pay out three dollars for badly written biographies. Every one of those readers put eighteenpence in my pocket, and the total of those eighteenpences surprised me when I received it. Oddly enough, the sales of those two really bad books were each of them equal to the sale of the one biography I have ever written with real enthusiasm and with devoted hard work – my life of Nelson which appeared a year or two ago.

So that while I was putting together the first of those two biographies, labouring through the hot summer days, *Payment Deferred* started on its rounds, following the route which had been mapped out years before by its predecessors. It was unlucky at first; it was summarily rejected by the two really 'highbrow' publishers to whom I submitted it; the third on the list nibbled at it, summoned me to an interview, suggested tentatively that I might reconstruct it to give it a happy ending (publishers have queer ideas) and finally parted from me with genuine sorrow at my indignant refusal. Once more there began the old painful waiting for the postman's knock, the old forced stiffening of my determination, the old hanging on desperately through a cloud of depressing circumstances.

There was, however, no need now for me to labour at Ideal Home Exhibitions and at the various other humiliating and wearisome jobs by which I had struggled through bad times before. I could earn some sort of living by my pen now. Magazine work was beyond me, just as it is now – I have never in my life written a story which would be looked at twice by a magazine editor. But there were other possibilities which I had never dreamed of before – I fancy my attention was called to them by a newspaper advertisement asking for articles for a trade paper. It was fun to write for trade papers. I wrote articles on the Diamond Necklace and kindred subjects for the *Goldsmiths' Journal*, and short stories about haunted motorbus drives for a road travel paper, and guidebooks for the Pullman car company – I fancy that when you travel even now to Scotland the Pullman attendant will bring you my description of the route to while away the journey. Only a little while ago I received a couple of indignant letters berating me for my tactless allusion to the Young Pretender (instead of Prince Charles Edward) in that classic monograph. As I say, those articles were fun to write; they were good work and historically extremely sound. The trade papers and the Pullman car company were the only people in England who were prepared to pay money for my best work, and I could find it a constant source of wry-mouthed amusement that a distinguished novelist and historian should be labouring with all his skill and talents to amuse the United Pawnbrokers or the Busdrivers' Association or the people who go to Scotland by Pullman.

The fees paid by these organisations seemed to me to be fantastically large. If only I had not set my mind on being a novelist I might have worked up a very fine connection among the trade papers and I could have earned a steady income about three times as large as what I can earn at present. Perhaps the most typical action of my life was my incontinent dropping of the whole business as soon as novels brought me in enough to live on. Even although it was not distasteful to me I could not bring myself to believe that I ought to write for trade papers. The last article I believe I sold was one to a cold storage magazine (largely bought by fishmongers) describing how the great kings of Persia in the old days obtained steady supplies of snow to cool their wine by maintaining a special fast dromedary service to bring the stuff from the eternal snows of the Caucasus to Persepolis – every word of it true and laboriously dug from the classics in the British Museum Library. It was to my mind excusable to do that sort of thing when I would starve if I did not. And I used to think in those days that when I was become famous and after my death my biographer would have an exciting time hunting out from those journals all the stuff I wrote therein in order to include their titles in my bibliography. Thoughts of that sort helped to enliven the sick period of waiting during that hot weary summer.

Finally, and just in time to save me from sinking into depression, there came the letter for which I had been waiting. Someone was willing to publish *Payment Deferred* – not merely willing, seemingly, but anxious. There was the usual routine to go through – to brush up my one shabby suit, to debate whether it would be less conspicuous to arrive hatless than to wear the battered relic which was my only hat, and to sally up to town for the interview. There was the Vigo Street office – how well I was to come to know that entrance in later years – and the encounter with the office boy (later he was to ask me for my autograph and thus confer upon me the brevet of distinction) and the ushering into the room where awaited me the partner whose particular job was to interview young authors. When I came out again the agreement was signed and the future was settled in a manner far more definite (as I felt in my bones) than ever it had been when I signed my first agreement with a publisher. My intuition was correct – that firm has published a dozen books for me since that date.

All that remained to be done was to fight off starvation for the next ten months or so until the royalty cheque drifted in.

Chapter Twenty

I DO not think it would be very profitable to continue this history in detail very much farther. As I have noticed when writing books about my travels, it is far more interesting to write and to read about difficulties than about anything else in real life. Besides, not long after the point to which this book has now reached I begin to lose interest in myself. Frankly, I am intensely interested in my memories of the lanky, shabby, hard-pressed young man I once was; it is quite hard for me to believe that that desperate individual was me. I look back on his adventures and his troubles and think to myself that I could never survive what he went through.

And yet, such is the cross-grained nature of mankind, no sooner do I get myself out of one kind of trouble than I feel compelled to go out and seek another. Nowadays when the possibility of starvation is fairly remote I must wander forth and run other risks. Early years as an author have given me a distaste for the peaceful and the ordinary – I try to make myself believe that there is nothing I like better, but I know inside me that I am trying to deceive myself. I try hard to be respectable. I have one suit of clothes which I wear once a month or so – which is really presentable. I have a bank account which I have not overdrawn for eight years.

Though in the old days it had some narrow escapes. There was at least one occasion when poverty drove me in to ask what my balance was – on the occasion I have in mind the piece of paper which the cashier handed me bore the significant figures 'four shillings and sevenpence'. And then and there I wrote a cheque for four shillings and sevenpence, and cashed it over the counter – it is silly to try and lunch on three halfpence when one has four and sevenpence in the bank. Life still has its disappointments and its excitements. *Payment Deferred* did not make its way home without meeting lions in its path. Only a week after it appeared the general strike came on and almost killed it dead – to this day I cannot understand how it survived that blow. And the postman's advent is still crammed with possibilities. Six weeks ago he brought me a fat envelope which I opened casually enough, to find that it contained page after page of letters and agreements. They concerned the dramatised version of *Payment Deferred* which I had, honestly, forgotten all about. All sorts of names met my eye as I ran through the covering letter 'Gilbert Miller', 'St James' Theatre', 'Charles Laughton', 'Jeanne de Casalis' and so on. Ten minutes before only a placid spring and summer lay before me with no special excitement in prospect. Now that unanticipated letter implied that I would be plagued before long into all the how d'ye do of rehearsals and first nights and so on, with the imminent possibility before me of earning more money in six months than I have made in all my life up to now – quite a large amount of implication for one single letter. And tomorrow's post may bring some other letter just as important to me, conveying, this time perhaps, bad news instead of good.

An author's life is one wherein anything is possible. My wife and I have had to make an agreement with ourselves by which we have promised – for fear of drifting – to alter our way of living for the worse when I find myself five hundred pounds in debt, and for the better when I find that I have five thousand pounds invested – either event may occur quite suddenly, and we must be ready to adapt our outlook. By the time the publication of this book arrives, even, I may be either a wealthy man or a pauper. And perchance I may merely be a swollen corpse, with my body rolling down the emerald green rapids of the Upper Loire, bumping gently against the golden beaches, being ground against the foam-bordered rocks, or rotating stiffly and grotesquely in the swirls and eddies of that queen among rivers – for as soon as this play business is under way (or come to a sudden end, as the case may be) I am starting out with my ridiculous little motor boat to descend the more dangerous half of the Loire.

171

On the other hand I may live to be full of years and honours, perchance a baronetcy, may come my way. I may grow a belly and become smug and self-satisfied and peaceful, and forget all about the restless years of my childhood and the unhappy years of my youth, and join in Sunday newspaper symposiums about what is wrong with the younger generation. Or my wife and child may come to know what a workhouse is like, and I may descend to become one of those shabby sly men who lie around theatrical bars, telling people whom I can induce to listen to me, 'Yes, I had plays of my own running in the West End once.' And the man I am addressing will notice my white hair and my watery eye, and my red nose, and my shaking hand, and will only half believe me, and will buy me a drink with contemptuous pity, and men who know me nowadays will shake their heads when they think of me, and say to themselves, 'Poor old Forester. He had a splendid chance once. Pity he threw it away like that.'

And if ever the best happens, the time will come when I am an old man, a nuisance to my children and a burden upon my wife, maundering in senility towards a grave which I alone will not regard as a merciful release. And when I die there may be a paragraph or two in the newspapers, and a few people yet unborn reading them will say to themselves, 'C. S. Forester? Oh yes, I've read one or two of his novels,' and turn to the sporting page. After that my name will linger in the British Museum Reading Room catalogue for a space at the head of a long list of books for which no one will ever ask. And all the hopes and sorrows and jaw-settings and artistic yearnings which I have tried to describe here will seem extraordinarily trivial; perhaps they will even seem trivial to me.

After all these very serious reflections I suppose it will be best to call this the end of the book. I have rescued a certain amount from the past, just in time, but the compass of a single book is not nearly enough to cover thirty-one years of a man's life. There is an enormous amount left out, largely from sheer necessity. To my mind this history appears complicated enough already although it is only a general broad outline. If I had brought in all the other things which seemed of enormous importance at the time and which actually did have some influence upon after events the narrative would have become too complex to read and far too bulky to publish – which is rather frightening, when I consider how often I have blithely set out to narrate the lives of two or three people in the course of a single novel.

Some Personal Notes

Here is an example of the author's original manuscript.
This particular material may be found in finished form on
pages 182 to 183 of this book

THERE are jellyfish that drift about in the ocean. They do nothing to seek out their daily food; chance carries them hither and thither, and chance brings them nourishment. Small living things come into contact with their tentacles, and are seized, devoured and digested. Think of me as the jellyfish, and the captured victims become the plots, the stories, the outlines, the motifs – use whatever term you may consider best to describe the framework of a novel. In the ocean there are much higher forms of life than the jellyfish, and every human being in the ocean of humanity has much the same experience as every other human being, but some human beings are jellyfish and some are sharks. The tiny little food particles, the minute suggestive experiences, are recognized and seized by the jellyfish writer and are employed by him for his own specialized use.

We can go on with the analogy; once the captured victim is inside the jellyfish's stomach the digestive juices start pouring out and the material is transformed into a different protoplasm, without the jellyfish consciously doing anything about it until his existence ends with an abrupt change of analogy.

In my own case it happens that, generally speaking, the initial stimulus is recognized for what it is. The casual phrase dropped by a friend in conversation, the paragraph in a book, the incident observed by the roadside, has some special quality, and is accorded a special welcome. But, having been welcomed, it is forgotten, or at least ignored. It sinks into the horrid depths of my subconscious like a waterlogged timber into the slime at the bottom of a harbour, where it lies alongside others which have preceded it. Then, periodically – but by no means systematically – it is hauled up for examination along with its fellows, and, sooner or later, some timber is found with barnacles growing on it. Some morning when I am shaving, some evening when I am wondering whether my dinner calls for white wine or red, the original immature idea reappears in my mind, and it has grown. Nearly always it has something to do with what eventually will be the mid-point of a novel or a short story, and sometimes the growth is towards the end and sometimes towards the beginning. The casualty rate is high – some timbers grow no barnacles at all – but enough of them have progressed to keep me actively employed for more than forty years.

Examination completed, the timber is dropped back again into the slime, to be fished out every now and then until the barnacles are found to be quite numerous. That is when the plot is really beginning to take shape; that is when the ideas relating to it recur to me more and more often, so that they demand a greater and greater proportion of my attention as the days go by, until, in the end, the story might almost be described as an obsession, colouring my thoughts and influencing my actions and my behaviour. Generally some real work is called for at this stage, to clear up some mechanical difficulty. At some point in the plot it may be essential for the *Lydia* and the *Natividad* to be at the same place at the same time – what forces (other than pure coincidence) can bring this about? What has happened earlier that makes it quite inevitable? A different kind of inventiveness has to be employed here.

This sort of difficulty is sometimes cleared up in a peculiar and often gratifying fashion – I have known it to happen half a dozen times. I have been developing two different plots, both of them vaguely unsatisfactory, and then suddenly they have dovetailed together, like two separate halves of a jigsaw puzzle – the difficulties have vanished, the story is complete, and I am experiencing a special, intense pleasure, a glow of satisfaction – entirely undeserved – which is perhaps the greatest reward known to my profession.

2

So at last the construction is completed, the beginning and the end are determined upon, and all the intermediate steps (with occasional exceptions, one or two of which will be noticed later in this essay), so that all that remains is to write the thing. Please do not think that I am laying down rules for the writing of novels. Other writers employ other methods. Some novels are begun without planning; the writer's invention carries him on to an end which at first he does not foresee. Sometimes characters in a novel take charge while the novel is being written and insist on developments utterly unanticipated. Yet, even so, I believe that basically there is no essential difference of method. Writers who work in these ways are doing on paper what I prefer to do – or must do – in my mind before I start on the paper. Characters of mine who take charge do so during the preliminary thought; those developments are new barnacles on the timber.

Now, with regard to this construction; clearly there are two extremes in the matter of procedure. The writer may first think of the deed that is going to be done, and then ask himself who would be the most suitable – and most interesting – person to do that deed; on the other hand the writer may think of a character and then ask himself what would be a likely – and interesting – deed for that person to do. On the one hand no one can imagine that Jonathan Swift first thought of the character of Lemuel Gulliver and then thought of sending him to an island populated by a race of people six inches tall. Swift must have thought about Lilliput first, and then developed the most suitable person to send there. Gulliver, with his shrewdness and simplicity, his knowledge of the world, and his ignorance – all quite human and believable – was the ideal person to observe and comment upon the cultures that he encountered. Without Gulliver the *Travels* would be pointless fantasy; without the *Travels* Gulliver would still be someone to be reckoned with; but all the same he owes his existence to the *Travels*.

There is a magnificent, an awe-inspiring example of this in *Hamlet*. It is hard to believe that Shakespeare conjured up that complex character and then arbitrarily made him a dispossessed prince in Denmark. It seems quite obvious that Shakespeare thought of (or read of) the situation first – the incest, the murder, the dispossession – and then built up Hamlet in his mind as the most interesting person to face the situation, alone, without a confidant, and hampered by his own complexities.

The most convenient example of the other method of approach, in which the character comes first, that I can think of, is *Madame Bovary*. I feel quite sure that Flaubert knew a great deal about her before he decided upon what she was going to do, and that he built her up in his mind before making the discovery that she was a suitable person through whom to exploit the 'realism' that attracted him after the *Temptation of Saint Anthony*. Then that discovery naturally dictated the things that would happen to her, the deeds she did; the story came into existence because of Madame Bovary, and not the other way about.

In any case, whatever the method of construction, the book still has to be written. The ideas formed in the mind have to be fixed on paper. First of all, a start has to be made – that statement of the obvious is justified by the magnitude of the truth it contains. The happy-go-lucky methods of the jellyfish have to be abandoned for the diligence of the ant and the endurance of the mule. For me personally, the change of state occasioned by beginning to write is abrupt and violent. It is the difference between standing at the top of the toboggan slide and starting the descent. It is taking the plunge, swallowing the pill, walking through the door marked 'Abandon Hope'. It means giving up the pleasant life of contemplation for a period of the hardest and most unrelenting work, because (as experience has long taught me) it is hard work, exhausting work. I am held back by the thought of what I am leaving behind as well as by the thought of what I am entering into. At some moment I have to sit myself at my worktable, write the figure '1' at the top of the first page on my pad, and then begin the opening paragraph; that is when the toboggan is pushed off, and there is no going back.

There are various devices to bring this about; the most usual one is to tell my publisher that I am contemplating a novel and to promise a date for delivery – promise it solemnly, with no ifs or perhapses. I have done this maybe twenty times, and I have never broken one of those promises. To do so would be like a reformed drunkard taking his first glass of whisky. My last safeguard against idleness would be down. Contemplation of the rapidly changing dates on the calendar, calculation of the number of days left to me in which to keep my promise, drive me into action sooner or later – not sooner, but later.

4

For me there is no other way of writing a novel than to begin at the beginning and to continue to the end, and that is not quite the statement of the obvious as it might appear. Other people have other methods; I have heard of novels started in the middle, at the end, written in patches to be joined together later, but I have never felt the slightest desire to do this. The end is in my mind, of course, and so are the intermediate passages, and I rush forward, leaping from one solid foothold to the next, like Eliza leaping from one cake of ice to the next on the Ohio River.

There is still need to think and to plan, but on a different scale, and along different lines. The work is with me when I wake up in the morning; it is with me while I eat my breakfast in bed and run through the newspaper, while I shave and bathe and dress. It is the coming day's work which is occupying my thoughts; the undemanding routine activities permit – encourage – my mind to work on the approaching difficulties, to solve the tactical problems which arise in the execution of the strategical plan. So, the day's work is clear, usually, in my mind as I stand screwing up my resolution to begin again. Then I find myself in my workroom, uncapping my fountain pen and pulling my pad towards me and glancing down the paragraphs written yesterday, and instantly I am swept away into composition.

Yet, surprisingly perhaps, it is hard work, exacting and exhausting work. For me (I know many novelists who feel differently) the pleasure to be found in the act of composition is overlaid by the physical and mental fatigue that it occasions. From one point of view I would rather be in the dentist's chair. This is largely the result of the defect in my temperament which will not allow me to work slowly. I have never learned restraint in all this time. I cannot bear to rest or to wait. Once started, the day's work must be done, and done it is, perhaps in an hour, perhaps in three hours, but always when it is finished there is the sick, weary, flat feeling of exhaustion. There is no pleasure left in life; I am drained and empty, and the rest of my day is lived by a different creature, mindless and spineless, who is creeping back to a resemblance to humanity only as the evening draws to a close.

It is the knowledge that this is going to happen to me that makes the initial plunge into work such a difficult step to take. But the reluctance that shows itself each morning afterwards is more easily overcome. First of all there is the knowledge gained by experience that one day's postponement is like the one drink of a drunkard. Tomorrow's postponement is easier still, and when I finally emerge from my bout of laziness three weeks have passed by, and the after-effects are so unpleasant that nowadays I have learned to maintain a firm front. Another factor is routine; after a few days' work I have slipped into the habit of starting work at the earliest possible moment each day, to such an extent that much as I dislike the thought of work, I dislike even more the present feeling of not having worked – and there is no stronger expression than that. And lastly there is the temperamental desire to finish the thing, not merely to rid myself of this burden that I am carrying, but in order to gratify my curiosity. There are certain things ahead to be done, there are certain moods to express, there are difficult corners to turn. Will the plans I have made prove adequate? Will I be able to find the right words to express the feeling I wish to convey? There is only one way to find out, and that is to go on writing.

5

SITTING at a table writing words on paper; what is it that forms those words? What is going on in my mind as I write them? I have no doubt that in my case it is a matter of a series of visualizations. Not two-dimensional, as if looking at a television screen; three-dimensional, perhaps, as if I were a thin, invisible ghost walking about on a stage while a play is in actual performance. I can move where I like, observe the actors from the back as well as the front, from prompt side as well as opposite prompt, noting their poses and their concealed gestures and their speeches. One might almost call it four-dimensional, because I am aware of their emotions and their motives as well. So I record what my judgment tells me are the essentials of the scene I am witnessing. I can run through a scene again, like a Hollywood director in his chair in a projection room, and when I have finished with a scene I discard it and conjure up another one, devised in my mind all those weeks ago in the happy period of construction. It is really reporting, for almost all the invention has already been carried out, but it is surprising what a high degree of concentration is necessary during the process; when the day's work is finished and I return to civilized life I am conscious of the same feeling of confusion – short-lived, fortunately – as one feels when awakened from a vivid dream. And it is possible to lapse, to sneak back, or drift back, into the secret theatre and on to the secret stage, from out of the workaday streets and the domestic life, so that my dinner partner eyes me with distrust or my bridge opponents exult in my lapses.

Almost all the invention has already been carried out, as I have just said, but not quite all. A minor sort of invention is necessary at the worktable – tactics rather than strategy. The words have to be chosen, the sentences devised, which most accurately and most economically – and most suitably – describe the scene I am witnessing. I have to ask myself continually if the paragraph I am writing will conjure up the same scene in the mind's eye of the reader, will make him equally aware of the emotions I am aware of. An awkward sentence may bring the reader back to reality, as a breaking stick may alert the feeding deer. An incorrectly worded sentence may convey an impression quite different from the one I wish to convey, so that each completed sentence has to be looked at objectively; the objective and the subjective have to work in unison – or at least alternately.

That is the great advantage of writing by hand instead of on a typewriter. Alterations are readily made, and not only in the sentences just completed. Sometimes it is necessary to refer back a page or two, to check whether the ship is under one reef or two, or who it was made the last report; one way or another every word is reread once or twice, and the self-critical mood is naturally adopted then. On a handwritten page it is easy enough to substitute one word for another, or to transpose phrases with a ring and an arrow. Faced by a typewritten page, and the necessity to re-align the carbon copies, it is possible to be lazy, to decide that the present wording will just do, even though conscience says otherwise. The self-critical impulse is easily enough diverted in any case, because it is distasteful to follow it, to face the fact that I have written something incorrectly, that my judgment has been at fault, or simply that I have been careless. To recognize my imperfections comes hard; to force myself to look for them comes harder still, but it is necessary – just as an ugly woman has to force herself to examine objectively her image in the mirror to see what can best be done about it, even if she hates what she sees.

So time goes on; each day brings its quota of words, its finished pages, and with each day the increasing desire to have the thing finished grows stronger. I have learned not to indulge it. Unpleasant experience has taught me that to work on and on through the day and to finish a prodigious amount at a sitting is ill-judged. (Remember, I am only discussing my own methods; other people successfully use other methods.) Next day I am sick and bone-weary and I *cannot* work. Not even the most objective and impersonal analysis of my motives brings me to the conclusion that I am being influenced by plain laziness, by mere distaste for exertion. It is *impossible* for me to work, and my loss today is greater than my gain of yesterday. In consequence I have to remain orderly and methodical, and there are few people in this world naturally less orderly and methodical than I am. I have to plod along from day to day, from the beginning to the end, even though my instinct is to act as if the beginning were a forest fire and the end some safe refuge of desert country.

Three months – four months – something in between those two limits, and then at last it is finished. There is no pleasure, even, in writing the final word; my mind is too numb to feel anything of the sort. Not even relief; for the next thing to do is read the completed typescript – a long-suffering secretary has been following me up, two or three days behind me, and within a day or two the final pages are typed. Naturally I have glanced at the typescript during the progress of the work, but now I have to read the whole thing through – out of curiosity, perhaps; I can think of no other reason. And there it is. The ugly woman, having completed her make-up, can now study the final result, of course with disappointment. Can a finished book ever be as good as the book the writer dreamed of before he started writing it? I cannot believe that to be possible, for obvious reasons; certainly it has never happened to me. Luckily the numbness and weariness take the edge off the disappointment. I am too tired to feel it deeply. And the mental attitude changes a little, so that I can reach the decision to send the typescript off to a publisher. Trying to be as objective as I can, I am ready to agree, reluctantly, that the book is as good as I could ever make it – there is nothing I can do to improve it.

The shortcomings that displease me are my own, and I have lived with my own shortcomings long enough to be callous about them. By the time I have finished a book I am callous about pretty nearly everything. Let it go – let me come back into the normal world which I left three months ago. Those three months have been devoid of every ordinary reaction; as far as my daily life is concerned I might as well have been under an anaesthetic.

7

YET my distaste for my own work lingers on surprisingly. A father looking down at his first-born for the first time may experience a sense of shock, but he generally recovers from it rapidly enough; after a day or two he thinks it is a very wonderful baby indeed. My life would be happier if I reacted in the same way towards my books – the odd thing being that even as it is there are very few people who lead a happier life than mine, despite all the feelings that I have just been describing. I must be like the princess who felt the pea through seven mattresses; each book is a pea. Inevitably, the proofs start coming in, set after set of them, English proofs, American proofs, serial proofs, and every set has to be read carefully and objectively for the literal mistakes it contains – different ones for each set. I approach the first set with distaste and the fourth or fifth set with horror. By the fourth or fifth reading the imperfections have grown huge in my mind; I feel, quite seriously, that no one will ever bother with this nonsense.

Because of this feeling, favourable reviews and kindly comments by friends do not bring the satisfaction I expected in the days when I first wrote. People who say or write nice things about my books must clearly be people with no perception whatever and their opinions not worth consideration. Luckily, the acute phase of this trouble does not last long. A feeling of amused tolerance replaces the distaste, and all troubles are forgotten in the delicious pleasure of not being exhausted each day. To recognize my children when I meet them in the street; to seek out once more that elusive difference (unnoticeable while I am working) between WHITSTABLES and COL-CHESTERS; to welcome the dawn as an old friend whether I am on my way home or on my way out; to bathe in the euphoria of having energy to waste; to undertake some of the myriad projects (unconnected with novel writing) left neglected during this little death – these are things that (thanks to my profession) I enjoy far more keenly than less fortunate persons.

8

AND, almost unnoticed, the next story begins to creep into this delightful life. The serpent enters into Eden, but without arousing apprehension, even when, eventually, it is recognized for what it is. There are the moments of solid satisfaction at each advance in construction, there is the pleasure experienced (greater, rather than less, in being entirely undeserved) when, during the course of an idle morning, the discovery is made that an awkward corner has been turned; these are all the innocent, and yet astonishingly acute, joys of creation to add to the pleasure of being alive and in Eden. Perhaps it is the best life that anyone could ever lead.

Even when serious work has to be done on the construction, when the final phase is reached, there is still no cloud to obscure the sun. This new book, if it ever comes to be written, will be as nearly perfect as any book can be. It will be easy enough to make sure that the imperfections that disfigure its predecessor will not occur in this one. And if ever I set about writing it I shall have some sense. I will work slowly and stay cheerful and free from fatigue. Perhaps this experience will be much better than the last – I can be sure that nothing could be worse, anyway. And if I delay any longer, with this story demanding expression, Eden will not remain quite the same Eden. And so I walk into my workroom, uncapping my fountain pen, and the doors of Eden slam behind me, not to reopen until I have suffered the whole cycle again.

9

I CAN remember how Hornblower started. It was buying a book that prepared the slime into which the first waterlogged timber would be dropped. The *Naval Chronicle;* this was a magazine published monthly from about 1790 to 1820, written largely by naval officers for naval officers. There were three volumes in a second-hand bookshop – six issues of each, bound together – and I bought them in 1927 because I was looking for books to supply a library for a small boat on which I was going to live for several months together. They were biggish books in small print, crammed with facts, and (within limits) covering a wide range of subjects – ideal for the purpose. The fact that they were of nautical interest gave them added attraction, although that was not the decisive factor. I might possibly have bought books about banking methods or law – in that case would I later have found myself committed to write a novel-cycle about banking? I suppose that is possible, but I cannot believe it.

Those volumes of the *Naval Chronicle* were read and reread during the months that followed, and perhaps I absorbed some of the atmosphere; certainly I became very familiar with the special mental attitude of naval officers at that time regarding various aspects of their profession.

And in one of the volumes was the actual text of the Treaty of Ghent signed in December, 1814, making peace between the United States and England. The general terms can be found in any standard history, but for me there is a special attraction about detail – how these things were actually expressed at the time, the exact wording, the moods hinted at in the words. Here was Article Two, defining when the war should legally end; in the North Atlantic, twelve days after the ratification, the interval increasing to forty days for the Baltic and so on up to a hundred and twenty days for distant parts of the Pacific.

This was an interesting illustration of the difficulties of communication, and gave rise to odd trains of thought. If you captured a ship off Java one hundred and nineteen days after the ratification, that ship was yours, but if you captured a ship one hundred and twenty-one days after ratification you had to hand it back. And if the capture took place after exactly one hundred and twenty days what happened then? And if it happened on the wrong side of the International Dateline? There were possibilities of all sorts of disappointments and heartburnings along these lines. Down into the slime went the waterlogged timber.

10

IN any case, there was more material for the subconscious to work on in dealing with the situation of the man who has to make unaided decisions. The man alone; he may have technical help, he may even have friends, but as regards the crisis he is facing he can only act on his own judgment, and in case of failure he has only himself to blame. The murderer, who, having committed his crime, dare confide in nobody and must plan his future actions without assistance, is one example of the single-handed man; at the ripe age of twenty-three I had dealt exhaustively (so I thought) with a murderer and his problems, but there was still a great deal not yet said regarding the Man Alone. There was the terrifying perfection of Hamlet; but in the world there are uses to be found for candles even after arc lights have been invented.

This Man Alone – the captain of a ship, and more especially of a ship of war, was very much alone in the days before radiotelegraphy. A captain like one of those I had been reading about – barnacles were growing apace on the waterlogged timber.

There was another interest at this time, besides the *Naval Chronicle* and the allied reading which it had led me into. This was the Peninsular War. Sir Charles Oman had just finished his *History* in several large volumes – one of the best histories, and certainly one of the best military histories ever written. The painstaking care it displayed left me in awe; the myriad details enchanted me so much that I had written two military novels dealing with the period. Even though those novels were now behind me, and other work occupied my attention, there were still lingering memories. The character of Wellington himself was fascinating – and he was certainly an example during the Peninsular War of the Man Alone, although not quite of the type that was taking form in my mind. Also in his family had occurred one of the most resounding scandals in a scandal-ridden age; his brother's wife had eloped with the cavalry general who was later to become Marquis of Anglesey. The repercussions of that elopement spread far through history; that was very interesting.

Another detail that held my notice was quite unrelated. When the war was at its height, and the Spanish Government was fighting for its life against the Napoleonic armies, Spanish troops were actually withdrawn from the struggle and sent across the Atlantic to repress a rebellion that had broken out in Mexico. The Spanish-American empire was beginning to fall to pieces, and communications were long and difficult. And barnacles were still growing on those sunken timbers, attaching themselves almost unnoticed while my conscious mind was at work on novels like *The African Queen* and *The General*.

11

Now came a coincidence, although its connection with Hornblower was not at that time apparent in the least. Hugh Walpole, whom I had never seen, nor spoken to, nor corresponded with, was at work in Hollywood; the Hollywood of the new talkies, at the height of its power and pride and wealth and insolence. Walpole was asked, inevitably, who among the young writers in England showed promise and might be useful in handling this new medium; it happened that he gave my name. So a letter arrived for me asking if, were I to be invited to come to work in Hollywood, would I accept the invitation? Would I cross the Atlantic and visit those outlandish United States? Would I commit myself to working in that Hollywood about which such fantastic tales circulated? If, at that moment, some novel had held me in thrall I might well have refused, but as it was I was momentarily preoccupied with a very minor interest – a mere marionette theatre. In any case it was common knowledge that Hollywood promised much and delivered little. I wrote back saying that I would accept the invitation if it came, but I was quite sure that the invitation would never come. Yet it came, charged with all the desperate urgency of Hollywood, so that after forty-eight hours of active visa-seeking and desperate packing I found myself sailing for New York in the old *Aquitania*.

Details of that first period of work in Hollywood are of no importance as regards this present discussion, except from one point of view. It has always been my experience that ideas do not form themselves in my mind when I am leading what might be thought a contemplative life, doing nothing whatever. Activity, violent interests outside a life of writing, a crisis twice a week and a catastrophe every Saturday, with neither the leisure nor the strength to do any serious thinking – a few weeks of that sort of life and when a breathing spell arrives I make the gratifying discovery that the subconscious ideas have developed and fresh barnacles have grown on the submerged timbers. And the newcomer to Hollywood in those days faced new crises twice a day, not merely twice a week; it needed experience to discover that not one of the crises mattered, and that emotions ran only skin deep. Encountering a new culture, seeing new sights, breathing a different air – and goaded into ever-fresh activity by a natural curiosity – I certainly had no time for contemplation.

The final crisis was personal to me. After going along from one job to another I found myself engaged by Irving Thalberg – perhaps the most prominent Hollywood personality at that time – to work on a screen play about Charles Stewart Parnell. No two people on earth, perhaps, were less suited to work together than Thalberg and me; and perhaps the spirit of Parnell did nothing to soften any personal difficulties. Then, idly, I noticed the announcement of the sailing next day from San Pedro of the Swedish ship *Margaret Johnson*, of the Johnson Line, with freight and passengers for Central American ports, the Panama Canal, and England. An idle reading, perhaps, but it brought about an immediate change. There was the instant realization that I wanted no more of Hollywood, that I never wanted to work under instruction again, that I wanted my freedom, that I was passionately anxious to see England once more. (I feel compelled at this point to interrupt the narrative by mentioning that since that time I have managed to work in Hollywood, without active unhappiness at least.) But this was the moment for action. Within the hour I was a free man, having tendered my resignation comfortably ahead of dismissal. Before the day was over I had engaged a passage, and, remarkably, had settled my income tax with Internal Revenue. And before the next day was well advanced I was standing on the deck of the *Margaret Johnson* watching the United States sink below the horizon.

12

THAT was an extraordinarily happy time. Central America in those days could only be visited by ship – such ships as the *Margaret Johnson* herself – and this was the time of the coffee harvest. We wandered about from one little harbour to another, from one open roadstead to the next, picking up fifty bags of coffee here and a hundred there, and if the harbour facilities – the rickety pier or the battered old lighters – were already preempted by another ship we dropped anchor and waited without impatience. When we steamed into the Gulf of Fonseca to find the port of La Unión already occupied, and had to anchor beside the island of Meanguera, the captain took advantage of the delay to put the lifeboats through their annual test; and when the big motor lifeboat was in the water the first mate and I persuaded him to let us go off in it on a long voyage of exploration into the inner recesses of the Gulf.

There were forgotten villages, lashed by the rain and roasted in the sun, where pathetic life moved on at a snail's pace, where old, old women squatted in the market place mutely offering for sale their entire stock in trade – a single egg held in a skinny hand. Back at sea again there were sudden violent storms that laid the *Margaret Johnson* well over on her beam ends, a hurricane wind that picked me up when I incautiously emerged on to the open deck and flung me twenty feet against the rail and very nearly through it. There was blazing sun, and volcanoes glowing at night, and the False Cross visible on the southern horizon. There was a civilized interval while passing through the Panama Canal, and then more beachcombing along the coast of the Caribbean.

For six weeks this went on, six weeks with nothing to do except to observe, to feel, and, vaguely, to think, while the tension that had built up in Hollywood gradually eased off. The captain was a shuffleboard enthusiast, an addict; for him shuffleboard was one of the important things in life, and he and I played hundreds and hundreds of games on the blazing upper deck – the *Margaret Johnson* had a long, easy roll, and there was a certain fascination about standing waiting to shove one's disc while keeping an eye out over the ship's side so as to pick exactly the right moment to send the disc slithering along on a curved path between two hostile discs laid as obstacles – with good timing the disc could be made to behave almost intelligently. Stabilizers have taken half the fun out of shuffleboard. All the same, shuffleboard made no extravagant demands on the brain; it provided healthy exercise for the body while keeping the mind just busy enough so that it could not act on its own account and the subconscious could have full play. Every now and then the results became evident as the submerged timbers revealed fresh barnacles.

That break-up of the Spanish-American Empire; twice at least while Spain was an ally of Bonaparte England had made common cause, disastrously, with malcontents in South America in the hope of detaching the Spanish colonies from the Spanish crown. It was odd to think of British forces fighting in Montevideo and Buenos Aires, but there had even been moments when the British flag flew in Manila and Java. And on the lost Pacific coast of Central America queer things could happen. Someone could set himself up as an independent, and in that enlightened country a leader could be an untrammelled tyrant, as the later history of the Central American republics amply proved. And a tyrant in that country? El Supremo began to take shape, and also began to dovetail in with the possibility of British support. Had not Nelson himself, as a young captain, nearly lost his life on some similar hare-brained expedition to the Mosquito Coast?

Nelson, of course, had been involved in the Nelson-Hamilton scandal which had preceded the Anglesey-Wellesley scandal. Did Wellington ever have a sister, and not a mere sister-in-law? Wellington's intensely interesting personal character would be more interesting still in the female line, and I already knew enough about the influence of politics on naval careers to guess what part the Wellesley clan might play in a novel of the period; clearly (as was once said in another connection) if a Wellesley sister did not exist it would be necessary to invent one.

13

THE *Margaret Johnson* went out through the Mona Passage from the Caribbean into the Atlantic, and with that change – quite probably in consequence of it – the vital step in the construction was taken. That first faint hint remembered from years back, which had been calling attention to itself and demanding recognition and incorporation – the difficulty in olden days of disseminating the news that a war had ended and a peace begun – applied with special and peculiar force to a Central American situation. For the change in the attitude of Spain in 1808 was not only rapid but especially drastic. Bonaparte's attempt to set his brother on the throne of Spain turned every Spaniard overnight from an enemy of England into an enthusiastic ally; there were few examples in history of such an instant political change – war was generally preceded by a period of tension, and peace by a period of negotiation. The results of such a complete reversal could be especially dramatic in Central America if a British naval expedition there had first encouraged a separatist movement and then had to aid in suppressing it. My gloomy tyrant on the shores of the Gulf of Fonseca would have opportunities of revealing himself first as an ally and then as an enemy. The presence of Barbara Wellesley (I believe she had already been christened) would be susceptible to explanation and would not result from too wild a coincidence. The novel now had a beginning and an end, and – to drag in yet one more metaphor – with the identification of the keypiece the rest of the jigsaw puzzle fell into place, without further effort, to reveal the whole picture.

That was a moment of enormous satisfaction, as the *Margaret Johnson* headed into the trade winds northeastward across the Atlantic, and the long roll which had added so much interest to the games of shuffleboard was replaced by a shorter pitch-and-toss that altered their character. My character changed too; now I was Tom o'Bedlam, gradually becoming surrounded by dream figures more real than those of this world. Blandly abstracted, I lived the routine life of the ship without giving it a thought; my mind was now actively busy. When and how would the news of peace be received? What must be the attitude of the frigate's lieutenants one to another? How could the drama of such-and-such a situation be best expressed? The person who spoke to me at noontime with the result of the calculations of the ship's run would be mildly puzzled at my careless – almost deaf – reaction; he had summoned me out of an interview with El Supremo, possibly; I looked – I am sure – like a man awakened from a dream even though I had been pacing the deck, apparently normal. At least I refrained (unlike Gray's character) from muttering my wayward fancies aloud – self-consciousness inhibited that ultimate exhibition of abstraction, likely though it was, in my state of excitement.

14

THE Azores drew near; the trade winds dropped astern, and Hornblower began to develop a personality; to a large extent he was already formed by the necessities of the story. As in real

life we are moulded both by heredity and environment, so in
fiction characters must have certain qualities in order to be able
to perform their destined parts, and then are given additional
ones in order to make the necessary ones more believable, or
to make the character himself more believable, or because he
could not endure what he is to undergo without these additional
qualities, or even – and ultimately – because these characteristics seem suitable, fitting, and right.

Hornblower was to be the Man Alone that I had sought. He
had a definite task, or series of tasks, to perform in the course
of this novel that I contemplated, but that task was only a part
of a greater whole – while fighting El Supremo he was fighting
for his country against the continental tyranny of Bonaparte.
And then he had another task as well, one of much longer
duration, and perhaps of greater importance to him, and of
greater importance still to me. Wars could reasonably be
expected to end; Bonaparte might reasonably be expected to
fall – at any rate such highly desired possibilities were at least
possibilities, but Hornblower's other struggle would go on as
long as he was to live, for it was the struggle with himself. He
was to be self-critical. Just as no man is supposed to be a hero
to his own valet, so Hornblower could not be a hero to his own
self. He would be too cynical about his own motives, too aware
of his own weaknesses, ever to know content; and he would
have to be a man of considerable character so that, even though
despairing – hopeless – he could maintain this struggle with
himself and not subside into self-satisfaction or humility.

So now a great deal about Hornblower was settled. He was
the captain of a British frigate – not a ship of the line, for naval
policy demanded that ships of the line should be kept in fleets,
or at least squadrons, and not dispersed in units. Nor would
Hornblower be captain of a mere sloop, for a sloop would be
too small for the task contemplated. This gave a measure of his
seniority, for as a general rule the more senior the captain the
larger his ship. Hornblower would be likely to have from three
to ten years seniority as captain. He was not a man of blue
blood – that would over-simplify his affair with Lady Barbara –
so that his promotions would have been due to merit and not to
influence; giving additional force to this would be the fact that
he had been entrusted with this single-handed mission – he was

a man of mark to some modest extent. So that as his promotion had been comparatively prompt he would now be in his early thirties – a convenient age for his entanglement with Lady Barbara, whose elder brother was indisputably thirty-nine in 1808. A convenient age, too, because I was in my late thirties and could look down on my juniors with Olympian neutrality.

Incidentally, he would have to speak Spanish well, in order to save interminable trouble with interpreters while negotiating with El Supremo, and the need for a reasonable explanation of this ability tells us one thing about his professional past – he was at one time a prisoner of war in Spain.

He was a married man, of course – otherwise there would be no difficulty with Lady Barbara; and what had already been settled went a long way towards fixing the character of the wife, about whom something had to be known, although she would make no personal appearance. She was hardly likely to be sensitive, or intelligent or experienced, because if she had been she might be expected to have done something to loosen some of the knots Hornblower was tied up in. Likewise, she was a woman of the people, for if she were of blue blood Hornblower's approach to Lady Barbara would be simplified. It was lucky that there would be no need to explain how a man like Hornblower had come to marry a woman like this Maria; the reader could be expected to know that mismarriages happened.

15

Now for the rest of Hornblower. He must be perceptive and imaginative, for otherwise he would not see the things and the possibilities that were going to be observed through his eyes. He was not going to be an utterly fearless man – that was implicit in his character already; besides, as he was going into danger he must recognize it as danger so that I, the writer, could record it as danger, subjectively and not editorially. We already know him to be a man of marked ability; he must also have the quality of leadership – that would develop out of his perceptiveness and sensitivity; it would be the kind of leadership that owes much to tact and little to animal spirits.

So, as the *Margaret Johnson* neared England, Hornblower's character was pretty well settled for him. The details had to be filled in. He would be a gangling and awkward man, because that would be an effective contrast with his mental ability, and would offer fuel for the fire of his self-criticism. But he would be an accomplished mathematician; I myself was constitutionally unable to make the leap from the binomial theorem to calculus, and it would be pleasant to have a hero to whom it was easy, especially as some of my close friends had been mathematicians. Yet, of course, in making Hornblower a mathematician I was indulging in shameless wish fulfilment, but it is only today, while writing these lines, that I realize it.

Besides being self-conscious he would be shy and reserved – those qualities are closely associated – so as to make his relationship with Lady Barbara more difficult, and there I would be able to help myself considerably; there was little I did not know about shyness and reserve from personal experience. And as regards his actual appearance, he obviously must have the indefinable good looks that a woman would notice and yet which he himself would under-estimate, and along with those good looks would go good hands, beautiful hands, perhaps; hands that are often associated with the temperament I had in mind, and, once again, Hornblower would not be aware of their charm.

Another development. Lady Barbara's father, the first Lord Mornington, had been musical, and in fact had been a composer of minor distinction, while Wellington, her brother, had played the violin for his own pleasure until it interfered with his military studies. Lady Barbara would certainly be musical, too. Yet music had passed me by. I knew more – far more – about the etiquette of the court of Hapsburg-Lorraine than I did about harmony and counterpoint. Something must be done to bar Lady Barbara and Hornblower from finding common ground in music, and for more reasons than one. The action I eventually decided upon was perhaps drastic, even cold-blooded; Hornblower had to be tone-deaf, barred for ever from the pleasures of music. And that would help to keep him more human despite his intellectual eminence; a man I once knew well, and heartily disliked, had been tone-deaf, and had given me many opportunities of observing this condition. But if he had been a friend I suppose I should have profited in the same way from his infirmity.

One final point, before the *Margaret Johnson* sighted the Bishop Light and we entered the English Channel. This odd character had to have a name – so far he had been merely 'he' in my discussions with myself. He had to have a name which the reader would remember easily, which would stand out on the page, and which would not be confused with any other name. *War and Peace* had, in my judgment, almost not reached perfection because of the difficulty I had experienced in identifying the characters by their names. It would be desirable, but not entirely necessary for 'him' to have a slightly grotesque name – something more for his absurd self-consciousness to be disturbed about. The consideration of least weight – the merest milligram – was that 'he' was a slightly grotesque character, too. 'Horatio' came first to mind, and oddly enough not because of Nelson but because of Hamlet; but it met an essential requirement because it was a name with contemporary associations. Nelson was by no means the only Horatio in late Georgian times. Then, from Horatio, it seemed a natural and easy step to Hornblower. At one moment he was 'he'; at the next 'Horatio'; and yet a moment later he was 'Captain Horatio Hornblower of His Britannic Majesty's Navy,' and the last awkward corner was turned and the novel practically ready to be written, and there was England fully in sight on the port bow.

16

THERE were things to be done before I could make a start. I had to get reacquainted with my wife and family; I had to re-adjust to the old environment; I had – most rebelliously – to deal with necessary business, and I had to do a great deal of reading to make sure of my facts. For once, in a way, there were so many obstacles to be surmounted that I even grew impatient. Instead of being driven, apprehensive and reluctant, into starting work, I was this time being held back from it, and with my natural cross-grainedness I chafed against the barriers. As always, there was the mounting curiosity regarding whether I could actually carry out the plans that were in my mind, especially as my reading progressed and the minor points were cleared up. The internal pressure reached a positively explosive point.

There was the constant slight irritation of having to explain myself, of having to make some sort of polite answer when asked, 'What's your subject this time?' That is a human enough question which I find extraordinarily hard to answer, even when I am actually writing, and practically impossible when I am not. There is one possible answer – 'Men and women' – but that can only be employed when rudeness has been amply justified. Why I should experience this difficulty is something I have never been able to explain to myself; there is some sort of mental cut-off system bringing about almost complete inhibition – something that functions nearly as efficiently as that which prevents a man from swallowing down his windpipe.

Michael Joseph was my publisher, and had been for years, and he had been my friend for years before that. He deserved an answer; I even *wanted* to answer him. For that matter there was the practical point that publishers have to plan their future production, and (I believe) prepare the ground for the books to come. So Joseph said, 'What next?' and I had to brace myself and splutter out a miserable answer. 'I'm thinking about writing a novel about a naval captain in 1808.' Joseph had read Henley, of course; he did not wince nor cry aloud. There was only a long pause and a blank stare before he answered, 'Splendid.' The magic of the year 1808 was imperceptible to him, and that was not his fault – to all except specialists, English naval history ended with Trafalgar, three years earlier. Even Joseph, as perceptive a man as I have ever known, could make no sense out of my tongue-tied efforts at explanation, not even when I added, 'I think I'll call him Hornblower,' and when we parted he was very little wiser and far more alarmed than before we met.

Nor could I blame him; the only person I could blame was myself, and I was nettled and irritated. It was only one more proof of the self-evident, of the fact that no book can be judged before it is written. So it came about that the very next morning I sat down at my table and pulled my pad toward me and wrote the words that had formulated themselves in my mind while I was drinking my breakfast coffee. 'It was not long after dawn that Captain Hornblower came up on the quarterdeck of the *Lydia*.' Perhaps it was a leap over the preliminary hurdle which I would not have taken in quite that fashion if I had not been goaded by that polite stare.

There followed the usual period of intense work, the inevitable fatigue, the loss of all sense of belonging to this world, which I had long ago come to expect and recognize, and then the thing was finished, sent off to the two publishers, and I could sink back into forgetfulness.

17

THE things that happened next make a puzzling sequence even to me. There is the matter of the lost novel, which I find almost inexplicable. The man I was then was different from the man I am now, and when I look back at myself there are numberless occasions when I find myself out of touch, experiencing the same hopeless feeling of addressing myself to a different kind of human being as fathers feel in discussions with their growing sons – for that matter I am old enough now to be a father to the man of those days, and I prefer not to think about what he would have thought of me if he had ever met me as I am now.

At any rate, there is this unsatisfactory matter of the lost novel, which demands a moment's attention at this point. Hornblower was finished, sent off, and forgotten. I cared so little about the book that when my American publishers suggested changing the title (American publishers always want to change titles) I agreed without thinking twice, so that the book was destined to be called *The Happy Return* in England and *Beat to Quarters* in America – a discrepancy which inconveniences me to this day. By the time the proofs came in I was deep in another novel – another set of waterlogged timbers had grown another crop of barnacles already; the fetid slime of my subconscious was seething with nutriment for low forms of life. And that novel was written, it was sent to London and to Boston, it was accepted, and was made the subject of signed agreements.

Then came the next development. There I was, recovering from my exertions, deep in a hundred activities all of them alien to literature, and enjoying ecstatically my hard-won freedom, when the old symptoms showed themselves again. They ran their course with feverish rapidity. Some time in 1809 or 1810, with the Peninsular War at its height, Bonaparte became concerned about the victualling of his garrison in Barcelona, which was in a state of semi-siege thanks to the activities of the Spanish *guerrilleros*. Land communications were difficult, and Bonaparte sent out a small squadron from Toulon under Admiral Cosmao with orders to break through to Barcelona carrying the necessary supplies. Cosmao met with the fate anyone could have predicted. His squadron was intercepted by a British naval force under Admiral Martin and destroyed. That was all, at first. That was the pioneer barnacle clinging to the timber.

Now came real life, horrible reality, unpleasant to remember and unpleasant to write about. General Franco had raised the standard of revolt in Spain, and the Spanish Civil War was tearing the country to pieces, and I was one of the men who went to try to find out what was happening. Fortunately I do not have to go into details about what I saw; all that it is necessary for me to say here is that it was an extremely unhappy experience, during which there was never a moment to think about anything except what was going on around me. Everything was in stark and dreadful contrast with the trivial crises and counterfeit emotions of Hollywood, and I returned to England deeply moved and emotionally worn out.

The reservoirs refilled in time, and the old promptings reasserted themselves, and the inventive impulses made themselves felt once more. While in Spain I had, naturally, referred continually to what I knew of the Peninsular War; there were analogies and parallels, and there was the consistent Spanish national character to bear in mind. In the Peninsular War, command of the sea had been a vital factor; victory depended upon it more than upon the admirable determination of the Spanish people never to submit to conquest. There was a possibility of a novel in this; when I started to come back to normal after my return I found that there had grown up in my mind a whole series of disconnected pictures of the feats the Royal Navy had performed during the war – the convoys destroyed, the signal stations blown up, the aid carried to the *guerrilleros*, the marching columns bombarded, the pin-prick raids upon the coast. Some sort of story – a story of considerable power, even – might be made of all this, with the underlying theme of the command of the sea.

And then – and then – here was the old surge of excitement,

the intense realization that possibilities were expanding, were exploding. Who could best perform those feats? Who was the thinking and sensitive man who would be aware of the influence of sea power? Who but the discarded character in my last novel but one, Horatio Hornblower? The framework of history was exactly fitting; he would have made his 'happy return' just in time to be appointed to a ship of the line and to be sent out to operate on the Spanish coast, where (the Admiralty might well believe) his knowledge of the Spanish language would be useful. Hornblower was both mentally and technically equipped for coastal operations, with their need for expert ship handling and rapid extemporization of plans. And that attempt on the part of the French to revictual Barcelona; that would provide a climax for the story – Hornblower throwing himself between the French and their goal. Surely all this called for close consideration.

18

OF course it is foolish to be dogmatic regarding matters of taste, regarding artistic conventions, but it seems obvious that a novel (I am sure there are exceptions, but I cannot think of a single example) starts at one moment of rest and finishes at another. The moment of rest may be extremely fleeting, but it is indisputably there. If the action should already be under way in the opening paragraph it is necessary to go back in some later paragraph to explain how the action started. The action continues, it may transform itself into some further action, but sooner or later the action ceases even though there may be consequences and potentialities obvious to the reader when the novel ends. The conventional ending of a love story with a wedding is a hackneyed example.

Hornblower had come to life at the end of a period of rest with his entry into the Gulf of Fonseca; at his parting from Lady Barbara he had entered into another period of rest. Now we could find him leaving a period of rest – fitting out his new ship – and carry him through to another; that would be his final battle against the French squadron. And that final battle would have to be a glorious failure, in a sense. Somehow I did not feel it to be fitting for Hornblower to be too successful; it seemed better, more appropriate, that the novel should end with his naval career ruined, with him parted, until the end of the war at least, from his Maria, and his Barbara.

There were momentary bursts of pleasure at this point of the construction. There would be the opportunity, in fact the necessity, of bringing Maria to life; so far she had only been hinted at, and it would be necessary to construct a real person from those hints, as a paleontologist is supposed to be able to build up in his mind an entire dinosaur from a single bone. It was an interesting challenge, almost an amusing one. And Barbara; she would have to enter into the story. Only if it meant straining probability too far could she be omitted, so my judgment told me. I wanted her there as badly as Hornblower did. It could be managed, easily enough. Nothing could be more natural than that Barbara on her return to England should marry a distinguished admiral. Nothing could be more natural than that this admiral, with the influence of the Wellesleys behind him, should be given this new command-in-chief set up as a result of the Spanish revolt against the French. And surely it would be natural for Barbara to call her husband's attention to Hornblower's talents. She had seen those talents demonstrated; she must surely have a soft spot in her heart for him, whatever had happened between them. He was momentarily unemployed and here was this squadron being formed for action on the coast of Spain; everything seemed to fit. In my construction I had thought of the cart before I thought of the horse, but in the novel the horse would take his place in front of the cart naturally enough.

Such are the pleasures of construction; now, once again, with the jigsaw puzzle half completed and the picture becoming clear, it became increasingly easy to fit in the remaining pieces; all the odd barnacles that had grown up on the sunken timber were found to have their uses. A few more delirious days of half-conscious work and the whole story was ready, from start to finish. It only needed (here was a grim reminder of reality, the skeleton at the feast), it only needed to be written.

19

Now we must go back again to the lost novel – it almost deserves that name already because it has disappeared from this narrative after only the briefest mention some pages back. The typescripts were lying in Boston and London, and soon they would be going to the printers. And I did not want that novel to appear yet, not if I were going to write *Ship of the Line*. It would not be fitting for it to be published between these two books. There was something inartistic (hateful though that word might be) about such a scheme. *Ship of the Line* was demanding to be written. There was one obvious course to take, and that was to postpone publication of the lost novel.

I wish I could remember more about that novel. It was contemporary, and it contained at least one murder and a hint of incest, and the principal characters (I think) were women, but I cannot recover any additional details. Every three or four years something reminds me of it, and then I forget about it again. Cynically, I suspect that it was a bad novel, which makes me content to continue in ignorance; presumably I was in my usual state of disappointment over finished work, but I do not believe that influenced me – consciously. However it was, London and Boston were informed that I had changed my mind about publication, that to fill the gap I was going to write a sequel to *The Happy Return*, and that I would have this ready for publication at the time originally planned for the publication of the discarded novel.

Looking back, I am astounded at the light-heartedness of all this. My publishers took it more seriously than I did; I distinctly remember the arrival of a long and solemn telegram from Boston in which the pros and cons were carefully debated, but it arrived after I had started the actual writing of *Ship of the Line* and I was no longer in a fit state to view mere practical matters with any balance at all. I was off in another world; and, as always at the moment of starting, this book would be far better than any predecessor, and who cared what happened to some other miserable novel already half forgotten? So the lost novel was really lost. It is just possible that the typescripts still exist, that they lie forgotten and gathering dust, in rarely entered storerooms in Boston and Bloomsbury; some day someone may find himself in one of those storerooms and wonder vaguely what is this wad of typescript he has stumbled over. I am perfectly content to let the matter remain like that. My literary executors can debate the ethics of publication.

So *Ship of the Line* was written, tumultuously, with a genuine reason for haste besides the invariable and inadequate one of my own impatience. The title was fixed from the start, but most of my titles are; knowing what will be the title of the book while it is being written is closely allied to knowing what the end of the book will be; it stands beside the goal faintly perceived in the mind's eye, as the writing makes its weary way towards the end. The ship herself, Hornblower's command, H.M.S. *Sutherland*, somehow won my special affection. Her Dutch build – like most of her contemporaries, she had entered the Royal Navy as a prize – was of considerable service to Hornblower and to me, and she was something of an ugly duckling of whom I grew fond.

There was a ridiculous incident just when I had begun the first chapter. I was dining in some Armenian restaurant or other – fatigue had not yet asserted itself to the extent of making all food indifferent to me – and had ordered the almost inevitable shish kebab. Here it came; pieces of bell pepper, pieces of lamb, pieces of mushroom, pieces of onion, a score or more items on a skewer. A firm grip on the skewer, a long push with a fork, and there it all lay in a tumbled heap on my plate. An analogy shot into my mind as I sat and stared at it. This book I was beginning to write (which I could not help being conscious of, whatever the business of the moment) was going to be something like this. Cutting out expeditions, convoy battles, shore raids would be the peppers and onion and bits of lamb. And the skewer which held them together and gave them form or reason? That would be H.M.S. *Sutherland* under the command of her renowned captain. I think that must have been the moment when my affection for that ship started to sprout; I know that from that time on I had to use restraint in my writing lest sentiment should creep in. And to this day, more than twenty-five years later, the sight of shish kebab on a skewer calls up to my mind's eye a three-dimensional picture of a blue sea and a hot sun and H.M.S. *Sutherland* standing in under easy sail to her rendezvous off Palamós Point. Sentiment, shish kebab, and *Sutherland*; an odd trio inextricably associated.

Hornblower and his *Sutherland* started from their moment of rest and went on to their moment of rest; the book was finished and the typescripts sent off comfortably in time for the promised day of publication, one year exactly after *The Happy Return*. It had been a full year and there was the usual numb bewilderment at the easing of the demand for mental activity. With the return of sensation, second thoughts began to creep in. The details of my day-to-day life at that time are naturally (perhaps mercifully) blurred in my memory; the only thing I can be sure of is that I was active (as always) domestically and socially; reading omnivorously; travelling and even writing (at that time I was under contract to deliver a weekly column to a newspaper); making up feverishly for the three months which had dropped out of my life on account of *Ship of the Line*.

21

THE second thoughts crept in insidiously. One of my bedside books (it is my habit to read dry factual books – even the *Encyclopaedia Britannica* – before going to sleep) was a volume of unedited letters of Napoleon I, letters which for obvious reasons had not appeared in the official collection issued by Napoleon III. Here was a letter to his brother Joseph, the intrusive King of Spain. 'The five or six persons who have been arrested at Bilbao by General Merlin, must be put to death.' Nearly all these letters revealed Bonaparte as utterly unscrupulous, and as utterly merciless when he thought his interests, his precious prestige, were imperilled. There could be found hints of his desire for vengeance – even though vengeance might be impolitic – perhaps traceable to his Corsican boyhood. And Hornblower was at this moment a prisoner in Bonaparte's hands – Hornblower, who had struck such shrewd blows at his dominion over Spain, who had fooled his generals and who had the audacity, the insolence, to violate the sacred soil of France. There were detestable examples in plenty of Bonaparte's mean indulgence in personal revenge. Alvarez of Gerona, Hofer of the Tyrol, had been done to death when generosity would have cost him nothing. Bonaparte must have hated the very name of Hornblower, and – on one occasion, on the coast of Spain, Hornblower had sailed under false colours, under the French flag.

This was a legitimate ruse of war; there were frequent examples in history, one notable one during the opening moves of the attack on Quebec in 1759. But to Bonaparte it might well supply an excuse for indulgence in his thirst for revenge, while he had in his power one of the very few English captains ever to be taken prisoner during the Napoleonic Wars. To have Hornblower shot would gratify Bonaparte's desire for revenge; to charge an English captain with a gross violation of the laws of war might help to explain to France and Europe why the Imperial Navy had not been over-successful lately. But perhaps something less than actual murder might satisfy Bonaparte, or at least might be deemed by him to be more profitable. To try Hornblower and condemn him, scare him nearly to death, and then pardon him with a great show of generosity, would be (in Bonaparte's judgment) an effective piece of theatre, like the celebrated incident of the burning of the letter in the presence of the Countess von Hatzfeldt. Perhaps Lady Barbara could make a personal appeal to Bonaparte on Hornblower's behalf? No. That was not quite right; or perhaps it was a theme not susceptible to sufficient elaboration. I was following a false scent.

That was a surprise to me; it seemed an admission that there was a scent to follow, and here I was in bed trying to go to sleep, and I knew from long experience that there was no surer way of inhibiting sleep than to dally with plots at midnight. Besides, I had left Hornblower a prisoner of war; the novel was about to be published, and I wanted nothing more to do with him. So I put down the *Lettres Inédites* and turned out my bedside light and composed myself to sleep, and an hour later I was out of bed seeking a drearier book still which might bring me some distraction from these nagging thoughts.

22

OF course the plot formed itself; if it would not show on the surface, it burrowed below it like a mole. If Hornblower was not to be formally pardoned, he would have to escape from captivity – there was a fairly extensive literature dealing with escape from Imperial prisons, but nothing I had read was either satisfactory or suggestive. Besides, by 1810 so much of Europe was under French domination that it would be impossible, were he to escape, for him to reach a neutral country. He would have to reach the sea. Of course he would have to reach the sea; there could be no compromise about that. I found myself actually yearning for it to come about; I wanted quite passionately for Hornblower to escape from the confinement that, with his temperament, he would find so insupportable, to escape from the treacherous land to the freedom of the sea. It would be a long and tricky journey.

Now came one of those sudden moments when one idea unexpectedly adheres to another apparently quite alien. I made the discovery at the usual neutral moment when I was glancing through the morning's letters, even though not one of those letters related to the business of Hornblower's escape. Some years before I had taken a motorboat down the river Loire; I put down an unread letter to face a new realization that Hornblower could use the same route to the sea. A small boat – and I had spent months, perhaps a total of years in small boats – on a river was a very convenient means of transport for a fugitive. It eliminated the possibility of losing one's way, it offered a convenient method of carrying necessary stores and equipment, and it would help considerably towards evading those inspections of passports and demands for papers to which travellers by road were continually subjected in Imperial France. Particularly would this be the case on the Loire, which I knew from personal experience to be lonely, unfrequented, apparently unnavigable, and yet practicable.

The blood was stirring in my veins; at the limit of deep sea navigation on the Loire was the city of Nantes. Seagoing vessels came up as far as the quays there – I could remember them. Perhaps Hornblower could – a sudden boiling over, and when the flurry had died down the mental picture was formed, of Hornblower recapturing the *Witch of Endor*; it was vivid and urgent in my mind. There were logical and interlocking corollaries, too. To perform such a feat Hornblower would need assistance, and skilled assistance. He would have to have Bush and Brown with him. That meant they would have to be with him on his journey down the Loire, and that called up further mental pictures; Hornblower in command of a ship's company of three; a twenty-foot boat instead of a two-thousand-ton seventy-four – there was a sort of wry and yet dramatic quality about that situation which demanded, insisted upon, consideration. Something was certainly happening to my prejudice against dealing with Hornblower again.

23

SOMETHING else happened. The proofs of *Ship of the Line* arrived, and I had set myself to read them, with all my usual reluctance. Then my small, but elder, son looked over my shoulder to see what I was doing. 'Oh, hurry up and finish that, Daddy,' he said. 'I want to read it. I liked the first one so much.' That son now has a son himself of just that age, but the gratification I felt at that moment is still fresh in my memory. It was compensation – overpayment – not merely for the trials of parenthood but for the labours of writing. And, sentiment apart (why was sentiment so distrusted by the man who was me at that time?) the incident inevitably helped to reconcile me to the notion of writing another novel about Hornblower.

Michael Joseph helped to stir the witches' brew. I was trying to explain to him about the turmoil that I was feeling, and I was struggling with my life-long prejudice against ever putting into words to a single soul, the half-formed ideas that were engrossing me. But somehow I was able to convey to him the tenuous theme I had in mind. 'You want to bring him back with flying colours?' said Joseph. This time it was his turn to be met with a blank stare, as if the remark had not raised a ripple. Nor could it; it had fallen, not into the liquid and lively river of polite conversation, but into the sluggish slime of the subconscious, sinking down and farther down to stimulate the barnacles into increased reproduction.

The effect was naturally contrariwise. Plain triumph, unadulterated success, was not the theme I was seeking. For that matter I had myself enjoyed considerable personal success, and I was acutely aware that 'enjoy' was by no means the correct word to use. The cross-grainedness of human nature meant that the gift horse had always to be looked in the mouth, and found to be long in the tooth; some rose leaf always to be found crumpled, while simple fate, and extraneous events, were bound to add bitter to the sweet, rough to the smooth, in addition to mixing the metaphors. It would serve Hornblower right if the same thing happened to him; but also (let us at all costs keep sentiment out of literature) there was the certainty that this would be artistically (that hateful word again) satisfactory.

The days went by, and the other ideas which had been

growing in my mind began to join on – ideas at first apparently unrelated, even regarded at first as the germs of some different piece of work. I had been observing the development of a theme of thwarted, transient love affair; hot passion gratified and yet cut short. Of course, it must have been Hornblower that it happened to. Why had it not occurred to me before? Hornblower making love, if not with one eye on the clock, then with his mind full of rival thoughts. Hornblower, as always, lucky and yet discontented, quite incapable of self-abandon; Hornblower, the sort of man with whom any woman might fall deeply in love, and yet whom a discerning or intuitive woman would recognize as one neither to hold nor to bind. It was bound to happen to him sooner or later, when he had a little leisure. And in France at this moment the *réfractaires* were beginning to make themselves felt, the young men who were on the run to avoid conscription; there had been a momentary consideration of the possibility that Hornblower might find help from some of them in his escape – and in France there had been also a growing body of more mature public opinion opposed to Bonaparte because of liberal convictions, or simply from contemplation of the disastrous results of Bonapartism. Half a dozen pieces of the jigsaw fell into position now. I knew where Hornblower would find the necessary help and how he would have his love affair.

There were some final decisions to be made. There was a death sentence to be passed – two, in fact. Poor Mrs Hornblower. Her death was decreed, not without hesitation, not without unavailing compassion; I seemed to know her so well. But there was no place left for her, and her death would be a very bitter ingredient in the cup of Hornblower's success. It would not be a difficult matter to arrange, for she was already pregnant in the last novel, and death in childbirth was common enough in those days to escape comment. She had been made pregnant to enable me to score a particular point in *Ship of the Line*, and now the fact was additionally useful, almost as if I had had the next development in mind at the time. I can affirm quite truthfully that this was not the case, but I suppose it is just possible that somewhere down among the barnacles, quite unrecognized, her approaching death had been planned. As for the death of Admiral Leighton – Barbara's husband – there would be no difficulty about that. He was a sailor in active service, and it was quite certain that he would be soon fighting his way into Rosas Bay to destroy the ships Hornblower had disabled there. I could be quite sure that few would shed a tear over Leighton's fate – perhaps not even Barbara.

<h2 style="text-align:center">24</h2>

So now it began to look as if the novel were ready for the writing. Certainly the old restlessness began to assert itself. There was the same lure, the temptation to discover if I could really fix on paper the complexities and moods that were circulating in my mind. There was the same quite unreasoning hope that this novel would be easier to write than the last. There was the same taking of the plunge. The day came when I wrote 'Page 1' and 'Chapter I', and Admiral Leighton launched his attack on Rosas Bay. The work went along well enough, if 'well enough' can be construed as including the inevitable daily exhaustion. Colonel Caillard and his gendarmes arrived to carry off Hornblower and Bush and Brown, just after Hornblower had learned enough about Leighton's fate to leave him in distressing uncertainty for the next few months. Everything was normal, until the shock came, almost as sudden and every bit as painful as walking into the edge of a door in the dark. One morning, while planning my day's work, I was filled with horrible doubts, and blindly ignored them; the next day those doubts were certainties and I was faced with disaster.

I cannot explain how it had come about, how I had been so incredibly careless, so blind, so inattentive. At this point in my construction of the story I had blandly said to myself 'here they escape', and had actually thought no more about it. I had left a gap and I had done nothing to fill it. By some unprecedented lapse I had not even realized that a gap existed until I found it yawning at my feet. They had to escape; they had to escape from an escort of twenty gendarmes in the heart of France, and Bush was only beginning to recover from the amputation of his foot – he could not walk a yard. How in the world could they possibly escape? There could be no question of leaving Bush behind – Hornblower would never have done such a thing, and in any case Bush would be badly needed in the remainder of the story. I had loaded myself with difficulties; I had made *l'affaire*

210

Hornblower so important that in addition to the escort I had put one of Bonaparte's ablest police officers in charge; Colonel Caillard would leave no opportunity for escape that I could avail myself of.

For me this was a moment of disruption. I was ashamed of myself, shocked at my behaviour, consumed with doubts as to my fitness for my chosen profession. But that was only the long view; the immediate and pressing future was momentarily more important.

The story had come to a complete stop, and there seemed to be no way out of the impasse into which I had hastened so blindly. I might have to back out and take another route altogether. But that meant recasting the whole story, beginning the construction anew, and, after reconstruction, rewriting; and it was fifteen years since I had rewritten one single chapter. So far in this book I had written five chapters. Must I rewrite them all? As usual my passionate and unreasoning prejudices against having anything to do with finished work were stirred up until I was in a state of panic. But how could a man with one foot newly amputated escape from twenty gendarmes?

Of course he escaped in the end. I was to find that my profession has its privileges as well as its burdens, and luck was on my side. Two days (I think) of the most anxious thought and I worked out the solution – two days of pacing up and down my workroom each morning, and of walking frantically through unsympathetic streets each afternoon and night. Not for nothing had Hornblower acquired the habit of pacing his quarterdeck when he had a problem to solve. I expect those two days were filled with moments when my children shrank from me in terror; I cannot believe that physical weariness would blunt my anxiety.

But the writer has the powers with which witches and warlocks were once credited. He can summon up storms and floods. Fortunately the weather was on my side in any case; *Sutherland*'s battle had taken place in late autumn and now it was winter, and a snowstorm was not only possible but actually likely. A snowstorm – a river – a boat – a flood – and my three characters had escaped, as anyone who troubles to read Chapter Six may see. And I had been through such an experience that I would never be the same again, or so I thought. Indeed, for a few days after that incident I would have grudgingly admitted (if I had ever discussed the subject) that there were worse things than the day-to-day writing of a novel, just as a man who has once tasted the strappado might admit there were worse things than the rack.

25

NOT so many days later there was another new experience, as clear in my memory even now as the one just recounted. Hornblower was on the move again; his love affair with Marie de Graçay was over – or at least in abeyance – and he was making the descent of the Loire with his two companions. There was trouble ahead of him, and trouble behind, but at that moment he was as free from trouble as he could ever hope to be. I know that feeling so well myself; I found myself envying Hornblower while simultaneously feeling in deep accord with him. Hornblower was happier at this time than a life of action and hardship had ever allowed him to be so far. He was still the Man Alone, but he was experiencing the comradeship and personal intimacy which – partly through his own faults of personality – had so far evaded him. He was experiencing the pleasures of the land, seeing beauty all new to him, like the dawn creeping mistily over a silent river, or a line of willows against the background of the different green of the hills. He was on the move, too – a necessity for the happiness of a restless fellow like him – but sedately, without pressure, and with a sufficiency of trivial incidents (such as finding a channel through sandbanks) to keep his active mind from racketing itself into discontent.

There were one or two mornings while I was writing these passages when I actually observed, with considerable astonishment – perhaps even dismay – that I was going eagerly to my worktable, that I was looking forward to a morning with Hornblower while he was, for once in a way, in a tranquil state of mind. There was a momentary temptation to prolong the voyage; certainly there was a faint regret that the Loire was not as long as the Amazon. But geography as well as history opposed any self-indulgence. So did something still more important; the necessity for keeping a balance, for obeying the dictates of my artistic judgment, my literary taste. (Those hateful words again, always seeking to creep in like disease bacteria into the human body.) The story demanded a certain modicum of happiness, but to increase it beyond a particular point would destroy the equilibrium. My taste and judgment told me that there should be so much, and no more. In a rather similar mood to Gibbon's, I sighed as a sentimentalist and obeyed as a craftsman; I found wry consolation in thinking of some *chef de cuisine* setting himself to compose a master dish, and exercising the necessary restraint regarding the herbs he personally favoured. So Hornblower went on to Nantes, to honour and distinction, and the wave of publicity which he found so distasteful.

26

Six years went by before he came back into my life again, to find me a changed man, physically at least. I have written about this experience briefly before, and so I approach this writing with my usual distaste for finished work. I was now an invalid, or I was told I was one, or thought I was one. One of the symptoms of old age had made its appearance, somewhat prematurely, twenty years or so before it might be expected. My arteries were closing up – please forgive these anatomical details – and the assumption was that the process would continue. I found myself limited in my walking, in my ability to climb stairs, and my distances diminished with the weeks, so that soon I could not walk more than fifty yards, or climb more than a single flight of stairs, without pain enough to make further effort impossible without rest. And the future was gloomy; soon my extremities would be starved of blood, and then would follow amputation and helplessness.

There was no comfort in the future at all. I could not guess – neither could the doctors – that I was a freak, a unique case, about whom articles (pleasingly impersonal) would be written in the technical press, that the disease was going to halt itself (in a way never before known) on the very brink of total disaster. The doctors were grimly advising me to find a house without stairs so that I could be wheeled about, and they said, also, that a life of complete inactivity, of doing nothing, of avoiding every kind of excitement and exertion (even mental) might postpone the worst for a brief while.

Naturally, I tried it, and inevitably I found it impossible. To sit in gloom and await dissolution is not a practice to be recommended to anybody. Moreover, there were the bomb ketches. I have to acknowledge – ridiculous though it may sound – a great personal debt to bomb ketches. In my recreational reading bomb ketches had shown up repeatedly – the curious and highly specialized craft that had been devised for the purpose of throwing shells from the sea at targets on land, especially (by virtue of the lofty trajectory of their mortars) targets in dead ground behind hills or fortifications. They were employed in frequent amphibious operations during the Napoleonic Wars, and in peacetime they often found a use in Arctic exploration, because their sturdy construction enabled them to withstand the stresses of the ice. Nelson himself had once made an Arctic voyage in a bomb ketch.

It would be interesting to work out some hypothetical campaign in which bomb ketches played an important role. Of course that would involve the employment of a whole squadron – the bomb vessels always needed cover from attack by more powerful ships of war. They had been employed repeatedly against Bonaparte's invasion fleet in the Channel ports, but without great success, even under Nelson's command. They were a weapon of surprise and opportunity, and even Bonaparte's admirals knew about the potentialities of bomb vessels, and could take elementary precautions against them.

Surprise and opportunity! Something was happening to me, something I thought was never going to happen again – and something which, according to the doctors, should not be allowed to happen. Here were the stirrings of invention, that pleasant feeling of recognition, like the pricking of the witch's thumbs. And here, too, was an enormous wave of relief that these symptoms were appearing, something normal in a grossly abnormal world. Those blessed words, surprise and opportunity, could be allowed to sink down into my subconscious and stir up things there. And if they brought amputation any nearer I was in the mood to say it was worth it.

Bomb ketches; they had been employed in the second British attack on Copenhagen in 1807; Wellington had seen action there as a divisional general. But that was a formal battle with due warning given – no room for surprise and not much opportunity. And Wellington had a brother-in-law, although

214

he was to live another fifty years and never know he even had a sister.

So now the gloomy mornings were no longer gloomy; they were enlivened by the entrancing discoveries of what had happened during the night without my volition. Additions came hurrying in, especially now that Hornblower had made his reappearance into the debate, although without formal recognition. He was barred from consideration, yet remembering him caused a twinge of regret, for I realized that I had finished with him on the threshold of an interesting period in his career, married at last to his Barbara, whom he respected and whom he would come as near to loving as his limited capacity would ever allow. Hornblower learning to be a country squire would make an interesting picture. On the other hand, following his public and personal triumph, he was bound to be given some important employment, for the Napoleonic Wars were by no means over. The Admiralty might find difficulty in discovering the right hole in which to put such a square peg as Hornblower, all the same. He was no more than halfway up the captains' list. Hornblower commanding a ship of the line, one of twenty or so enduring the endless monotony of the blockade service, might make an interesting psychological study. But as Hornblower was finished as far as I was concerned there was no satisfaction – rather the reverse – in these speculations about his later career. Much better to return to our bomb ketches.

Of course, there was the Baltic. That was where the next vital developments in the world-wide war were going to take place. That was where bomb ketches could be employed – shallow waters, and important coastal trade, while repeated and rapid changes of national policy might offer the necessary surprises and opportunities. There was the burning question as to whether Bonaparte would actually go to war with Alexander of Russia. British diplomacy had worked hard to maintain Alexander in his obstinate attitude towards the French Empire; and where British diplomacy was at work the Royal Navy was not far behind.

Of course! Of course! (The really gratifying moments of construction are always introduced by 'of course' instead of by 'perhaps'). Bonaparte was trying to enforce his Continental System along every mile of coast, and, while he was planning

215

his surprise attack on Russia, and eventually when he launched his left wing in an advance on St Petersburg, he had an immensely long and very vulnerable line of communications along the southern shore of the Baltic. That was the ideal scene of operations for bomb ketches. I knew a British squadron in actual fact had pushed its way up into the Baltic. There was need for an active and ingenious naval officer there, not afraid of responsibility, capable of understanding a diplomatic problem, capable of stiffening the moody and incalculable Alexander, capable of threading his way through the convolutions of neutrality laws – and with bomb ketches under his command ready for instant employment. And, of course, that officer would be Hornblower.

He was of just sufficient seniority for it to be quite reasonable for him to be appointed commodore of a small squadron – say a ship of the line, a couple of sloops, a couple of bomb ketches – and entrusted with the immense responsibility which, however much he might worry about it, sweetened the air he breathed. Of course it would be Hornblower. The fragments joined up as if endowed with minds of their own. Spring, and the opening of navigation in the Baltic, would come just when Hornblower had had long enough leave, after his last adventures, to discover what it was like to be a country squire and the husband of Lady Barbara. There was the curious and involved question of the neutrality of Swedish Pomerania – and the behaviour of the French troops who eventually overran the province constituted a classic example of what happens when soldiers unpaid and unfed break loose from the control of generals devoid of feelings. There was Sweden, now under the rule of a Marshal of the Empire.

And (of course!) the left-hand prong of Bonaparte's attack on Russia, directed against St Petersburg while he himself marched on Moscow, had been held up at Riga – there had been a desperate amphibious, and unsuccessful, siege, and the subsequent retreat of the French had been marked by the defection of the Prussian contingent, which presaged the disintegration of the Empire. If Hornblower needed troubled waters in which to go a-fishing he could ask for nothing more troubled than the Baltic in 1812; there he would carry as much responsibility as any man could desire. At Riga he could use his precious bomb ketches, and, for once, justice could be done him by allowing him to be actually present at the moment when the French Empire reached its farthest point of conquest. Lastly (had we come as far as 'lastly'?) if Hornblower were not safely employed up the Baltic there was the danger (which I did not like to contemplate) that it would be his bombs that burst in the air over Baltimore.

So the decision had been reached without my even knowing that a decision lay ahead. It only remained to complete the work of construction, to perform all the pleasant, logical tasks of deciding on a beginning and an end, settling the sequence of events within the framework of history and geography – it was fifteen years since I had last breathed the keen air of the Baltic, but my memory still served – to invent and then to select, to exercise my judgment and taste; all this was so completely different from the miserable attempt to live the life of a cabbage in grim resignation that, really, only the hackneyed metaphor of the change from hell to heaven could adequately describe the difference.

27

THERE was at least one important change in technique. I was quite surprised to find out how much thinking I had always done before on my feet. When a special piece of construction had been called for in the old days – when, for instance, it was necessary to provide adequate means for some expression of Hornblower's feelings, or, more desperately, to invent the circumstances in which he could escape from Colonel Caillard, it had been second nature to walk about so as to set the mechanism of thought to work. It was while I was walking, sometimes deliberately for that purpose, sometimes merely because I was walking to arrive somewhere where I needed to be, that ideas generated themselves, and not merely these lesser ideas, but sometimes whole major pieces of invention.

Now walking was impossible; I had to find other ways of allowing my mind to act. The habit of thinking while walking had begun in boyhood and had established itself during a creative life of more than twenty years. I could no more deliberately think out a new system than I could deliberately invent a new plot; the substitutes came by fortunate accident.

There were the little mathematical puzzles; nothing very advanced, almost pure arithmetic, exercises in logic rather than in algebra, which I used to invent and then set myself to solve. It called for some small ingenuity and considerable patience to prove, beyond dispute, that A could only be seven and X could only be nine in the example I had before me. And in the little intervals of thinking about the puzzle I could think about the plot; arithmetic carried construction along with it as a sponge carries water.

And the absurd, ridiculous game I devised related to the drinking of soup. I have never spoken about this to a soul; this is a first and public confession. Dinner begins, and a bowl of soup is put before me. Then I must estimate the amount of soup in the bowl, and the capacity of the spoon, and calculate how many spoonfuls it will take to finish the soup – all this, of course, while carrying on the polite chatter that goes with soup. Then the spoonfuls must be counted, one by one, while maintaining at least the outward appearance of a sane and normal person. Dr Johnson on a stroll could keep count of the beats of his walking-stick and still go on talking; I can do the same with spoonfuls of soup, even during the mounting excitement resulting from reaching the twenty-fourth spoonful and observing that only about three more remain when my original estimate was of a total of twenty-eight. Why that should help Hornblower devise a means of bringing his bomb ketches within range of the French siege batteries I cannot imagine, but luckily it did.

28

So construction was completed and the book was ready to be written, and the eternal question as to when, or whether, to start, presented itself in aggravated form. I had been warned under dire penalties never to incur fatigue, to do nothing that might cause a rise in blood pressure, and I knew only too well how laborious was the process of composition, of visualization. I told myself that a sensible man would be content with all the pleasure of construction and would now go back to the life of a cabbage and carry with him to the grave the secrets of Hornblower's campaign in the Baltic.

That was just the point. Putting it into those words made it instantly and abundantly clear that I could not bear to do anything of the sort. The thing simply had to be written. I had to face the unsavoury fact that I was an exhibitionist at least. Until that moment the logical sequences of construction, composition and publication had gone unanalyzed. It had never occurred to me that those sequences were by no means fixed and immutable, but could perhaps be broken off by a mere exercise of will. I think I had even told myself, on occasions, that a piece of work could not be considered completed until it was in print and presented to the public; now I realized that I was only finding an excuse, that really I urgently wanted to publish my work, to exhibit it. However much, and however genuinely, I disliked personal appearances; however much I disliked meeting strangers, I yet wanted to do so vicariously. I make my fleeting personal entrances into the literary world with almost the same reluctance with which I would take my clothes off in Trafalgar Square, but there was a decided and definite pleasure – more than that, a positive need – in regard to pushing Hornblower out into the world.

This admission introduced a new factor into the situation; bluntly, the fear of death. I had to contemplate the possibility that I might die before the *Commodore* was finished, and – especially from the point of view of the Commodore – I disliked the idea intensely. It was not so much that I would be sorry if the world were to miss a masterpiece, but rather that the masterpiece would miss the world. To leave it unfinished would be perhaps even worse than leaving it unwritten altogether – all the old discussion about Edwin Drood used to irritate me profoundly. Hornblower had attracted sufficient attention by now for it not to be a wild impossibility for an unfinished *Commodore* to call up some considerable speculation as to how he would have been finished, and the thought of someone else trying it, the thought of the silly things that might be said, drove me into a panic. There were now most pressing reasons to begin the writing, and even more pressing reasons to complete it. But while the writing was going on there were also definite reasons for moderation; I felt in exactly the same situation as if I were driving a car low on gas in an effort to reach a filling station – to drive too fast would simply defeat my own object, however great the temptation. There was a certain optimum speed that would have to be maintained, and, luckily, with a long experience behind me, I knew all about that optimum speed; it was what I had always tried to maintain while writing some twenty-odd books previously, when the matter was not of such desperate importance.

There was a mingling of regret and satisfaction when I contemplated the fact that there were no written notes for some literary executor to look through. I had never made written notes in my life; it had always been too much trouble, and I was certainly not going to start now. Moreover, I was quite sure that written notes – like conversations with a publisher across a luncheon table – could not convey anything like the impression I wanted to make, and I am equally sure of that to this day. Only on the evidence of the finished book could the book be judged.

So there was my mind made up for me. I sat myself at my work-table and sat Sir Horatio down in his hip bath, ready to go to take command of the precious bomb ketches which had triggered all this off, and the work of composition began. It ran its usual course, hardly different from its predecessors. A change of method was necessary in the writing as in the construction. I discovered – what I had never realized before – that it was my habit to get up from my work-table and pace the room at quite frequent intervals. Partly, this was to ease my stiff joints, partly to allow my mind to debate some minor point. Would it be better if someone's mood were to be expressed editorially, or revealed by his speeches? Should the text of a written order be given, or should it be summarized? I was surprised to find how often I took a turn around the room in order to settle these questions of taste. Yet walking was a hundred times more tiring than it used to be – at the end of two hours' work I would now have walked the equivalent of fifty miles to a fit person. It could not be done, and it did not take more than a day or two's experimenting to prove it to me. Luckily, supremely fortunately, trial and error (mostly unconscious) supplied a solution. Now I stand up, as the result of the habit of years, and then have to decide whether the point is serious enough to justify walking, and that in itself will clear up the difficulty as often as not. Otherwise I stand erect and gaze into space long enough to loosen the sitting-joints, until the already written work lying before me attracts my attention so that I sit down again and glance through the earlier paragraphs. The mere act of doing so will carry me over the momentary difficulty, like a horse who has refused a fence but who will make the leap at the second attempt if he is allowed a good look at the obstacle and then given a fair run at it.

29

THE book was finished. During the hours of visualization I had been living in a world in which arteriosclerosis played no part; during the other hours of the day there had been, first, the usual numbness when the personal troubles lost their edge; to be succeeded by the irrepressible interest in the approaching day's work. Three months had gone by, and I still lived – more important, the accursed disease had made no progress – and I had learned that it was perfectly possible to face the rest of life as a handicapped person. Hornblower had brought inexpressible benefits. In later years I was able to estimate the magnitude of those benefits by re-reading the book, disregarding the inevitable distaste with which I approach past work. There it is, a book of adventure, sometimes of tension, an analysis of action and responsibility. Its literary merits do not enter into this discussion (I will not say fortunately), but the interesting conclusion is that it is not an unhappy book; I really do not believe that anyone could guess that it was written by a man going through a period of profound gloom – I must add here that at that time I was experiencing all sorts of other violent personal troubles which I shall not mention further. The fact that no hint of them is apparent in its pages is the clearest proof of the intensity of feeling occasioned by the act of writing, and, as I have already said, it is also a proof of the debt I owe to that book.

One small incidental point; the *Commodore* appeared as a serial in the *Saturday Evening Post*, to which I had become a frequent contributor. This was always with the feeling that my work was not quite suited to such a medium – not quite that I was a fish out of water there, but more as if I had strayed by accident into some strange house filled with unfamiliar furnishings. And in the *Commodore* there was a certain small amount of adultery. Not even very profound adultery, if such an

221

adjective is permissible. But it was adultery, all the same, and never before, not since the days of Benjamin Franklin, had adultery made any appearance at all in the pages of the *Saturday Evening Post*. It really caused quite a flutter. Many American newspapers commented on the fact; so did innumerable readers. It was the first rift in the dike of convention, and there was no little boy handy to put his finger into the hole. Before very long topics that had been barred for a century and a half were being freely discussed in the pages of the *Post*. The commodore was not the cause of all this, but he certainly was the *Saturday Evening Post*'s first adulterer.

There was an odd reason for that adultery, too – I suppose there is an odd reason for most adulteries, but this one I consider odder than most. Hornblower was destined at the end of the book to come down with typhus, the jail-fever that killed off whole armies that winter, and typhus is a disease transmitted by lice. I knew – more than one volume of memoirs mention the fact – that dignitaries of the Russian court were usually carriers of body vermin, and I wanted to show Hornblower with at least a flea, and he had to be provided with ample opportunity for acquiring a minimum of one. He also, like many mercurial souls, did not carry his liquor well; and the bond that united him to his Barbara was as frail as any bond would prove to be when applied to Hornblower; so that one way and another that adultery was pretty inevitable. But I fancy that Hornblower picked up the louse that gave him typhus at some moment when he was helping to defend the village of Daugavgriva, that place whose name might well have become historic if it had not been so unpronounceable.

30

By the time the *Commodore* was finished the world was a happier place for me, and, incidentally, the clouds were lifting all over the world with the victories of the Allies over Germany and Japan. I had discovered that it was perfectly possible to live a full life without ever walking more than fifty yards at a time – and I will take this opportunity of saying once and for all that for twenty years I have lived under that handicap and have never ceased to enjoy myself. But, equally important, the disease had somehow halted, despite the fact that I had done some heavy work. Optimism was beginning to creep in, and I could return to life.

The first piece of work I was given to do under these new conditions was commissioned – naturally – by the Allied governments, and the terms of reference were, in themselves, highly optimistic along certain lines. Mr Churchill and Mr Roosevelt were quite certain that the Hitler government and the defences of Germany were about to collapse. That collapse seemed imminent to anyone reading the newspapers, but it was reassuring to be told that the highest authorities thought so too. But those same authorities also expected that Japan would put up a long and desperate defence even after the fall of Germany. It was something I did not clearly understand, for my geography lessons at school had emphasized that Japan, like England, was an island power which would be forced into rapid surrender on losing command of the sea, but the authorities believed differently now, and said so. Of course it was only one half of the authorities' mind that believed this – the other half knew about the progress of the atomic bomb without a great deal of confidence in its efficacy.

What Washington and London feared was that the public both in England and America, over-confident with the fall of Germany, would be set back by the prospect of a long and bloody campaign in the Pacific, and would insist on a premature, unsatisfactory peace. So my task was to prepare public opinion for this next development, and to set about it even while the Allied armies were poised along the Rhine, gathering strength for the final blow. As a result I was established in Washington with a free run through the departments of the Department of the Navy, having all the secrets revealed to me as to the difficulties of delivering a massive attack against Japan across the vast distances of the Pacific. There was the magic word 'logistics', which I heard on every side. In dazed fashion I read through vast lists of the necessary shipping and specialized equipment that would be called for. I listened to serious – desperately serious – debates as to what would be the reaction of the United States Army when it would be summoned fresh from the conquest of Germany, to undertake the even more difficult conquest of Japan.

I went here and there to see these things with my own eyes.

Does anyone remember nowadays the system of priorities in air travel? With every plane crowded, anyone holding a higher priority could wait at an airport, and on the arrival of a plane destined for the place he was ordered to, could 'bump off' some unfortunate with a lower priority, and fly off happily, leaving his miserable victim waiting disconsolate – perhaps for days – for the chance to board another plane. And in wartime Washington society this priority was the exact, vital measure of personal status. At all the innumerable parties deft questioning was directed to discovering other people's priorities, and I had a No. 2, like four-star generals and admirals, and was treated with corresponding respect. That was not nearly so pleasant as it was to go to sea again, and to discover – what should have been obvious – that with my handicap I could still live on board a ship of war as long as it was no bigger than a destroyer; the distances in a carrier were quite beyond me. There was an occasion (of subsequent importance) when my ship passed through the tail of a typhoon and I experienced the worst weather I had ever seen at sea.

Hornblower had no chance of asserting himself in those conditions; but those minor and seemingly unrelated experiences were, I fancy, storing themselves away in my subconscious even while I toiled at writing the articles about the war in the Pacific – not very good ones; logistics for the common man – while Germany fell and while I was preparing to join the British naval force in the Pacific. And then the war ended, and there was Hornblower demanding attention in a way that could not be denied.

I had been preoccupied with the fall of empires – Hornblower would have recovered from his attack of typhus just in time to be available when the French Empire was falling. There were the political considerations, the peace conferences, the question of a new government for France – as well as for Japan. There had been the crack-up of Mussolini's power under Allied attack; Hornblower had seen in the last days of the Empire the interesting secession of Bordeaux from Imperial rule. I often had wondered – somehow my reading had never led me to the discovery – what had happened to the Royalist Mayor of Bordeaux, Lynch, when Bonaparte returned to power during the Hundred Days. A great many people during that wild moment must have discovered that they had backed the wrong horse.

These considerations were more urgent in my mind because at the same time as the Nuremberg Trials the trials of the misguided traitors, Lord Haw-Haw and others, were fresh in my memory; I did not remember reading anywhere that, after the fall of the French Empire, England instituted any intense pursuit of the numerous deserters, even traitors, who must have hidden trembling in France awaiting apprehension. Now what really happened to men of this sort at that period? The mutineers of the *Hermione*, a generation earlier, had been hunted down and hanged without mercy. And, of course, what happened to the Comte de Graçay and his daughter-in-law Marie, when Bonaparte during the Hundred Days had them in his power and was aware of the assistance they had given to Hornblower? And Hornblower? With the least pull from the front or push from behind he would plunge again into his affair with Marie. He could certainly, in that case, find himself in a difficult situation during the Hundred Days. Previous to that he must have played an important part in contributing to the fall of the Empire. And those mutineers?

There presented itself in my mind the problem – an interesting mental exercise – of how to deal with a crew of mutineers who had seized their ship and threatened (as had once or twice happened in history) to hand her over to the enemy unless given a promise of immunity. Fight them? Impossible, if the mutineers chose their cruising ground with care. It was amusing – not quite the right word, that; stimulating was a better one – to work out a plan which might be successful. Then there was that storm; I would like to find Hornblower at sea again, contending with dirty weather. And there was the peace-making, and the remodelling of Europe at the Congress of Vienna. Wellington attended that as Ambassador Extraordinary; surely his only sister, if not his brother-in-law, would be involved too, especially as it was notorious that Wellington was not on the best of terms with his Duchess? And Marie de Graçay, to whom I had nearly lost my heart? Earthy and yet sweet; intuitive as well as shrewd; sensible as well as generous; what, if anything, did the future hold for her?

It was a strange jumble of ideas as well as emotions, but

there was a solid scaffolding of actual history to provide framework with which to build from these assorted materials. The two systems of construction discussed in Chapter 2 were available simultaneously this time; there were the deeds to be done and yet here were the doers already at hand, and luckily the two methods were mutually self-supporting instead of antagonistic. Things fell into place, and the moment came, and I was off again into a world of Channel gales, and petty but tiresome disagreements between Hornblower and Barbara, and black contrasting tragedy, and moments of profane love balanced against an idyllic village wedding, with Hornblower climbing to the uttermost peak of professional recognition while suffering intense personal loss. War has many dreadful aspects; people are killed in war, and the survivors are changed people – brief words, but charged with tragedy.

But now Lord Hornblower was finished, and I could return to my own world. This is the moment perhaps for me to insert one more personal note; if I were ever to be asked (and, obviously, even without being asked) what was the best ten minutes' work I had ever done, which page of all the thousands I have written displeases me least, I should single out the last, concluding page of *Lord Hornblower* – a complexity of action and emotion expressed as nearly exactly, in the most economical and fitting wording, as I believe I could ever be capable of.

31

Now, with sincere reluctance, I have to allow my physical health to intrude again into this account of the writing of Hornblower, the *enfant terrible* breaking into the polite conversation of his betters. Some years had gone by; other novels had demanded my attention, and (of course) life had been lived between them. Then, suddenly, life nearly left off. The heart attack struck at two in the morning; a coronary occlusion of a severe type, extremely painful. Fortunately my yells for help attracted attention; and Dr Fox, in the best traditions of his profession, instantly turned out of his bed and drove along foggy roads to the rescue. I knew, after the first few seconds, what had happened to me; one of my closest friends had died, three months before, within an hour of experiencing a coronary occlusion. There was time to review the situation, to recall with fair satisfaction that my will was made and my affairs in some sort of order. There were the most bitter regrets, naturally – regrets at leaving this pleasant life, sharpened by thinking about all the things I had not done, and even sharpened by the thought of all the half-formed ideas which I would not have the chance to develop to completion.

Here was Dr Fox standing at my side; little need to tell him what was the matter with me. The pain was severe, and I was shifting my position in bed in the endeavour to find a posture less uncomfortable – it was then that I suddenly realized, with singular clarity, that what I was actually doing was writhing in agony. I had seen it before, both in men and in animals, but I had never writhed in agony myself and it had not occurred to me that I should ever do so. With the realization I tried to lie still; without overmuch success. The needle went in and the plunger was pushed home. 'Aren't you *ever* going to react?' asked Dr Fox, turning back from the telephone after calling for an ambulance. Then the reaction came, the blessed relief of morphine, the dulling of the pain and the lifting of anxiety. Pink clouds of positive (even though unexplainable) happiness began to billow round my bedside. And out of the clouds came three words. I am quite certain that Dr Fox did not utter them – they were much too unprofessional – nor did anyone else at my bedside. But the three words formed in my mind as clearly as if I had heard them. An Even Chance. That was it; an even chance. In the happy illogicality of morphine those words could even raise a smile.

In came the ambulance men with their stretcher, and I was carried out into the night, the pink clouds rolling along beside me and those three words somehow following me up, all the way to the hospital. Weeks of compulsory helplessness followed (I believe nowadays they treat coronary occlusion with less ceremony), accompanied by prolonged struggles to breathe in an oxygen tent, and bewildered efforts to think logically and deal with mundane affairs while the thinking apparatus was clogged by soothing drugs.

Clarity came back accompanied, naturally, by boredom, and for perhaps the last week there was every opportunity to think, and little else to do; the nice nurses were so easy to tease that the sport soon surfeited – it was too much like shooting sitting birds – and having once worked out mentally that I could have exchanged this hospital room for a suite de luxe in the *Queen Mary* (or the wing of an oriental palace complete with dancers) and still be money in hand, there was the tendency to think about other matters. It was still too physically tiring to hold up a book for long; thought it had to be.

32

THERE was that queer memory about the even chance. Perhaps it had been my own subconscious estimate of my chance of survival. Possibly it was a breaking through from down below of the germ of a story too young to be recognized for what it was – a sudden bobbing up of a waterlogged timber bearing an immature barnacle, under the stimulus of morphine. But there was the phrase, and inevitably it began to sprout, upward and down, as a seed will send out shoots.

It was a phrase which might perhaps apply to a duel. No, it would not. All the rules and etiquette of the duel were directed towards eliminating chance, towards making sure that the more skilful would not suffer as the result of accidental circumstances. The measurement of swords, the choosing of even ground, all this had a specious appearance of trying to be fair, but actually it really meant that the better shot, or the better swordsman, had a better chance, in a matter of honour which really had nothing to do with marksmanship or skill in fencing. An inexperienced duellist with a grievance might well complain at the dice being weighted against him like this. He might seek to give himself a chance – an even chance.

So there grew up in the mind the picture of someone so angry, or so unhappy, that he would be willing to risk his life if in exchange he had an even chance of putting an end to his troubles. Most likely that would be a young man – it has been observed ever since civilization (and formalized murder) began that young men, with far more to lose, are the more ready to risk losing it. A young man, suffering from intense troubles which he could directly attribute to one other man, presumably also young. A schoolboy might feel that way, except that duelling was unusual among schoolboys.

But a midshipman in the old navy – horrible things went on in the midshipmen's mess in the old days, and duels were frequent enough to be not unusual. Someone might easily make a mathematical calculation, weighing an even chance of survival against the certainty that his misery was otherwise incurable. A mathematical calculation! Now whom did I know, and on whom had I once (in a fit of self-indulgence) bestowed a mathematical talent? The answer did not even have to be put into words. All that I knew about the later Hornblower seemed to fit in with the picture of the younger Hornblower who began to grow up in my mind. And the later one was such a diversified character that it would be fun to work out how he came to grow up like that.

All this was a major development, clearly. Hornblower had been out of my thoughts for years; I had taken him to the top of the tree and left him there – not too comfortably – with every intention of never looking back at him. There were dozens of other projects in my mind, dozens of other eggs hatching in the nest, and I was extremely doubtful about introducing this sort of cuckoo. I left the hospital, so that all the projects came to be forgotten in the excitement of learning to live again.

33

THIS odd profession of mine has brought me a great deal of happiness, even though I feel shamefaced about confessing it. That was a remarkably happy period, up in the clear, delightful air of the High Sierra, which – so the cliché runs – is like champagne. Perhaps because of that the ideas came bubbling up as well. The gangling, thoughtful youth who was taking shape in my mind began to win my affection – he was inclined to take things over-seriously, and yet he was learning to laugh; he had a great deal of ability, and his addiction to self-analysis called his attention to his own weaknesses so that he would make the effort to eliminate them, or at least render them ineffective, and that would enable him to profit by the intensive training given a young officer in those busy days.

Busy days they could certainly be, with those ideas bubbling up in endless succession. That duel with the even chance could easily lead to transfer to a more lively field of endeavour, with plenty of activity. In 1794 there was commerce destruction in the Bay of Biscay; absurdly young officers frequently found themselves called upon to navigate prizes back to home ports – and here was the idea of a cargo of rice swelling up because of a leak. His rather solemn priggishness could lead to his condemning himself to the penalty of failure. In early 1795 there was the disastrous expedition to Quiberon; in 1796 would come – as so often in history – a change of sides by the Spanish Government, leading, of course (while I was cautiously rowing a boat over the blue waters of Fallen Leaf Lake) to a skirmish with the Spanish galleys that still survived centuries of nautical development.

There were endless things that could happen, and yet not quite endless. Cassandralike, I was aware of the doom that awaited Hornblower. A dozen years before, that doom had been pronounced. He was going to be taken prisoner by the Spaniards, because he had to learn the Spanish language so that in 1808 he would be able to converse with El Supremo. But that imprisonment must not hinder this advancement, so that it must come to an end long before the natural end at the Peace of Amiens in 1801. Capture was easily arranged – he could be carrying dispatches in a small vessel and, through no fault of his own, he could fall into the hands of the Spanish fleet at sea before the Battle of Cape St Vincent in 1797. This very misfortune could be used to help along his necessary promotion to lieutenant. But then he must be set free in some way. Escape? Oddly, he had escaped from imprisonment once already – true, that was a dozen years later, in 1810, but we could not have him doing so again in 1798. Some distinctive reason had to be thought up that would give good grounds for his regaining his freedom. There was singularly little trouble about thinking out the necessary mechanism; that was really too strong an expression – it sufficed to realize the necessity, and the solution presented itself. It was almost worth having had weeks in a hospital bed if afterwards the mind worked so readily.

Naturally, there was nothing to do except to write all this. It was going to be quite easy because the stories had presented themselves as separate episodes, so that a sensible man would be able to write one and then stop and recover before starting the next. In fact, it was most convenient that this should be so, with a coronary occlusion not so far in the past. Sheer nonsense, of course. With each story bubbling up from below the instant the dead weight of its predecessor was lifted from it, it was impossible to hold back from starting again. There was always that will o' the wisp – this story is not as good as I hoped it was going to be, but I am quite sure this next one will be. So story after story flowed from my pen, each one begun in hope, and it was not true that each was finished in despair – the next one was demanding too much attention for any thought to be given to the last.

Partly because of this, but largely because of other circumstances, the act of writing was not quite as laborious as usual. There was a genuine pleasure in watching my young man growing up, acquiring some sense and some ballast. In the tense sessions of visualization I was going along with a young fellow to whom everything was new, who enjoyed all the resilience of youth – it was ridiculous, but true, that he could confer some of it on me. Lastly, there was satisfaction in achievement; the parts were falling into place. If I had ever stopped to think beforehand, I might have contemplated with dismay the necessity for creating a youth who had to grow into someone already well understood in his prime, but that difficulty had really never occurred to me in the excitement of the moment – the thought had merely been added spice to the prospective dish – and it was only later that I could look back on it and grudgingly agree that at least it had been something worth attempting.

34

THERE was other work to be done when the *Midshipman* was finished; there was life to be lived, possibly more urgently still, as a result of recent events. Hornblower was now some sort of public figure. He had made me innumerable friends. On a dozen different frontiers I could arrive with my baggage and present myself to a customs officer, and, with my name noted, the officer would say 'Not—?' and I would say 'Yes,' and my baggage would be instantly chalked or labelled or waved through. Hornblower was a kind of perpetual travelling companion, even though he was far removed from the new thoughts that occupied my mind regarding my new work. Letters came in steadily; and a surprising proportion of them demanded more news of Hornblower. Letters from readers are frequently what I call 'but' letters – 'I liked your book but—'; yet these were mostly friendly letters. I do not believe they exerted any direct influence on me; except as a wartime duty I had never written a word I did not want to write, and the only person I have ever attempted to please by my work is me – or I, if it is necessary to be grammatical. Yet when every mail delivery brought letters like that; when I could hardly ever have conversations with acquaintances (friends came to know me better) without Hornblower's name coming up in the opening sentences, it was hard to keep him entirely out of my mind. That is a practical explanation of why it all started again, but there were other factors.

There was the continual lure of trying to explain Hornblower's marriage to Maria. All those years back in *The Happy Return* it had been easy, and I believe not inconsistent, to pass it off as one of those things that happen to people, but an actual word-for-word description of the process was tempting in its difficulty. Technical problems have their allure; they are most definitely seductive. And – here comes the confession – I wanted to know, I wanted to find out the details for myself, I wanted to work out how it came about.

There crept up in my memory pictures of another young man, incredibly lean and lantern-jawed and earnest, who through an unfriendly winter had spent his days writing *Payment Deferred* and his nights in playing bridge professionally, who ate well when the cards came his way and remarkably poorly when they did not. I remembered that young man very well indeed; it was as if he were a friend of my youth who had died years ago, and I suppose he really was dead, and the present me inhabited the changed body he had left behind. It was interesting how these memories haunted me.

Another problem. Hornblower had emerged from his midshipman's chrysalis to become a lieutenant. But how had it happened that he had received his next step to commander, over the heads of hundreds of his seniors? How had it happened without his achieving a blaze of glory? How *could* it happen in a way that would leave Hornblower the rather cynical and dissatisfied individual he developed into? Time flies; in 1808 he was a captain of some years' seniority – much would have to be crammed into the intervening years, and those events would have to be crammed into the intervening years, and those have to have a special and particular quality. Besides, there was the Peace of Amiens to be considered – nearly two years of peacetime without any chance of achieving distinction. Two years probably of half pay – and we already knew that Hornblower was a whist player of merit.

Something also happened – something as hard to explain as any of these. How did the *Artillery Manual* for the British Militia for 1860 ever arrive in a second-hand bookshop in San Francisco? A copy certainly showed up there, because I bought it. In 1860 the British militia was concerned about the possibility of invasion by the armies of Napoleon III, but their artillerymen still manned guns exactly like those that were used against Napoleon I. And the special concern of militia artillery was coastal defence, and coastal defence against wooden ships – the day of the ironclad was only just beginning to dawn. What the artillery militia proposed to use was red-hot shot, the same as had been used in the defence of Gibraltar nearly a century earlier. A good half of the manual was devoted to the drill for the employment of red-hot shot – it was a drill that had to be carried out very punctiliously, with lumps of red-hot metal being carried about amid barrels of gunpowder. That *Artillery Manual* made good bedside reading for several nights; I had never before studied details of the handling of red-hot shot. It was a remarkably substantial morsel to come within reach of the jellyfish's tentacles.

There was another point. If ever – as was most unlikely – I were to write about Hornblower again, and deal with this portion of his life ending in his marriage, it would be desirable – necessary – to write from another angle. That was what my taste or judgment dictated to me, in a way which, as in most matters of taste, is more easily felt than described. Someone had to observe Hornblower's future wife more objectively than Hornblower himself could be expected to do. For that matter it was time that Hornblower himself was put through an objective examination. This, if ever, would be the right moment, while Hornblower was still a junior officer and subject to command. And, of course, as soon as that decision was reached the writing of the book became more desirable still, because of the added attraction of the difficult technical problems it would present. The right moment; there was pleasure in admitting that phrase into my thoughts.

Somehow, at this time another fragment of a plot made its reappearance. There was the question of a mad captain; junior officers in a ship, and especially a ship of war, find themselves in a terribly difficult position when they have reason to believe their captain is insane; my attention had been pointedly called to this two years before, when thinking about the mutineers in *Lord Hornblower*. Under the Articles of War any discussion between even two men regarding their dissatisfaction with some aspect of their service was mutinous and criminal and liable to terrible punishment. Reading that Article of War had started a train of thought that still nagged and demanded attention.

So there we were; red-hot shot and marriage; promotion and professional card-playing; a mad captain and a different point of view; there were a dozen different elements (I have no doubt there were several which I discarded and have now forgotten) all elbowing each other and trying to push their way into the picture. Luckily, as ever, all I had to do was to be patient. The details sorted themselves out and arranged themselves in order, and I could indulge in daily and unjustified self-congratulation when each morning revealed further progress towards the completion of this process. It was only at the end that I had to intervene personally, to make my own arbitrary decision between rival claimants, to do a little honest work in the matter of studying my sources for confirmation of my theories. Then, at last, it happened. Not only was the course of events clear in my mind but it had been clear for a couple of weeks or so; at that moment I made a series of discoveries about myself. One was that although there was as usual the genuine distaste for plunging into fatiguing work, it was almost counterbalanced by my desire to put my theories into practice, to turn my ideas into words on paper. Worse still, I brought myself up before the stern judge who was myself and found myself guilty of something unheard-of heretofore. I was actually savouring these pleasures in anticipation, and, like a child with a plate of food before him, I was saving up the best until the last, as if the actual writing could be considered as having any desirable aspects at all, let alone being the 'best'. Fortunately I had long ago ceased to be surprised at any new inconsistency I might display. The judge's sentence was, of course, that I should sit myself at my writing pad on the spot, and sure enough, it only called for a day or two's real work to dissipate all these odd notions, especially as very early, as soon, in fact, as a minimum amount of work was completed, the old bogey presented itself – the fear that I might die with the book incomplete, with the final developments never to be revealed. That, more than any other consideration, drove me to write the book in the usual desperate haste burningly anxious to show Hornblower in his cross-grained moods, by refusing to rejoice in his own successes, refusing to truckle to authority when truckling was obviously called for and might be exceedingly profitable, and, above all, by allowing his silly temperament to draw him into a silly marriage, all this under the puzzled eyes of his friend Bush.

35

INEVITABLY, I suppose, it all happened again, this time after a much smaller interval than of late; about eighteen months, in fact – a period spent in all sorts of activities, from a prolonged visit to the West Indies to writing a minor history textbook for children. Here were the ideas creeping in again. Someone gave me a vivid account of the methods of the pearl divers of Ceylon in the old days. Something else again; it may have been with advancing years that my own memories of past experiences kept returning with renewed clarity; once I had taken a motor-boat clear across England and back again, from London to Llangollen, by canal, and I frequently found myself recalling incidents in that peculiar voyage. On another occasion I had had to navigate a small boat on a stormy day through London, up from the Pool, through wild river traffic – that voyage ended in disaster at Vauxhall Bridge, with safety almost in sight.

Seeing that the Hornblower novels always were about Hornblower (another statement of the obvious) it was interesting that, to a great extent, the old method prevailed of thinking first of the thing to be done and then selecting the right person to do the deed. It was a coincidence (is that the whole truth? I fear I am not being entirely honest, even while trying to be) that the right person should turn out to be Hornblower. The bare bones of history constituted, appropriately, a skeleton framework on which a story could be constructed. Hornblower must have been 'made post', promoted to captain, sometime in the spring of 1805; October, 1805 saw the battle of Trafalgar, and the following January saw Nelson's funeral procession up the Thames from Greenwich to Whitehall. There were plenty of accounts of this extraordinary display; there were numerous contemporary prints to illustrate them. I knew from personal experience what the Thames was like on a bad day – those ceremonial barges must have been horribly difficult to handle. There was the mischievous notion that perhaps the barge containing Nelson's coffin might have sunk in mid-procession. And what would be more natural than that Hornblower, a very junior captain, should be given the duty of organizing the procession? It would be onerous, highly responsible, and devoid of glory – certainly it was a duty that would be thrust upon the captain least able to evade it. Hornblower would be posted to a very small ship – small enough to be fitted out in the river at Deptford, so that he would be on the spot, readily available. Fitting out for what mission? What about those pearl divers?

So the development was instantly in full swing. By what route had he come to London? By canal, of course – somewhere or other I had read about the express passenger service that was maintained on the canals during their brief heyday before the coming of railways. Maria would certainly accompany him. But here were the germs of tragedy. Fifteen years ago, as mentioned in *The Happy Return*, but two years in the future as regards the present Hornblower, his two children died of smallpox. Here were chickens coming home to roost; the comparison must be made, despite the frivolity of that wording when applied to the horrible truth. The children had to be born, they had to bring Hornblower some brief happiness, and they had to die. The dates served, very fortunately; Hornblower's marriage was in April, 1803, and here we were in January, 1806. Time enough for two pregnancies. But those pearl divers?

And *The Happy Return* had found Hornblower with a sword of honour presented him by the Patriotic Fund for boarding the *Castilla*; it was certainly time that he should board the *Castilla* and win that sword, pearl divers or no pearl divers. And time was hurrying by; the summer of 1808 was to find him in command of the *Lydia* in the Gulf of Fonseca. There was plenty to be done, especially as somewhere about this time my attention had been called to the Continental usage of putting a crossbar on the figure 7 when writing it. That had to be attended to somehow; also how did it happen that Hornblower was transferred from his present ship – name unknown at the moment – to the *Lydia* in a way that would help to give some bitterness to his temperament?

It was a delightful life, sitting back and letting these tangles sort themselves out. There was that tour of the West Indies, flying from island to island, chartering a motor car in each, and driving up into the innermost recesses through enchanted forests or barren hills. Those islands were fiercely insistent upon displaying their freedom from ordinary international convention; an international driving licence meant nothing to them – I had to pass a dozen different driving tests and earn a dozen different licences, which I really believe helped those pearl divers to come to life; construction is an odd business. Then home again, to the familiar work-table and the familiar fatigue. My method of visualization while writing has its disadvantages; tragedy strikes the harder. I had to kill two children. It was on the last page of the manuscript that they had died, leaving Maria heartbroken and Hornblower desolate. I can remember sitting with the final words written, feeling not exactly heartbroken, but certainly desolate, and most desperately sorry that I had had to do that to Hornblower.

36

So it seemed as if the cycle of novels was now complete. Owing to my lighthearted beginning of *Hornblower and the Atropos* in late 1805 there was a gap of two and a half years during which Hornblower must have gained promotion from commander, but, except for that, his career had been described throughout the period of the French Wars, from the declaration in 1793 to Waterloo in 1815, and I could look upon this aspect of my work as completed, and I thought (vain thoughts) that now I could call my soul my own. I could do the other work I had long been anxious to do. The rough with the smooth; there was a nightmare period of reading the evidence given at the Nuremberg trials – a casual turning of the pages of the interminable

volumes was like the first step into quicksand. There was a
novel about the United States Navy in action which I had long
been anxious to write; with Hornblower out of the way it
demanded my attention in the usual fashion. There was sober
history to be written, and – as I have pointed out before,
perhaps without laying sufficient stress upon it – there was life
to be lived. There was an interval of sailing a yacht in the
Caribbean, to fall once more under the spell of the West Indies.
There was a moment when I clumsily drove a motor car over
a small precipice in Mexico, and had to spend some days (they
might have been weary days, but of course proved not to be) in
the earthquake-shattered city of Colima; it had not been much
of a city before the earthquake. There was this to be done, and
that to be done, and something else to be thought about.
Anyone might have believed that Hornblower would have left
me alone now, with all these preoccupations, happy and otherwise, but he would not. Perhaps I can blame it on my correspondents, who would not let him rest; two or three times each
week at least there came letters asking for news of him;
certainly that kept him in my mind when I might otherwise
have forgotten about him. I was even moved to write a ballade
abusing him – the vital line was 'I hope you roast in hell,
Horatio' – which was not merely published but paid for; I had
written almost no verse since my discovery at the age of twenty
that (for me, at least) prose was a more suitable medium.

Needless to say, the ideas began to creep in. The first
impulse came when I found myself wondering about Hornblower
and his Barbara. I came to the conclusion that after the frightful
tragedy of Marie de Graçay, and his own terrifying experience,
Hornblower must have gone back with considerable relief to
Barbara, who, undoubtedly, would have enough understanding
and kindness to make him welcome. I could well imagine it; I
could imagine those two proud people, both of them reluctant
to merge their personalities, finding that such a thing was at
least possible, with mutual respect coming to reinforce mutual
attraction. But Hornblower was never a man to know complete
happiness, and he was the kind of cross-grained individual who
would distrust it when it was waiting for him. Barbara had
been married once before; it would be just like Hornblower to
brood about that, to allow his vivid imagination to conjure up

mental pictures that would rouse a feeling of jealousy, to confuse the flesh and the spirit, the past and the present, if only to provide a base on which to build a new discontent. Undoubtedly that would be just like Hornblower; fortunately Barbara would be discerning enough to be aware of it, and tactful and clever enough to keep the discontent down to a minimum.

This was a small enough germ to begin with, but of course others made their appearance. Hornblower would fret if he never saw service again. He had been 'made post' in the spring of 1805; the usual miraculous coincidence came to my assistance here, for that made him senior to all the captains who attained that rank in the spate of promotion following Trafalgar. He would probably attain flag rank in 1820 or 1821, and with his record he could count with some assurance of employment even in the attenuated navy of those lean years. It was an interesting coincidence that Napoleon died in 1821. The Spanish empire was still breaking up at that time; that was another interesting coincidence, seeing that it was the beginning of that convulsion which had called Hornblower into existence in 1808 – or 1936, to use another reckoning. There was plenty of fighting going on in Mexico and Central and South America at the time Hornblower would be promoted to rear admiral, while the Royal Navy kept the ring and the United States put forward the Monroe Doctrine. There was the suppression of the slave trade, too – the Royal Navy had undertaken the enforcement, and the Spanish and Portuguese colonies constituted the main market for the trade. Undoubtedly, if Hornblower were to be employed, it would be in the West Indies.

What would he be like? What sort of a man would he have grown into? His peerage and his flag would do something to mellow him, surely, however much he would distrust distinctions that he had not conferred on himself. But even though mellowed he would not lose his old restlessness, his desire for action, his quickness of thought. He would be witnessing rapid changes at sea, the development of the clipper ship, the beginnings of steam, and he was a liberal-minded man who would not be in accord with the conservative attitude of the navy towards these innovations. For me, there was a great deal of appeal about these considerations; down in my subconscious ideas were struggling towards maturity. In Jamaica to this day there is a small area – the Cockpit Country – still inaccessible, still the scene of a different culture, whose impassable boundary is hardly half an hour's drive from the glittering palaces of Montego Bay. I had gazed down into it myself, repeatedly, from precarious roads on rainswept hillsides. The Cockpit Country began to haunt me.

Somewhere or other – I have quite forgotten where – I came across a curious historical item; after Waterloo a large number of Napoleon's Old Guard had organized themselves into an association that had seized, and attempted to colonize, an area of Texas, at a time when Texas was still part of Mexico and Mexico was still fighting for her independence. What was likely to happen to them? There was room for conjecture – and I must remember that Napoleon's death occurred about that time. And all sorts of hotheads, from all sorts of motives, came to take part in the struggle for independence. I could picture some of them; I could picture Hornblower's attitude towards them, both official and personal. But I must not overlook, among all these distractions, the original wonderings about the relationship between Hornblower and Barbara.

Now a woman comes into this story, a real flesh-and-blood woman, not a mere character in a novel like Barbara and Marie and Maria. Flesh and blood, but really a saint – a truly good woman, so good that I dare, without permission, to tell this story about her and still hope for forgiveness. A saint with one pardonable weakness, and that is a complete inability to resist the appeal of flowers. The streets in Californian cities in the springtime are made beautiful by flowering trees, in hundreds, in thousands. How could anyone resist the temptation to snip off a few sprays so as to make flower arrangements? How could anyone resist? Nearly everyone does, as far as I know, except my saintly friend. Of course it is against the law, and so I have made up my own version of the story of the miracle of St Elizabeth of Hungary. My friend is out with her secateurs and her little bag, snip-snip-snipping. Up drives a policeman. 'What is in that bag?' he asks. 'Only groceries,' replies the poor little saint. 'Show me,' says the policeman. And she opens her bag, and, of course, it is full of groceries.

It was odd how that story haunted me. Then it began, the

old familiar stirring of the emotions, the feeling of recognition, the knowledge that something was about to take shape. And so it did – with everything coming at once. That had happened before, and would happen again. I do not understand why it is, that when I am constructing a story which is quite episodic, the episodes should all take form at once, or as nearly as my capacity allows. One day all the episodes are chaotic, formless, and then on a later day, not so long afterwards, they have all taken shape and are arranging themselves in order – I had had the same experience with the *Midshipman* as well as with other books.

There have been occasions when psychologists have questioned me to discover the mechanisms of these processes. They call them 'creative', but that is a misnomer; the eventual result is creation, if such a self-satisfied word can be tolerated, but the processes are to a large extent – are almost entirely – involuntary. Does a chicken lay an egg because she wants to or because she has to? Just possibly the writer may assist, or speed up, his processes by making himself receptive, by offering hospitality to the wandering idea, but I not only do not believe it but I am inclined to think the opposite is true. Certainly there is a danger point at which there is a sharp transition between being receptive and trying to force the process; if ideas are forced the result is nearly always – let us say invariably – hackneyed or unnatural or pedantic. The average Hollywood story conference is a deliberate attempt to force the formation of ideas.

So far in my life I have flinched from going more deeply into this question; when the psychologists have started to probe I have always remembered how easy it is to take a watch to pieces and how hard it is to make it go again. Maybe my ideas come because, deeply rooted, there is something wrong with me, which analysis might cure. If this is so I cannot think of a better example of the remedy being worse than the disease. I have no desire whatever to be cured of something which has piled interest into my life from boyhood until now, and I hardly expect to grow so old that I shall decide that there is sufficiently little in the future to lose, and submit to analysis to discover the cause of the flow.

A few paragraphs back *Hornblower in the West Indies* had

just formed itself in my mind, and from there to the writing it was only a step – the usual step on to the toboggan slide. Precipitately the stories ran on; is it of any interest that in my opinion the story about Hornblower and St Elizabeth of Hungary (which owes its existence to my flower-snipping friend) is the best story I have ever written? My opinion may be of academic interest, at least. As a digression I may mention that it was in the middle of that story that a Hollywood producer telephoned to me. I will not give his name, but it may be sufficient to add that he was of Greek extraction. Plans were forming, he said, to make a film about the sinking of the German battleship *Bismarck*, and would I help? It would have been a tempting invitation from every point of view, except that I was well started on the book and quite immune to temptation. There is nobody in the world less like a bulldog than myself, I suppose – except in this one respect. Once my teeth are clenched into a piece of work no inducement will make me unclench them – that, again, is nothing to be proud of, any more than the bulldog should be proud of what has been bred into him.

So to the pleadings of Hollywood I turned a deaf ear – that analogy being very close to the truth, for I hardly listened to the arguments, being so preoccupied with my current work. I could only say that I would not be available for another two months. No, I was not under contract to anyone else. Yes, I liked the idea, but I simply could not leave off what I was doing. If the need was urgent (as Hollywood needs always appear to be) they had better get someone else. Good-bye.

When I hung up the telephone I thought about the Greek extraction of the producer to whom I had been talking, and I remembered the story about Archimedes. He had been prominent in the defence of Syracuse against the Romans, and when the city was stormed, Marcellus, the Roman commander, gave orders that he was to be taken alive. But Archimedes was deep in some geometrical problem, and only gave an angry answer when a Roman soldier interrupted him to ask who he was, and so the soldier killed him. It seemed as if I had acted in the same way.

Of course Hollywood had not been in nearly so much of a hurry as Hollywood had believed itself to be, and two and a half months later I walked into the first conference that eventually resulted in the filming of *Sink the Bismarck*. There the producer hugged me like a bear (he rather resembled a bear) and said (to my utter astonishment and delight) 'I'm glad to meet you, Archimedes.' Nowadays in my mind St Elizabeth of Hungary is not only associated with my saintly friend, and with Hornblower's pursuit of Cambronne down the Caribbean, but also with the *Bismarck* and with Archimedes – the sort of mixed association which sometimes gives rise to plots, although none has made its appearance in this connection so far – unless this is it.

37

THERE was that gap in Hornblower's life, between the renewal of war in 1803 and his appearance on the Thames-Severn canal in 1805. It was really remarkable how many correspondents wrote to me and pointed it out – but, as before, I cannot lay the blame for the result on the shoulders of the kindly people who wrote to me. I was intrigued about that gap myself, even though I had not given it a thought when I began to write the *Atropos*. Now, not quite against my will, I found myself working out what must have happened. I had left him on the verge of getting married, newly promoted to commander, and about to serve in the renewed war; on his next appearance he was a captain and the father of a child with another one about to be born. So certain points were settled for me without any need for invention. He had distinguished himself – although that could have been taken for granted in any case, seeing that Hornblower was Hornblower; and also because there had to be a story about him. He must have been home on leave, too, to account for that second child, and that was by no means the general rule in the old navy.

The explanation was obvious; he must have served in the fleet blockading Brest – the ships of that squadron frequently had to put back into home ports to refit when damaged. As he was a commander his ship would be a small, light vessel – the kind of ship that would be employed in close observation of Brest; plenty of opportunity to gain distinction, then, and plenty of chance to receive damage compelling a return to port, even though Cornwallis in command was chary about giving permission to return. And so construction was off to a flying start.

One point to bear in mind. Hornblower, in later life, had been notoriously unlucky in the matter of prize money, so that however much he was to distinguish himself at Brest he was not to capture prizes; the ships he was to fight must either be destroyed or must escape. Unless – a sudden memory sent me hurrying to my history books. There it was. The incident of the captured Spanish treasure fleet, which convulsed with mirth the whole Royal Navy except for the participants, had occurred in the autumn of 1804, just when Hornblower could have taken part in it. That was one more of the convenient coincidences which studded Hornblower's paper career; I can quite be conscienceless about history if it is necessary – I might have made use of the treasure fleet incident even if it had actually occurred in 1801 or 1807 – but as it was I was not even put to the test. The actual course of events fitted exactly into *Hornblower and the Hotspur* without any straining – an imitation of Art by Nature that might have delighted the heart of Oscar Wilde.

Relative to this subject I might mention as an aside something I forgot to mention when I was dealing with *The Commodore*, for in the writing of that book I imperilled – almost ended – a valued friendship. For an eminent historian – a friend for years – wrote to me on reading *The Commodore*: 'I knew there were British forces engaged at the siege of Riga, but I have never been able to find out much about them. What were your sources?' I could only reply lamely that I had no sources, that I had decided that Riga could not have been besieged without British forces arriving to help, and Hornblower (as usual) had been handy. No one would believe, without reading the letter I received in reply, how hard was the rap on the knuckles that historian administered to me. It smarts to this day, even though I know it was undeserved.

There were some cheerless aspects about the usually pleasant work of construction. There was poor Maria; here she was on her honeymoon, entering into married life, having children. I knew the fate in store for her, and the fate in store for those children. Surely now I could impart a little joy into her otherwise joyless life? Almost none. There was a war on; Hornblower was serving in the Channel Fleet; and Hornblower was Hornblower. In the face of that combination of circumstances there was little that I could do for her. At least I saved her from disillusionment, I could help her in a negative kind of way, but I could not allow sentiment to spoil the story. Already we knew the sort of man Hornblower was to grow into; already we knew how the marriage was to develop. There was a Calvinistic predestination about the whole affair; for that matter the moving finger had already written. Maria was a butterfly (was there ever anyone quite so un-butterfly-like?) crushed between the grinding surfaces of fact and fiction.

38

ANOTHER thing I have not mentioned so far. It is a superstition of mine that dull moments come to an end when construction finishes and I address myself to the task of writing. Presumably during the happy time of construction I am not sensitive to the ordinary small disasters of ordinary life, and when I am writing I am liable to be highly sensitive to them. It always seems to me that the moment I write 'Page One' and start honest work, things begin to happen, and there is never a dull moment. During the writing of *Hotspur* the coincidences were quite uncanny in their occurrence. I had not written half a dozen pages before construction work of another kind began across the road, not fifty yards from the window of my secluded and usually tomb-like workroom. Every pneumatic drill, every concrete mixer, bulldozer, and air compressor in California went to work there. The noise was hideous and ceaseless. In other circumstances I would have moved away, but how could I at that moment? With an effort I could have taken fifty books of reference with me, but only in the certain knowledge that it would be the fifty-first that I would need, when suddenly I would have to to have the weight and dimensions of a hogshead of pork, or the maximum range of a French field how-itzer. I could only try to lose myself in my visualizations and work on through the noise. While the noise was still going on a friend fell seriously ill, ill enough, and lonely enough, and enough of a friend for my personal intervention to be called for to deal with doctors and hospitals. The ink was hardly dry on the letters I had to write about all this before I lost my secretary and had to find another; the truest words Abraham Lincoln ever said were those warning against changing secretaries while writing a novel. Then, as if they had been waiting for the perfect moment, Internal Revenue leaped upon me with a request for a special investigation, demanding facts about my sources of income that I never had troubled to know and that the new secretary could not possibly know, and morning after morning I had to get up dazed from my desk, leaving Hornblower at grips with French frigates, and answer questions about matters of which I knew even less than I knew (as I remarked earlier in this book) about harmony and counterpoint. The providence that looks after sleepwalkers and drunkards came to my rescue, and I can proudly boast that I am one of the few men who have emerged from a special investigation with the Internal Revenue owing me money instead of the other way about. If I had not been so involved with the *Hotspur* I should have had that final letter from Internal Revenue framed and hung on my workroom wall – I still have not had time to arrange for that.

All this was during the summer months, and it is mostly during the summer months that visitors come to stay. Never has my house been so full of visitors as it was while I was writing *Hotspur* and training a new secretary and dealing with Internal Revenue and the hospitals. Friends were sleeping everywhere – there was a period when a charming young woman was sleeping on a hired bed made up in my workroom, and sleeping late, as young women will, so that I had to turn her out of bed each morning before I could settle down and sail with Hornblower to attack the Spanish *flota*. It seemed as if we could never manage to sit down with less than six to lunch and eight to dinner, all very light-hearted except for me; because of Hornblower and Maria – and perhaps because of Internal Revenue – I was a skeleton at fifty feasts during that lively time.

Despite all these handicaps there was an additional and weighty reason for finishing the book. Not only had I made my usual promises of delivery, and not only was I in my usual condition of panic awaiting the end, but also I was due to make a journey round the world. The reservations were all made, the passages all booked, and in a tiny area in southern Portugal the hoop-petticoated daffodil was due to bloom in the early spring, ten thousand miles away, and I was anxious to arrive there at exactly the right moment, even though to the unprejudiced eye the hoop-petticoated daffodil (one of the great aunts of the cultivated daffodil) is a miserable object barely two inches tall and not worth crossing the street for, to say nothing of going round the world for.

So *Hotspur* simply had to be finished; it did not surprise me in the least to discover that the full development of the story called for more words than I had calculated upon at the start. I had left ten days in reserve, and nine of them were consumed in dealing with Hornblower's promotion to captain. So that the day the typescripts were put into the post and started off eastward to the publishers, I started off westward to the hoop-petticoated daffodil via New Zealand. There was not even time for the usual feeling of disappointment; there was hardly time for the realization to sink in that I had finished with Hornblower for good and all.

39

IT was sixteen months ago that I wrote the last words of *Hotspur*. Of course Hornblower has troubled me since then, occasionally. It might be thought that with all the gaps in his active life filled up there would be no chance for invention to find anything to work on, and yet it does. Here is an example, which I am writing to show how a story presents itself to my mind, ready to be written. I am curious, myself, to see how the next paragraph or two will appear when completed (I can hardly guess), because I suppose that if ever I were to write preliminary notes they would take this as yet undetermined form.

The story is called *The Point and the Edge*. The time is 1819, with Hornblower a senior captain on half pay. His restlessness, as always, demands exercise, and he has been for long taking fencing lessons; his memories of a dozen hand-to-hand fights are now coloured by the strengthened realization of how the point will always beat the edge when skilfully used. England at this time is in the depths of a postwar slump; people are starving through lack of employment, and despite the savage laws, which enact that a man may be hanged for the theft of five shillings, crime is rampant. Hornblower has been invited to dine at Portsmouth on the flagship of a friend – say Lord Exmouth – who is fortunate enough to have employment in the exiguous navy that England still maintains. Hornblower travels down with Barbara, and puts up at the George. In the late afternoon

Barbara looks him over, sees that his civilian clothes are in good order, that he is wearing his gold watch and chain, and carrying his gold-topped ebony walking-stick, and sees him off, while she spends – like a dutiful wife – a dull evening alone.

Exmouth and Hornblower, of course, spend a pleasant evening, discussing the state of the nation and naval policy; Exmouth, rubbing his hands with glee, tells Hornblower of the revolution in recruiting methods nowadays. No flamboyant posters, no press gangs – starving seamen stand in line, waiting for the chance to enlist in the Royal Navy. Captains can pick and choose. Dinner over, Hornblower, fashionable clothes, gold-topped walking-stick and all, starts back to The George. At a dark corner a man springs out at him. He is bare-footed, wearing only a tattered shirt and trousers, and starving. In his hand is a branch torn from a tree – his entire stock in trade, his entire working capital. Threatening Hornblower with this improvised club he demands Hornblower's money. This footpad is actually risking his life, risking hanging, for a meal. Hornblower's liberal feelings have no time to assert themselves. He reacts violently against compulsion, and without a thought he lunges with his walking-stick, a quick, instant thrust. The point beats the edge – it lands on the footpad's cheek, half stunning him, so that he reels back momentarily incapacitated. Hornblower cracks him over the wrist so that he drops his club and is at Hornblower's mercy. Hornblower could now call the watch and have this man seized and taken away to certain death, but he naturally cannot bring himself to do so. Instead he drives him before him back to Exmouth's ship. 'My Lord, would you please do me one more favour? Would you be so kind as to enlist this man into your crew?'

There is the completed story – five days of methodical writing and it would be ready for publication. With the usual flurry of excitement it has presented itself in this form, unsought, adapted to this particular period – and only this period – ready for writing. Long novels take shape in exactly the same way, adapting themselves to the times. It has happened scores of times, possibly hundreds of times, in my life, and I still do not know how or why, although the adaptation to the necessary period is explainable, perhaps, because the ideas are necessarily canalized into it.

248

40

IT is a curious ability to be born with. Like the freaks in the circus sideshows, I earn my living by my freakishness, although with a great deal more physical comfort, I am sure. And – there is no way of evading the conclusion – I have exploited my own freakishness as Barnum and Bailey exploited General Tom Thumb. There is an excuse which I can offer – the same defence as is put forward every day in criminal trials. Undoubtedly there is an irresistible impulse. It is almost impossible, having formulated an idea, to resist putting it on paper, and, once it is on paper, it is just as impossible to resist presenting it to the public.

That was an additional reason for writing about *The Point and the Edge* in the preceding paragraphs. There are other ideas stratified underneath that one – ideas come in groups, as I think I have already mentioned. There might be another book, but what I have just written may – I fancy – head it off and cause it to be unwritten; there are other books I would prefer to write, books with more adventure and difficulty for me personally. That book (now here is another ridiculous reaction) would be too easy.

So perhaps these final paragraphs that I am writing are the last I shall ever write about Hornblower. I have tried to explain all the other Hornblower books, so I must try to explain this present one. It started with the idea of the maps; that idea had been with me for several years. It was remarkably tempting. I wanted to find out if the novels would pass the rather searching test of actual analysis as regards geography as well as history. To gratify my curiosity I was even willing to suffer the discomfort of picking up the novels again and turning the pages over one by one and going through past work while plotting out courses and battle charts. From there it was only a step to remembering the circumstances that caused the books to be written. Most of those memories – as I hope has been apparent – were happy ones, and the decision came to write about them, to resavour the happiness. Just for once I would write a book that needed no planning, no construction. For the actual writing no visualization would be necessary; only a simple recording of facts.

That did not prove to be true; while writing this present

book I have had to get up on to the stage and watch the antics of the young man who was me just as I once watched the performances of Hornblower. I cannot say it has been good for me; it has certainly been oddly pleasant. And for this pleasure I must thank my friends, not those of my everyday life, but the unknown numerous friends who have borne with Hornblower during the past twenty-six years since I began writing about him. And that word 'friends' is written in all sincerity, not just as a convenient formula, in the way that a politician might use it on the rostrum, or an actor after the final curtain. It is a remarkable, an extraordinarily pleasant feeling, to know, with comforting certainty (for once) that my work has won for me the friendship – even something like the affection – of people whom I have never met, and never shall meet. I thank them, and it is to them that these words are addressed. There is no need for the formal tag: *Plaudite et valete.*

41

AND so this book is finished; in five minutes I shall be recapping my fountain pen and rising from my chair to stretch. As always it is in the nick of time. A week from today I shall be driving a motor car in the Atlas Mountains, and if an explanation is needed as to why an elderly gentleman not in the best of health should be doing such a thing, I must point out that this is the second day of March and very soon the wildflowers will be blooming in the Atlas Mountains. I shall write one final line; I have always been faintly puzzled about why other writers have ended their books in this way – I have never done so myself until now – but I discover I have a real reason. This book is about writing books, and this is the ultimate item of data.

Berkeley, California. January 12–March 2, 1963.
Good-bye.

42

POSTSCRIPT, March 5, 1964

THE date which I wrote on the preceding page has its uses after all; it enables me to know that a year and three days ago I thought I had finished this book, finished everything. During that year there has been some delay over the illustrations, and instead of this book being published (as I expected) in the autumn of 1963 it will be quite surprising if it even appears in the autumn of 1964.

This delay enables me – or compels me – to insert this postscript, which presents an abrupt change of point of view, like most postscripts. With the printer waiting I must write these lines without being quite certain, but to wait until I am certain one way or the other would mean I would not be able to squeeze them into this book. I have an uneasy feeling that history is going to repeat itself. That is one more example of how these things happen. Hornblower is on the move again.

When I finished *Hotspur* Hornblower had reached captain's rank, and it was early in 1805. I chose that date for my own convenience. I did not want to face the complications of involving him in the Trafalgar campaign. And in the next volume – *Atropos* – he suddenly reappears in December 1805 on the Gloucester-London canal, and the lapse of time made it conveniently unnecessary to explain how in the world he got there and what he was doing in the interval. I did not know – I did not even want to know, as I have just said. I wrote those final lines, which appear on the page before this, and went off to the Atlas Mountains (the wildflowers, by the way, were surpassingly lovely) happy in the knowledge that Hornblower was finished, done with, buried.

Now during this past year the ideas have been stirring. It was forged orders that started it. The possibilities of forged orders were exercising my mind – military or naval or air force orders written on the right paper in the correct form and with a convincingly forged signature. I suspected that this basic idea might expand in the usual way, that it might be the parent barnacle of a family of barnacles; it seemed a fair start for a novel in a modern setting. Never in my simplicity during the first happy weeks of liberty did I dwell for a moment on the development which anyone who has read this far in this book probably thought of at once. I completed my visit to Morocco, and went on living my life as inoffensively (in my own opinion) as possible. It was sometime in the autumn of 1963 that the first misgivings assailed me, when the pattern of the barnacles began to assume an ominous shape, or when (to use another and equally hackneyed metaphor) I opened a cupboard door and found a skeleton inside – I saw it plainly despite the speed with which I slammed the door on it.

It was the most singular coincidence, and I declare it to be a coincidence even though I am certain that the psychologists (and psychiatrists) would shake their heads pityingly over my self-deception. There were only seven or eight months, in the latter part of 1805, of Hornblower's life unaccounted for, and I was thinking about forged orders. Yet there it was; forged orders could play a vital part in the campaign of Trafalgar, particularly in the opening moves of that campaign, and here was Hornblower unemployed. There was a certain need to tell what Hornblower was doing during those vital months when Britain's fate was being decided at sea – and here was a job simply ready-made for him, even though I had once thought the job might be done in Scapa Flow in 1916 or 1940 or in the Pentagon in 1953. As far as the Napoleonic Wars were concerned the idea fitted into 1805 and into no other time, and at no other time was Hornblower available to be involved in it, and there was no one more suited to the occasion than Hornblower. Surely the most sceptical psychiatrist, the most cynical reader, will agree that there was a considerable element of coincidence about all this.

It was with actual apprehension, it was with a reluctance never before observed, that last autumn, as I shaved or ran my eye along my library shelves to select a book, I found the barnacle-grown timbers rising to the surface to mock me with a display of new growth. All that growth – which normally would have occasioned vast pleasure – was now a source of bitterness because every new barnacle was another nail pulled out of Hornblower's coffin. In fact he was out of his coffin altogether; his was the skeleton in the cupboard, and while it was there, until he was decently buried again, his ghost refused exorcism. Every added fragment of plot made it the more necessary to include him in it; it was a plot that could only revolve around Hornblower, and could only apply to 1805.

New Year's Day, 1964, found me in Maui and it was there – in a place as far removed from the Trafalgar campaign in space and time and atmosphere as it is possible to conceive – that I had to give up the struggle and abandon the other work which

I had undertaken and allow events to take their course.

Since that time they have done so in the usual fashion. The stage has now been reached where it is necessary occasionally to refer to my reference library to check up on facts so as to decide whether some new turn in the plot is technically possible. This morning, before I began today's work (the second day of work on this essay) I found myself turning the pages of encyclopaedias, and taking down Boswell's *Life of Johnson*, in the endeavour to increase, and renew, my small knowledge of the Rev. Dr Dodd who was hanged for forgery in 1777; what Dodd did then has some sort of bearing on what Hornblower might do in 1805 and on what I might do in 1964.

Now, at this very moment of writing, I begin this paragraph having returned to my desk after taking a turn round the room, and the fact that I actually walked instead of just standing up is an indication of the intensity of my present feelings. The future hangs in the balance; another novel is becoming a possibility. Nor is that all. I have to finish this essay today in order to insert it in this book – not only is the printer waiting but the Greek Islands are waiting; I am, when present work and future work leave anything over for sane thinking, making preparations for an immediate departure to the Eastern Mediterranean. The poppies of Greece are intruding themselves upon my mental vision and the siren song that Ulysses heard is stealing on my inward ear. But how much of the one will I really see, and how much of the other will I really hear? This is the period of the deepest abstraction. Fresh links in the chain will be presenting themselves, and (judging by long experience) there will be times when selection has to be made, when one link will have to be, reluctantly, discarded in favour of another, and links that had once appeared tried and true will have to be tested against the standards of real history. What will I care about the Street of the Knights when it is essential that I should know, immediately, how many ships of the line accompanied Nelson to the West Indies?

All this sounds as if I were going to write the novel, but of course that is quite uncertain. Plots have presented themselves before, to be discarded in the end, when the novel finally appears to be not worth writing, or distasteful, or too fragile. That may easily be the case with this one; I would not have written this chapter about it if it were not a matter of now or never.

Supposing I were to write the novel? Supposing (that old doubt – one of the few things that grows stronger with age) I live to complete it? Then somewhere soon after the first week in July, when I am home again, I shall find myself sitting here, where I am sitting now, with this same pen in my hand and this same writing pad in front of me and I shall be writing the figure '1' at the top of the page and launching myself once more on to the toboggan slide, committing myself to the daily hours of visualization and the months of fatigue. Perhaps then – it is an odd thought – I shall look back with envy on the pleasant hours I have spent in this current exercise. Perhaps some time in October I shall recap my pen and rise stiffly from my desk and come hesitatingly back to life. Until then – perhaps —

The last word I wrote at the end of the last chapter was 'good-bye'. Now I have written it again, with feelings equally strong.